DONEGAL

ALSO AVAILABLE IN THIS SERIES:

Sligo, Michael Farry (2012)
Tyrone, Fergal McCluskey (2014)
Waterford, Pat McCarthy (2015)
Monaghan, Terence Dooley (2017)
Derry, Adrian Grant (2018)
Limerick, John O'Callaghan (2018)
Louth, Donal Hall (2019)
Kildare, Seamus Cullen (2020)
Leitrim, Patrick McGarty (2020)
Antrim, Brian Feeney (2021)
Roscommon, John Burke (2021)

Donegal

The Irish Revolution, 1912–23

Pauric Travers

FOUR COURTS PRESS

Set in 10.5 on 12.5 point Ehrhardt for
FOUR COURTS PRESS LTD
7 Malpas Street, Dublin 8, Ireland
www.fourcourtspress.ie
and in North America for
FOUR COURTS PRESS
c/o IPG, 814 N. Franklin St, Chicago, IL 60610.

© Pauric Travers and Four Courts Press 2022

A catalogue record for this title
is available from the British Library.

ISBN 978-1-84682-978-9

All rights reserved. No part of this publication may be reproduced, stored in or introduced into a retrieval system, or transmitted, in any form or by any means (electronic, mechanical, photocopying, recording or otherwise), without the prior written permission of both the copyright owner and the publisher of this book.

Printed in England
by CPI Antony Rowe, Chippenham, Wilts.

Contents

	LIST OF ILLUSTRATIONS	vi
	LIST OF ABBREVIATIONS	vii
	ACKNOWLEDGMENTS	ix
	The Irish Revolution, 1912–23 series	xi
1	'Seod glas san fharraige mór': Donegal in 1912	1
2	The home rule crisis, 1912–14: promised land or Armageddon?	16
3	'As much Ireland's war as England's'?: the First World War, 1914–18	32
4	'The squabble in Dublin': 1916 and its aftermath	49
5	'All changed': Sinn Féin, 1916–18	65
6	The victory of Sinn Féin: the 1918 general election	79
7	'Rendering government impossible': the political war, 1919–21	87
8	The storm: the War of Independence, 1919–21	101
9	Cogadh na gcarad: the Civil War, 1922–3	114
10	Donegal and the Irish Revolution	133
	NOTES	141
	SELECT BIBLIOGRAPHY	166
	INDEX	173

Illustrations

PLATES

1 Roger Casement and Úna Ní Fhaircheallaigh (Agnes O'Farrelly) at Cloghaneely, c.1905.
2 Bishop Patrick O'Donnell (1856–1927).
3 Edward Carson at Raphoe, 2 October 1913.
4 Charles Clements, 5th earl of Leitrim (1879–1952), commander of the UVF in Donegal.
5 UVF training camp in Donegal, 1914.
6 Patrick MacGill (1889–1963).
7 Joseph A. Sweeney (1897–1980).
8 Constable Charles McGee (1892–1916).
9 Peadar O'Donnell (1893–1986).
10 Joseph Murray and members of the 1st Battalion, No. 4 Brigade (SE Donegal), IRA.
11 Alice Cashel (1878–1958).
12 Donegal members of the Irish Republican Police.
13 Eithne Coyle (1897–1985).
14 Members of Cumann na mBan, Annagry, 1922.
15 'The Drumboe Martyrs' – Charlie Daly, Dan Enright, Timothy O'Sullivan, Seán Larkin – executed at Drumboe Woods, 14 March 1923.

Credits
1, 2: National Library of Ireland; 3, 5: Deputy Keeper of the Records, Public Record Office of Northern Ireland; 4, 12, 14: Donegal County Museum; 7, Pearse Museum, Rathfarnham; 9: Emmet O'Connor; 11: Humphrys family; 10, 15 and cover photo: Donegal County Archives; 13: UCD Archives.

MAPS

1	Places mentioned in the text	xii
2	Railways in Donegal	3
3	Parliamentary constituencies	11
4	Local government divisions	89
5	Distribution of Crown forces	97
6	IRA battalion, brigade, divisional areas	109

Abbreviations

AOH	Ancient Order of Hibernians (Board of Erin)
ASU	Active Service Unit
BL	British Library
BMH	Bureau of Military History
BN	*Belfast Newsletter*
CAB	Cabinet Office, TNA
Cd.	Command paper
CDB	Congested Districts Board
CI	County Inspector, Royal Irish Constabulary
CO	Colonial Office, TNA
CÓFLA	Cardinal Tomás Ó Fiaich Memorial Library and Archive
CSO	Chief Secretary's Office
DATI	Department of Agriculture & Technical Instruction
DA	*Donegal Annual/ Bliainiris Dhún na nGall*
DCA	Donegal County Archives
DCC	Donegal County Council
DD	*Donegal Democrat*
DÉ	Dáil Éireann
DI	District Inspector, Royal Irish Constabulary
DIB	*Dictionary of Irish biography*
DJ	*Derry Journal*
DN	*Derry People & Donegal News*
DPRA	Donegal Protestant Registration Association
DV	*Donegal Vindicator*
FH	*Fermanagh Herald*
FJ	*Freeman's Journal*
GAA	Gaelic Athletic Association
IAOS	Irish Agricultural Organisation Society
IFS	Irish Free State
IG	Inspector General, Royal Irish Constabulary
IHS	*Irish Historical Studies*
II	*Irish Independent*
IMA	Irish Military Archives
INTO	Irish National Teachers' Organisation
IPP	Irish Parliamentary Party
IRA	Irish Republican Army
IRB	Irish Republican Brotherhood
IT	*Irish Times*

ITGWU	Irish Transport and General Workers' Union
JP	Justice of the Peace
KC	King's Counsel
LGB	Local Government Board
LS	*Londonderry Sentinel*
MP	Member of Parliament
MS	Manuscript
MSPC	Military Service Pensions Collection
NAI	National Archives of Ireland
NAUL	National Amalgamated Union of Labour
NLI	National Library of Ireland
O/C	Officer Commanding
PRONI	Public Records Office of Northern Ireland
RDC	Rural District Council
RIC	Royal Irish Constabulary
TCD	Trinity College Dublin
TD	Teachta Dála
TNA	National Archives, London
UCDA	University College Dublin Archives
UDC	Urban District Council
UIL	United Irish League
USC	Ulster Special Constabulary
UUC	Ulster Unionist Council
UVF	Ulster Volunteer Force
UWUC	Ulster Women's Unionist Council
WO	War Office
WS	Witness statement to the Bureau of Military History

Acknowledgments

Writing a history of Donegal during the Irish Revolution has been for me a labour of love. The task has been facilitated by many people and institutions whose assistance I gratefully acknowledge.

The existence of an active county historical society has contributed to a lively local historical community in Donegal and a burgeoning historiography. My understanding of the revolutionary period in the county has been informed by the work of, among others, Seán Beattie, Anthony Begley, John Cunningham, Richard Doherty, Kieran Kelly, Jim Mac Laughlin, Helen Meehan, Pádraig S. Ó Baoighill, Liam Ó Duibhir, Okan Ozseker and Frank Sweeney. The volumes on the adjoining counties in the *Irish Revolution, 1912–23* series have helped provide a comparative dimension. More generally, I am grateful for suggestions made at an earlier stage in the process by friends and colleagues, including Marie Coleman, James Kelly, Theresa O'Farrell, Francis Devine and the late David Fitzpatrick.

I am indebted to the various libraries and archives in which I fossicked and especially the Donegal County Archives, the National Library of Ireland, the Public Record Office of Northern Ireland, UCD Archives, the Cardinal Tomás Ó Fiaich Memorial Library and Archives and the Cregan library, DCU. Their assistance was all the more appreciated given the vicissitudes of Covid lockdowns. My research has benefitted greatly from the assistance of Caroline Carr in the County Museum and Niamh Brennan, the county archivist, as well as the far-sighted digitization programme of the Donegal County Archives.

I owe a particular debt of gratitude to Mary Ann Lyons and Daithí Ó Corráin for their patience, encouragement and support, and for their painstaking comments on the text. Their facilitation of access to digitized material during lockdown was invaluable. My thanks also to Mike Brennan for creating the maps in this book and to Martin Fanning and the team at Four Courts Press for their customary professionalism in its production.

As ever, my greatest debt is to Mary Moore to whom I dedicate this book.

The Irish Revolution, 1912–23 series

Since the turn of the century, a growing number of scholars have been actively researching this seminal period in modern Irish history. More recently, propelled by the increasing availability of new archival material, this endeavour has intensified. This series brings together for the first time the various strands of this exciting and fresh scholarship within a nuanced interpretative framework, making available concise, accessible, scholarly studies of the Irish Revolution experience at a local level to a wide audience.

The approach adopted is both thematic and chronological, addressing the key developments and major issues that occurred at a county level during the tumultuous 1912–23 period. Beginning with an overview of the social, economic and political milieu in the county in 1912, each volume assesses the strength of the home rule movement and unionism, as well as levels of labour and feminist activism. The genesis and organization of paramilitarism from 1913 are traced; responses to the outbreak of the First World War and its impact on politics at a county level are explored; and the significance of the 1916 Rising is assessed. The varying fortunes of constitutional and separatist nationalism are examined. The local experience of the War of Independence, reaction to the truce and Anglo-Irish Treaty and the course and consequences of the Civil War are subject to detailed examination and analysis. The result is a compelling account of life in Ireland in this formative era.

Mary Ann Lyons *Daithí Ó Corráin*
Department of History *School of History & Geography*
Maynooth University *Dublin City University*

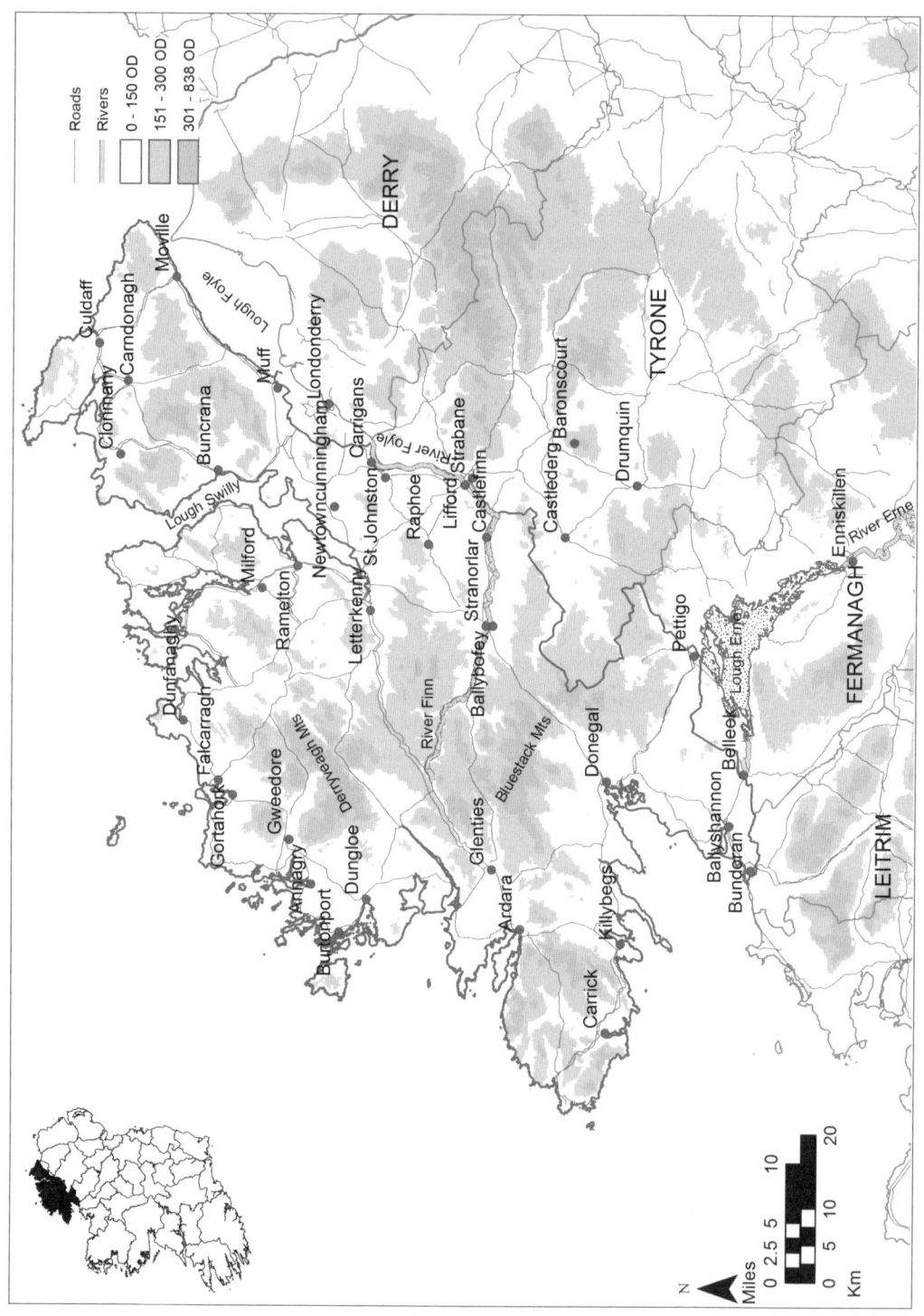

1 Places mentioned in the text

1 'Seod glas san fharraige mór': Donegal in 1912

Writing to a friend in July 1916, shortly before his execution, Roger Casement recalled sadly that his last view of Ireland before the outbreak of the First World War was of Tory Island in Donegal. In late summer 1914, he travelled through the remote Irish-speaking regions of the north-west.[1] No stranger to the area, having visited during a previous period of ill health, Casement had attended Coláiste Uladh in Cloghaneely to learn Irish and generously supported the college financially. Exhausted from his efforts to reveal the atrocities inflicted on the indigenous population of the Putumayo region in the Amazon and disillusioned with the destructive impact of colonialism, Casement's visit in 1912 confirmed a reorientation in his political outlook and helped set him on a fateful path. He became convinced that only an independent country, free from colonial interference, could ensure the preservation of a distinctive Irish cultural identity.[2]

For Casement, as for Patrick Pearse who also visited Coláiste Uladh, the Irish-speaking areas of the west of Ireland were both a spiritual oasis – a 'green jewel in the great sea' – and a reminder of what once was and what might be again. However, neither man would have envisaged the area as being an active participant in the coming upheaval. Donegal was not in the vanguard of the Irish Revolution, however that revolution is defined. Geographical location, historical development, and social and economic conditions militated against this north-western county playing a leading role. Neither were the inhabitants of Donegal uninvolved and disinterested bystanders. This book addresses the question of how the Irish Revolution was experienced by the people of Donegal.

With an area of 4,861 square kilometres, Donegal is the fourth largest county in Ireland. The Derryveagh Mountains and the Bluestacks dominate the interior of the county, with the iconic Mount Errigal the highest peak at 751 metres. Its mountainous terrain and remoteness have shaped Donegal's history and development. Tirconaill was the last of the independent lordships subdued as part of the Tudor conquest. The area was officially shired in 1585: the mutation of Tírconaill into County Donegal was the hallmark of the new political dispensation. This was entrenched by the plantation that followed and left an enduring impact on the county, not least in terms of land ownership, religious diversity and anglicization.

Writing about the Laggan area of east Donegal in 1908, Revd Alexander Lecky observed that there were two Donegals – an outer and an inner: the part to the east was fertile and strongly Protestant; the other to the west was predominantly mountainous, poor and Catholic.[3] This is broadly true, although it could equally be argued that there were four Donegals which in 1912 coincided roughly with the four parliamentary constituencies. East Donegal from the Finn to the Bann rivers is more fertile and contains a large Protestant population. The average farm size was larger and agricultural production more diverse. While Protestants were outnumbered by their Catholic neighbours, they were closely inter-connected with their co-religionists in the neighbouring counties of Derry and mid-Ulster. This had a considerable bearing on their experience during the decade of revolution. West Donegal was under-developed, contained the largest concentration of Irish speakers and was the focus of intensive efforts by the Congested Districts Board (CDB) from 1891 to combat poverty and emigration. North Donegal stretches from Letterkenny to Inishowen. It was marginally more industrialized and was economically oriented towards the city of Derry, a factor that influenced its experience in these years. As in east Donegal, the linen industry was an important part of the local economy. Finally, south Donegal was part of a distinct region which included north Leitrim and Sligo and west Fermanagh. It was part of the extensive Trinity College estates from the time of the Ulster Plantation and had an active Protestant farming and business community.

Despite the lack of fertile land, particularly in the centre of the county, in the early twentieth century Donegal had the highest density of rural population to agricultural land in Ireland.[4] Conversely, it had relatively little urban development. In 1911 only three towns (see map 1) were classified as urban or 'civic areas' with a population of at least 2,000: Letterkenny (2,194), Ballyshannon (2,170) and Bundoran (2,116). Donegal differed from other comparable counties such as Mayo which had four towns over 3,000.[5] The urban centres of Derry, Enniskillen and Sligo in adjoining counties played a significant part in the social, economic and political life of Donegal.

Donegal has the longest mainland coastline in Ireland at 1,134 kilometres and historically much of the external trade was by sea. In 1912 there were weekly steamers from Burtonport, Milford and Mulroy to Derry with onward sailings to Scotland, England and the United States. The coming of the railways to Donegal from the 1860s transformed internal communication and acted as an agent of change (see map 2). Between 1863 and 1903, a series of mainly light rail lines were built, linking formerly remote parts of the county with Derry, Belfast and Dublin. The final piece of the jigsaw came with the opening of the 50-mile Letterkenny to Burtonport extension in 1903.[6] By then the narrow-gauge rail network extended to 225 miles, the longest in the United Kingdom. While the railways damaged ports like Ballyshannon, they contributed to the development of trade and the emergence of a cash economy.[7] The railways played an important role during the Irish Revolution.

In 1911 Donegal's total population was 168,537, a decline of 43 per cent from the 296,448 recorded in 1841.[8] Some 59,313 or 35.2 per cent were able

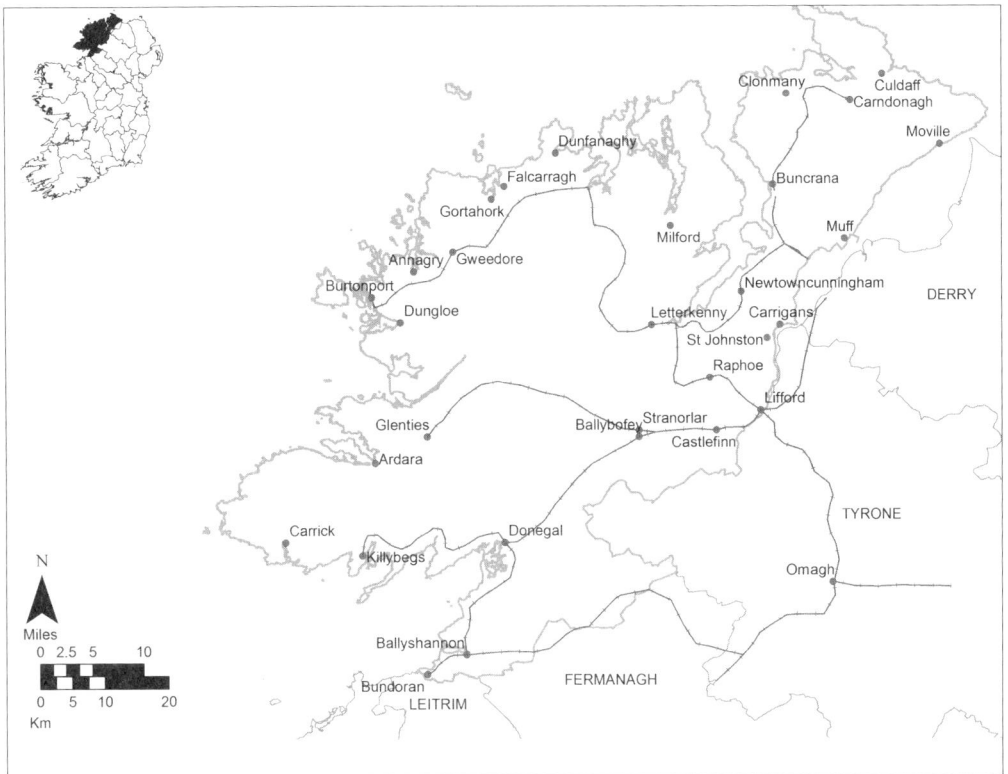

2 Railways in Donegal

to speak Irish. Of these 4,733 spoke Irish only and 54,580 were bilingual Irish and English speakers. The strongest Irish-speaking areas were in the west and north-west of the county but not exclusively. Dunfanaghy rural county district had the largest number of Irish-only speakers with 2,234, followed by Glenties (1,787), Milford (402) and Stranorlar (204). The distribution of bilingual speakers followed a similar pattern.[9] During his 1912 visit to Tory, Casement was impressed by the cultural distinctiveness of the islanders and the number of monoglot Irish speakers.[10]

In 1911 Donegal had a relatively large Protestant population: 10.7 per cent were Protestant Episcopalian (18,020), 8.9 per cent were Presbyterian (15,016) and 1 per cent were Methodist (1,698). Roman Catholics comprised 78.9 per cent (133,021).[11] Donegal included the Catholic diocese of Raphoe as well as parts of the diocese of Clogher in the south, while Inishowen was in the diocese of Derry. The personalities of the three bishops shaped the Donegal experience during the revolutionary decade in different ways. Bishop Patrick O'Donnell (1856–1927) of Raphoe was the most significant prelate and the dominant figure in Donegal social and political life.¹² Born at Kilraine in west Donegal, the son of a small tenant farmer, he was appointed bishop of Raphoe at the unusually young age of thirty-two. Horace Plunkett, who knew him well, considered O'Donnell the most intelligent of the Irish bishops.¹³ His episcopacy saw a growth in church building and a notable increase in the number of clergy. By 1911, the ratio of priests and nuns to people in Donegal was 1:652.¹⁴ Unlike other members of the hierarchy, who recoiled from political involvement after the Parnellite split, O'Donnell identified closely with the Irish Parliamentary Party (IPP) and became its treasurer and an influential adviser and power broker. By 1912, he was at the height of his power. Augustine Birrell, Irish chief secretary, considered him 'frankly a nationalist politician' rather than a bishop.¹⁵ Birrell consulted O'Donnell in relation to senior appointments in the Dublin Castle administration and his support was regularly solicited by election candidates, locally and nationally.¹⁶

George Alexander Chadwick (1840–1923), Church of Ireland bishop of the united dioceses of Raphoe and Derry, was no less formidable than his Catholic counterpart. Born in Cork, he was educated in Trinity College where he won the gold medal for oratory, a skill that he deployed to great effect during the home rule crisis. Appointed to Derry and Raphoe in 1896, he had a reputation as a preacher and was influential within the Church of Ireland General Synod. Chadwick promoted closer unity between Protestant denominations. He believed firmly in the right of Ulster unionists to resist home rule by force, if necessary, signed the Ulster Covenant and acted as grand chaplain of the Orange Order.¹⁷

Great landed estates were another legacy of the plantation in Donegal. At the turn of the nineteenth century, four landlords continued to own estates of over 39,000 acres, although some transfer of ownership had taken place under the land purchase acts. The duke of Abercorn's estate in east Donegal was one of the first sold to tenants. Despite the Wyndham Act (1903) and the Birrell Act (1909) which facilitated land purchase, the transfer of ownership remained slow. In 1912 the CDB reported that no proceedings for sale had been initiated for more than 600,000 acres of available land in Donegal.¹⁸ In January 1912 Donegal County Council (DCC) endorsed a call for land purchase to be completed without delay. The process was disrupted by the First World War and did not regain momentum until after the passing of the 1923 land act.¹⁹ Between 1879 and 1927, the ownership of fifty-five larger estates had been transferred to tenants.²⁰

For most small holders in Donegal, land purchase and land ownership were irrelevant. In 1910 there were still 1,966 holdings of less than an acre in Donegal, the owners of which subsisted through seasonal migration. Another 2,922 were between one and five acres. Over 73 per cent of holdings were less than 30 acres. At the other end of the scale, there were 188 holdings of more than 500 acres in 1910.²¹ The land acts gave the CDB power to acquire land for redistribution to small holders and evicted tenants. Expectations were high but progress was painfully slow.²² By 1916, thirty-three estates had been sold to the CDB, in whole or in part.²³ The process was disrupted by the war, and afterwards the political situation added another element to an explosive mix. By 1922, the Board was still fending off accusations of dilatoriness and complaining about the 'terrorism of the landless sons of tenants'.²⁴ A problem for the CDB was the persistent objection to land being given to 'outsiders', even when they came from the next parish. By March 1922, 117,000 acres had been purchased and re-sold by the Board to tenants.²⁵

Agriculture was the dominant industry in Donegal but in much of the western part of the country it was largely subsistence farming. Potatoes remained the staple food. Production increased in the early twentieth century with support from the CDB: the proportion of land devoted to potatoes was among the highest in the country.²⁶ In the east of the county, where the land was better and farm size larger, farming was more intensive. Tillage was more common, generating a demand for farm labourers. In 1912 the area of land ploughed per thousand acres of crops and pasture was 270 acres, compared to 140 in Mayo and 92 in Kerry. Oats was the dominant crop, but barley, rye, wheat and flax were also commonly grown. Cattle and sheep were important parts of the agricultural economy. The number of cattle in the county was 170,000 in 1910 and the number of sheep slightly less.²⁷

Although sometimes accused of paternalism, the CDB had a significant impact on all aspects of the social and economic life of Donegal.²⁸ Areas of the west of Ireland with a rateable valuation of less than 30 shillings and unable to sustain their current population were designated as 'congested'. Initially half of county Donegal was so designated but from 1909 the entire county came under the aegis of the CDB. Fishing was potentially a valuable source of additional income for subsistence farmers. Investment in equipment, training and the expansion of the market paid dividends before 1914.²⁹ The quality of the herring caught off Donegal was high and the CDB supported the introduction of decked sailing boats.³⁰ Bumper herring seasons contributed to a rapid increase in the number of boats fishing in Downings Bay and other areas around the Donegal coast and attracted buyers from Germany and Russia.³¹ Efforts to promote mackerel fishing were less successful.³²

Curing and other ancillary activities generated much needed employment. Small curing stations operated at Tory and five other locations. Mounting and repairing nets provided an additional source of income out-of-season as did barrel making and burning seaweed to make kelp. Barrel-making factories at Teelin and Burtonport were closed by 1912, but the CDB expanded its factory at Downings, which produced herring barrels.³³ Such modest interventions in the market benefitted the poorest communities but they attracted criticism from fish merchants who were hostile to suggestions of cooperatives for the marketing of fish.[34] Other initiatives were more welcome. Boat building yards were established at Killybegs and Mulroy Bay. Between 1910 and 1912, grants were awarded for improvements to sixteen piers or harbours in Donegal.[35] The introduction of power fishing vessels had revolutionized the fishing industry elsewhere by facilitating year-round fishing and following the fish further from port.[36] By 1914, the Board had five steam drifters in operation off Donegal and the fishing industry looked set for significant expansion.[37]

The ancillary activities associated with fishing provided opportunities for female workers. In 1911 just over 15,000 of the total female population of 84,000 had specified occupations: a surprisingly large number of those (6,804) were classed as industrial; 3,706 were classed as agricultural and 3,603 were employed in domestic service.[38] These figures probably underestimate the number of women engaged in cottage industry – one estimate puts the total in the textile industry at 20,000.[39] Most of the female 'industrial workers' were employed in spinning, weaving, knitting, and working with textiles. In Inishowen, shirt-sewing for factories in Derry was common, while in the south-west knitting was popular and small factories made carpets and other textiles. Alexander Morton who opened a carpet factory in Killybegs in 1898 later established smaller factories in Kilcar, Annagry, and Crolly in the Rosses. At full capacity, the four factories employed more than 600 workers.[40] It is estimated that around 10,000 people in Donegal were employed in shirt-making, which contributed as much as £100,000 to the local economy. Good road and rail connections facilitated a network of outstations in Inishowen and as far afield as Letterkenny, Raphoe and even Ballyshannon. Rates of pay and conditions were a source of criticism, but skilled machinists were in high demand and commanded good wages. Desmond Murphy has shown that household income was 30 per cent higher in Inishowen than in west Donegal, in part because of proximity to Derry and the shirt industry.[41]

By 1912, lace schools were flourishing throughout the county and income from lace making rose substantially until disrupted by the war.[42] West Donegal had a well established cottage industry in knitting which had been promoted by local entrepreneurs. Women were provided with yarn and paid by piece work. Travel writer Lavinia Edna Walter, who visited Donegal around this time, observed that it was common to meet groups of women on the roads carrying bundles of socks that they were delivering to the agent who would pay three halfpence a pair and provide yarn for more of the same.[43] However, payment was sometimes made in kind and any cash received was used to pay off debts to the shopkeepers. A similar cottage industry flourished in the embroidering or sprigging of linen handkerchiefs, blouses and bedspreads. The linen was sent from Belfast and distributed by agents.[44] Weaving was also an important part of the economy of west Donegal. To improve the quality, the CDB employed a travelling weaving instructor, supported the introduction of new handlooms and erected a roofed market house in Ardara for the sale and storage of the rolls of tweed and flannel. Sales at Ardara tweed fair and at nearby Carrick more than doubled in the following years.[45]

The dominance of merchants and shopkeepers in the economy of west Donegal did not go unchallenged. With encouragement from George Russell, who visited the area to preach the gospel of the cooperative movement, Paddy 'the Cope' Gallagher (1870–1964) established the Templecrone Agricultural Cooperative Society in 1906. Gallagher's personal story followed the well-established west Donegal trajectory from the hiring fair to farm work and labouring in Scotland. On his return to Donegal, his first venture was bulk buying of fertilizers for local farmers. The Irish Agricultural Organisation Society (IAOS), established in 1894, had made some progress in establishing cooperative creameries, particularly in south and east Donegal. Bishop O'Donnell was a member of the first committee of the IAOS and both he and Hugh Law MP promoted the movement. By 1905, seventeen cooperative creameries had been established but only ten survived in 1920.[46] With recognition from the IAOS, Gallagher's cooperative grew rapidly, despite opposition from vested interests. It successfully challenged the existing monopoly of merchants and shopkeepers and the dominant position of the 'gombeen man' or local moneylender.[47] In contrast, the labour movement made relatively little progress in the county before 1916 with the exception of the areas closest to Derry.[48] Some trade union branches were established in the main towns and sporadic attempts were made to organize farm labourers in the east of the county without much success.

In common with most western counties, Donegal suffered from emigration. Between 1851 and 1900, total net emigration was 122,566. The rate then fell but between 1901 and 1910 net emigration was 12,559. Contrary to the well-established stereotype of the young male emigrant, female emigration outnumbered male emigration in all but two years in this decade. During the period 1911–20, emigration fell to 7,044, reflecting the disruption of the war. The decline in emigration during the revolutionary decade was less marked than in other parts of the country. This highlights the extent to which Donegal functioned as an integral part of the labour market of Scotland and the industrial midlands of England.[49]

The diaspora in England and Scotland and further afield formed part of the Donegal world. The £300,000 cost of building St Eunan's cathedral, Letterkenny, opened in 1901, was raised largely from that diaspora. An important aspect of Donegal migration was the level of seasonal movement eastwards in the province of Ulster and to Scotland. As well as its contribution to the economy of west Donegal, this migration played a part in many of the political developments in the revolutionary decade. An unexpected consequence of the strong connection between Donegal and Scotland, in particular, was the part played by both nationalist and unionist cross-channel networks in supplying finance and arms to their respective groups.

In all, almost 21,000 children were in receipt of educational instruction in Donegal in 1911, with boys and girls attending school in almost identical numbers. The rate of illiteracy in Donegal was high but declining: 31.1 per cent of 5-year-olds and older were recorded as illiterate in 1891 and 22.6 in 1911.[50] This placed Donegal alongside Galway, Mayo and Waterford as the counties with the highest illiteracy – the national rate was less than half that of Donegal. Unlike primary education, which had been transformed through the introduction of the national school system, secondary education was conducted in private, fee-paying institutions and remained predominantly a middle-class concern. By 1911, almost 41,000 Irish children were attending superior schools (defined as secondary schools that taught a foreign language). In Donegal only 241 children attended such schools. A tiny proportion of Catholic children went to secondary schools in the county: 41 girls attended the convent school in Letterkenny and 87 boys were pupils at St Eunan's in Letterkenny.[51] There were higher numbers of Protestant children in secondary education in part due to the presence of endowed schools in Clonleigh South (Lifford) and Raphoe. Vocational classes by itinerant teachers were initiated in different parts of the county by the Donegal Technical Committee chaired by Bishop O'Donnell. This led to the establishment of the first technical schools in the county in Ballyshannon and Letterkenny in 1914.[52]

The only option for most well-to-do parents, the professional and merchant classes of the towns, and strong tenant farmers was to send their children outside the county for further education. Many Protestant children went to Portora in Enniskillen or Derry, Belfast or Dublin, while their Catholic contemporaries who could afford it were also sent to boarding schools in other parts of the country. Edward Kelly, MP for East Donegal, was a case in point. Born in Ballyshannon in 1883 to a landowning family who had a small brewery in the town, he went to the Vincentian Castleknock College in Dublin for his secondary education. He later attended the Royal University and became a solicitor and barrister.[53]

The gradual emergence of a confident Catholic middle class was a feature of the quarter century before 1912 in Ireland and contributed to social and political change. Some of this is reflected in the census figures for Donegal. In a county that was 79 per cent Roman Catholic, 301 or 80 per cent of the primary teachers were Catholic in 1911. The respective figures for secondary school teachers were 26 (66 per cent), merchants 160 (67 per cent), shopkeepers 336 (85 per cent), commercial travellers 39 (64 per cent). In medicine and the law, Catholics were significantly under-represented. Forty-five per cent of physicians (64), 36 per cent of solicitors and barristers (42) and 41 per cent of civil engineers (17) were Catholic.[54] In all cases, the proportion of Catholics had increased. The rate of movement was related to the availability of secondary and higher education.

The Established Church, land, and control of local government were the tripod on which Protestant ascendancy rested in Donegal. By 1912, all three had been significantly eroded. The Local Government Act (1898) which created new more democratically elected county, borough, urban and rural district councils foreshadowed the emergence of a new, mainly Catholic, nationalist class. In the DCC elections of 1911, 26 of 32 successful candidates were home rulers. Early in 1912, standing orders were suspended to welcome the home rule bill which had not yet been published; it passed with only token opposition.[55] That reflected the political balance in the council since 1899. James Dunlevy, a prominent solicitor from Donegal town, was the long-serving chairman. An active supporter of both the United Irish League (UIL) and Ancient Order of Hibernians (AOH), he was highly regarded on all sides as a fair and able administrator.[56] One of those elected in 1911 was Paddy 'the Cope' Gallagher. Although a member of the UIL, his election followed a stormy campaign and represented a challenge to the dominant conservative nationalist orthodoxy.

Between 1899 and 1912 a *modus vivendi* of sorts was reached between the old order and the new, and there was an unexpected level of practical cooperation on most local matters. As in neighbouring counties such as Fermanagh, relations between nationalists and unionists in local government were relatively good until fractured by the home rule crisis. The retention of boards of guardians alongside new rural district councils (RDCs) charged with responsibility for housing, roads and sanitary services may have been cumbersome, but it did ease the transition. Nationalists were happy to avail of the modest opportunities for patronage provided by the new arrangements. Liberal unionist figures complained about the neglect of local issues and the profligacy with ratepayers' money, while nationalists occasionally railed against the survival of symbolic relics from the old regime.

Local control over law and justice remained elusive, despite a growing number of Catholics being appointed as magistrates. High sheriffs were appointed by His Majesty's lieutenant – in 1912, Captain Henry White of Lough Eske Castle was appointed by the duke of Abercorn who resided at Baronscourt, County Tyrone, and in London.[57] There were four deputy lieutenants, only two of whom were resident in Donegal. Hugh C. Cochrane, the sub-sheriff from Lifford, had responsibility for selecting the grand jury of the county. A motion of protest was unanimously adopted by DCC in 1912 when no Catholics or Presbyterians were appointed.[58] F.S.L. Lyons's description of local government after 1898 as 'a shift to the democracy of farmers, shopkeepers and publicans' echoes the verdict of one of those who lived through the transition.⁵⁹ Looking back on the growing importance of the Catholic middle class, Captain John Hamilton of Brownhall questioned whether there was much point in replacing the aristocracy with a shopocracy.⁶⁰

There were three resident magistrates who theoretically sat alongside lay magistrates at petty sessions but in practice they often sat alone. The county court judge and chairman of the quarter sessions was John F. Cooke KC. Policing in the county was in the hands of the Royal Irish Constabulary (RIC), which was centrally controlled from Dublin by an Inspector General (IG) and locally by a county inspector (CI), based in Letterkenny. A long-standing member of the force, H.B. Morrell, the CI in 1912, was periodically absent due to illness. His monthly reports were detached in tone and complacent. In 1912 there were nine police districts in Donegal, each headed by a district inspector (DI): Ardara, Ballyshannon, Buncrana, Dunfanaghy, Dungloe, Moville, Raphoe, Rathmullan and Letterkenny. Each district contained several sub-districts and there were sixty RIC stations dotted across the county, some very small.⁶¹ Reflecting the relatively peaceable nature of the county, the total number of RIC in Donegal had fallen to 345 by 1913 or one policeman for every 488 residents. This level of policing was higher than most other Ulster counties but well below the south and west of the country which was more heavily policed.⁶² British military camps were located at Finner, near Ballyshannon, and at Derry, and in Omagh, County Tyrone. There were also naval bases at Lough Swilly, coastal forts at Dunree and Lenan Head in Inishowen, and coastguard stations at Killybegs, Rathmullan and Moville.

In 1912 Donegal comprised four single-seat constituencies, North, South, East and West (see map 3). The sitting MPs in 1912 were Philip O'Doherty (1871–1926), J.G. Swift MacNeill (1849–1926), Edward Kelly (1883–1944) and Hugh Law (1872–1943). All four were home rulers with legal backgrounds. Swift MacNeill and Hugh Law were Protestant nationalists, which suggests the necessity for caution in conflating religion and political affiliation. Law converted to Catholicism in 1912. By age and experience, MacNeill was the senior of the quartet but his connections with his constituency were more remote. Kelly and O'Doherty were natives and Law maintained a house in the county. All four were assiduous in contributing to debates in parliament and in asking questions about local issues on behalf of their constituents. Between 1885 (when the constituencies were revised) and 1921, all Donegal parliamentary seats were held by nationalists who were often returned unopposed. Only in East Donegal was there a record of contested elections with keen battles between Unionist and IPP candidates in 1900 and January 1910.⁶³

The two main nationalist political organizations were the UIL and the AOH. Established in 1898, the UIL was essentially the grassroots constituency organization for the IPP. While it sometimes became involved in

Donegal in 1912 11

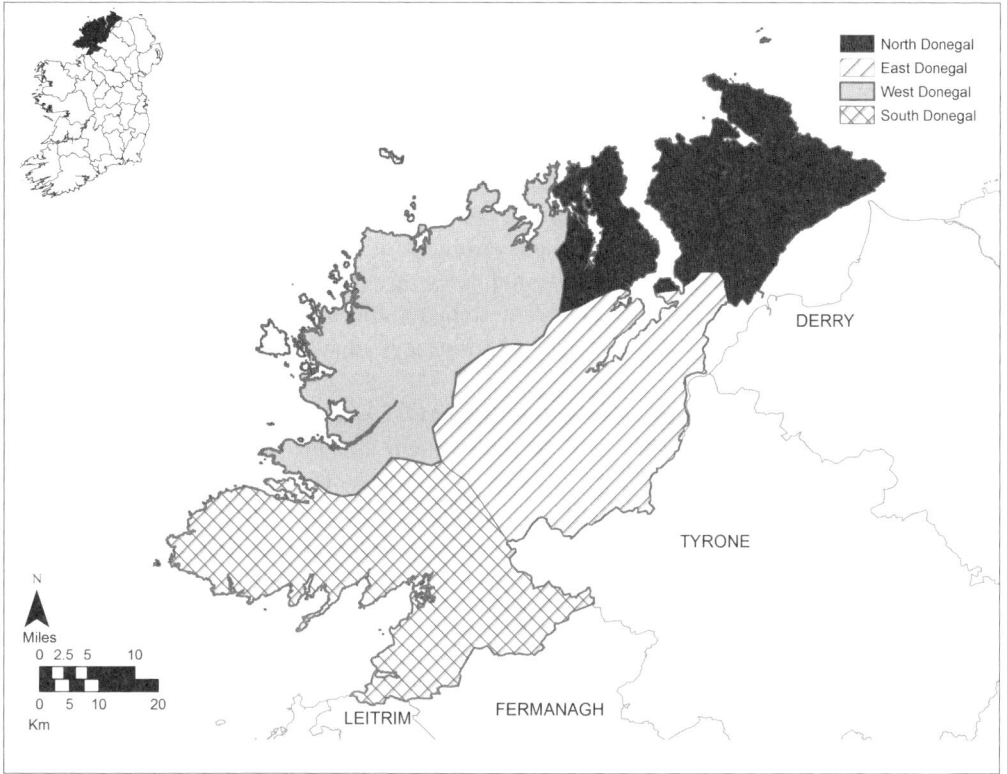

3 Parliamentary constituencies

local agrarian issues, its main function in Donegal by 1912 was to galvanize support at election times and to raise funds. Given the lack of contested elections, electioneering was not onerous. The motto of the UIL was 'the land for the people', a reminder of its agrarian roots, which was sufficient to ensure that it was strongest in areas where congestion and the slow pace of land purchase and distribution was most acute. The UIL was actively supported by Bishop O'Donnell. Aspiring parliamentary and local election candidates required the league's endorsement to have any hope of success.[64] Despite the anticipated introduction of the home rule bill, the RIC reported in early 1912 that the UIL was not particularly active.[65]

That was not the case for the AOH, a fraternal society with roots in Ribbonism and the desire to protect the Catholic peasantry. Membership was confined to Catholics of Irish birth or descent. The AOH was sectarian in the literal sense of being denominationally exclusive. Its motto was 'faith and fatherland'. The Board of Erin wing grew strongly in Ulster in the early twentieth century under the leadership of Joe Devlin, MP for West Belfast.

It complemented the UIL in electioneering.[66] Donegal was a bastion for the AOH (Board of Erin) and had the second-highest membership after Tyrone of any county in Ulster. This may be explained by the benign attitude of Bishop O'Donnell, who had been instrumental in persuading the hierarchy to lift the ban on the AOH in 1904.[67] Several of his priests, including Fr John McCafferty, the administrator of the cathedral, occupied senior positions.[68] Political tensions associated with home rule contributed to the increased popularity of the AOH in Donegal. It was strongest in areas such as east Donegal where cultural identity was contested, serving as a counterweight to the Orange Order. Although there was a considerable overlap in membership between the AOH and the UIL, the Hibernians gradually overtook the league in popularity.[69]

As well as its political dimension, the AOH was a friendly society that supported its members in securing employment and provided sickness and death benefits. From 1911, it experienced a noticeable increase in branches and membership as it cleverly moved to take advantage of the Insurance Act of that year.[70] This resulted in the building of AOH halls in many Donegal towns and villages.[71] Like the Orange Order, it had a penchant for public spectacle with ceremonial banners and other regalia and organized parades led by bands. St Patrick's Day and 'Lady Day' (on the Feast of the Assumption in August) were occasions of public celebration. The home rule demonstration jointly organized by the UIL and the AOH in Letterkenny in January 1912 was attended by twenty-five bands.[72] There was also a small number of branches of the Irish National Foresters in Donegal. Established in 1877 as a breakaway from the AOH, the Foresters supported constitutional nationalism but had little political visibility in the county.

On the unionist side, there were a small number of unionist clubs in 1912 but they had been relatively inactive since the second home rule crisis. A new unionist club was established in Ballyshannon on 7 March 1912 and other towns in east and north Donegal followed suit. The Orange Order had a strong presence, particularly in the south of the county with lodges, halls and bands. In the decade from 1912, there were about seventeen lodges affiliated to the Donegal Grand Lodge with a small number affiliated to the City of Londonderry Grand Orange Lodge. The number of lodges was considerably below that of Cavan and Monaghan.[73] They had been engaged mainly in parading around the twelfth of July but with the advent of the home rule crisis, drilling was added to the repertoire, which attracted recruits in greater numbers. Like the AOH, the Orange Order played a fraternal role and helped reinforce a common sense of identity among its members. Not all Protestants approved of the Orange Order. James Sproule Myles, who later played a leading part in unionist politics, came from a well-known Presbyterian business family in Ballyshannon and although an active Freemason, he did not join the Orange Order.[74]

There was an established tradition of involvement by Protestant women in Ulster in social and political activity and this was revived dramatically with the formation of the Ulster Women's Unionist Council (UWUC) in January 1911. The UWUC quickly became the largest women's organization in Ireland, claiming a membership of over 100,000 by the autumn of 1912. Four branches were established in Donegal. The involvement of prominent members of the Protestant gentry, including the duchess of Abercorn, who was first president, and the marchioness of Londonderry, gave the movement respectability and access to the senior echelons of the anti-home rule movement. The marchioness of Londonderry was a friend and patron of Edward Carson and a friend of Bonar Law. The UWUC operated on a professional basis with a full-time organizer and branches paid an affiliation fee of three guineas to fund its activities. While it was influential and effective, it never managed to transcend its aristocratic and upper middle-class origins.

There was no equivalent nationalist women's political organization in Donegal in 1912: notwithstanding their active role in the cultural nationalist movement, it was not until the emergence of Cumann na mBan after 1916 that nationalist women in the county mobilized in significant numbers. There were some unsuccessful attempts to promote the cause of women's suffrage. Despite the strength of the suffrage movement elsewhere in Ulster, it was conspicuously weaker in Donegal, Cavan and Monaghan. Periodic meetings were held, including one at Donegal town in July 1912, addressed by Margaret Cousins. The Irish Women's Franchise League had embarked on a militant campaign against the exclusion of women's suffrage from the proposed home rule bill. A petition in favour of women's suffrage was circulated in the county and efforts were made to establish branches of the league. However, the unsupportive attitude of the leadership of both the IPP and the Unionist Party, and the hostile attitude of the churches militated against any significant progress.[75]

The press played an important part in the dissemination of political messages and galvanizing support. The tone of the newspapers circulating was reported by the police to be 'distinctly moderate'.[76] There was no local newspaper serving all of Donegal. The *Derry Journal* catered for readers in Donegal as well as Derry, especially those in north and east Donegal. Originally a Protestant newspaper, it increasingly supported constitutional nationalism. J.J. McCarroll, the long-time managing editor, was an ardent supporter of the cultural nationalist movement and opponent of partition.[77] The *Derry People*, established in 1903, incorporated the *Donegal News*. It was nationalist in tone and was strong on the Irish language and Catholic issues. The *Londonderry Sentinel*, established in 1829, was unionist in outlook and served north and east Donegal as well as Derry and parts of Tyrone. Two nationalist newspapers were based in Ballyshannon in the south of the country and had the same publisher. The *Donegal Independent*, edited by Samuel Delmege Trimble, served south Donegal, Leitrim, Sligo and Fermanagh. It was taken over by John MacAdam, the owner/editor of the *Donegal Vindicator*, which claimed to be Donegal's first nationalist newspaper. Born in Scotland, MacAdam established the *Vindicator* during the Land War but took the anti-Parnellite side after the Parnellite split and this won him support from Bishop O'Donnell. He continued to follow O'Donnell's line on politics. MacAdam also established or acquired two other newspapers – the *Derry Weekly News* and the *Tyrone Herald*. Both were nationalist in outlook, becoming more so after 1916. The *Donegal Democrat* was established in 1919 by John Downey and Cecil Stephens: Downey had been a printer with the *Vindicator* but identified a gap in the market for a newspaper with a republican outlook. Both he and Stephens were active supporters of the Gaelic League, the Gaelic Athletic Association (GAA) and the Irish Volunteers.[78] Fermanagh newspapers such as the *Impartial Reporter* (established in 1825 by William Trimble) and the *Fermanagh Herald* also circulated in south Donegal, the former among unionists.

Sinn Féin (SF) and radical nationalism (discussed in chapter 4) had a relatively small presence in Donegal in 1912. The Gaelic League attracted support, initially with the blessing of Bishop O'Donnell. While GAA clubs had begun to appear as part of the growth of cultural nationalism, and hurling and football games were being played sporadically, Conor Curran has argued that the early attempt to create a county structure had limited success and the real upsurge post-dates 1916. The development of Gaelic football was 'a tough, slow struggle'.[79] Surprisingly, hurling initially made more progress but it quickly declined and became mainly confined to a small number of areas. After an initial flurry of activity, the GAA did not become firmly established until after the re-formation of the Donegal County Board in 1919. Soccer was played in some areas, particularly in the north and east, often associated with the presence of the British army or proximity to Derry, and in the west, associated with migration to Scotland; but a sustainable county organization had not yet emerged. Cricket was played in south and east Donegal on a haphazard basis. Rugby had no significant presence – occasional games were played, and teams appeared and disappeared. Sproule Myles, who played the game at school in Derry, toured with an Irish international team to Canada where he broke his leg. He organized both soccer and rugby teams in south Donegal but neither took hold.[80] Athletics enjoyed a period of popularity around this time but lacked an organizational structure. More traditional activities such as regattas were popular in polite society but for the majority in a still largely peasant society, entertainment remained mainly local and self-generated.

All of these social and economic contexts are crucial to understanding the Donegal experience between 1912 and 1923. Donegal was a large, disparate county, the various regions of which were at different stages of development in 1912. This disparity presents a challenge for those who would seek to apply a simple model to explain the upsurge of radical nationalism, whether in terms of modernization or intermediate zones of development.[81] The east and south of the county differed greatly from the west, while the semi-industrial areas of the north, closer to Derry, were different again. History, geography and religion all shaped the Donegal experience (or experiences) of the period 1912–23. Landlessness and poverty undoubtedly fuelled discontent but paradoxically also constrained the progress of radical nationalism. Religion and the spectre of partition loomed large, especially in east Donegal. As an Ulster Protestant, Roger Casement would have been acutely aware of how cultural and religious diversity might determine the responses of local communities to the prospect of political change.

This book examines the emergence of rival paramilitary groups of Irish and Ulster Volunteers in response to home rule, which threatened to spill over into communal conflict. This was averted at least temporarily by the outbreak of the First World War, considered in chapter 2. The radicalization of opinion in the county as a result of 1916 and the victory of Sinn Féin are then examined followed by an assessment of the fundamental shift in allegiances occurring between 1918 and 1921, and the successful military and administrative challenge to the legitimacy of British control locally. The imposition of partition had a deep and abiding impact in Donegal and contributed to the bitterness and intensity of the split in the nationalist movement and the Civil War which are considered in the final chapters.

2 The home rule crisis, 1912–14: promised land or Armageddon?

Both nationalists and unionists viewed home rule in biblical terms. For nationalists, it represented the long desired 'promised land'; for unionists, it threatened Armageddon – an existential threat to the union, their economic well-being and their identity. During the protracted passage of the third home rule bill through parliament between 1912 and 1914, both communities mobilized with intense political and paramilitary activity. The emergence of partition as part of a possible compromise settlement with all or part of Ulster excluded from home rule only added to the agitation. The crisis generated countless meetings throughout the county organized by branches of the UIL, the AOH, the Ulster Unionist Council (UUC) and the local unionist clubs. The diversity of responses to the crisis and the pervasive growth of militarization will be central themes of this chapter.

With the IPP holding the balance of power in parliament and the veto of the House of Lords removed, Herbert Asquith, the prime minister, agreed to legislate for home rule in Ireland. A cabinet committee was established in October 1911 to draft the measure and, following extensive discussion with the nationalist leadership, a bill was introduced on 11 April 1912. This seemed to mark the final chapter in a struggle begun by Donegal man Isaac Butt forty-two years earlier. However, under the Parliament Act (1911) the Lords could still delay legislation, which meant a protracted passage through parliament was guaranteed. The initial focus of attention was on Westminster but as the bill wound its way back and forth between the Commons and Lords over the next two years, the focus shifted to Ireland and particularly to Ulster in a manner that energized large sections of the population of Donegal.

A striking feature of Donegal in this decade was the lack of outstanding political leaders on all sides. An exception was Bishop Patrick O'Donnell who dominated nationalist politics in Donegal until December 1918. On the unionist side, there was no equivalent figure, although Charles Clements, 5th earl of Leitrim, and Charlotte Agnes Boyd of Ballymacool House were prominent. Liberal unionist figures such as James Sproule Myles also became increasingly influential. As an Ulster bishop and an influential adviser of Redmond, O'Donnell was consulted about the various drafts of the home rule bill. He shared the nationalist concern that the initial draft based on the idea of 'home rule all round', that is devolution for the different parts of the United Kingdom, would inevitably lead to delay. The approach was quickly dropped but reappeared temporarily as part of a compromise floated by Lord Loreburn in late 1913 to address the opposition of Ulster unionists when it proved no more palatable to the nationalist leadership.[1] O'Donnell took a keen interest in the educational and religious aspects of the bill and the various proposals to address Protestant fears.[2] He contributed actively to discussions about the financial clauses, favouring the recommendation of the Primrose committee that Ireland be given control over her own revenue and expenditure. In the event, the government opted for a more cautious financial scheme and this was further watered down to meet objections in parliament. O'Donnell was disappointed but pragmatic and, not for the last time, reluctantly accepted Redmond's recommendation for compromise.[3]

The eagerly awaited home rule bill was prematurely celebrated at a 'monster meeting' in the Market Square in Letterkenny in January attended by an estimated 5,000 people and twenty-five bands.[4] Bishop O'Donnell was not present but sent a message of support. On St Patrick's Day 1912, the AOH organized a series of fund-raising meetings for the IPP, including one at Carrick, which was attended by 2,500 people and addressed by Swift MacNeill MP.[5] When the home rule bill was finally published in April, the UIL held a convention in Dublin, attended by 5,000 delegates. O'Donnell sent a message welcoming the measure but indicating ways in which it might be enhanced over time. He expressed the hope that unionists would support home rule but felt that it should go ahead with or without their backing.[6]

With the home rule bill before parliament, it was not in the interests of the IPP to have agitation in Ireland. Under the influence of O'Donnell, a policy was informally adopted in Donegal of avoiding political conflict and potential flashpoints. This approach may have been too effective because during the rest of the year and for much of 1913, the police reported that the UIL seemed 'practically non-existent', except in localities where there was agrarian friction. By contrast, the AOH was increasing in strength by the day and eventually displaced the UIL as the pre-eminent nationalist organization.[7] The quietude of the UIL was replicated in neighbouring Derry and Tyrone.[8] By the middle of 1913, it was estimated that there were 36 branches of the UIL in Donegal. Most had only a nominal existence, whereas the AOH had 72 divisions with a membership estimated at 5,400.[9] A circular from AOH headquarters to all divisions in Ulster prohibited any demonstrations during the month of August and advised members to avoid any acts that might be prejudicial to the home rule bill.[10]

Those opposed to home rule took a different view of the need for agitation inside and outside parliament. In Ulster, anti-home rule meetings were organized. More ominously, there was an increase in drilling. A memorandum prepared at the request of Dublin Castle in February 1912 reported drilling in all Ulster counties except Donegal and Monaghan.[11] A week later, DI John Shankey, deputizing for the county inspector, reported that the people in Donegal were 'a peculiarly quiet, law-abiding community … insurrectionary methods are foreign to their nature, unless convinced that their personal and religious liberty was imperilled'.[12] In March he remained sanguine, reporting that there was little local interest in home rule. For the first time drilling on a small scale was noted to have been carried on in the Orange lodge at Carrigans but the police were not concerned.[13] Notwithstanding this complacency, the early months of 1912 did see a stirring among loyalists. On 7 March a well-attended meeting of unionists in Ballyshannon unanimously adopted a motion proposed by the local Methodist minister to establish a unionist club to defend the legislative union and render assistance to those carrying out this policy. A twenty-member committee was elected with Alfred Stubbs, a local solicitor, as president and James Sproule Myles JP as vice-president.[14]

The home rule bill increased the political temperature in the north-east but, outwardly at least, Donegal remained calm. In Ulster, 26,000 men were reported to have been involved in drilling in April and an estimated 300,000 attended a meeting at Balmoral showgrounds in Belfast. In Donegal, CI Morrell reported that the home rule bill was 'not much talked about', the county was peaceable and, while drilling continued at Carrigans, it was 'in a quiet and unobtrusive way'.[15] More detail of what was happening at Carrigans emerged over time. Some seventy Orangemen attended practice drill on two evenings each week under the instruction of two former soldiers. The drilling took place openly on the public road. Two home rule meetings held in Raphoe, presumably in response, passed off peacefully.[16]

The slow passage of home rule through parliament inevitably caused tension to rise in Ulster and led to disturbances in Belfast during the summer of 1912. The nationalist press in Donegal were exercised about attacks on Catholic workers in the shipyards by 'hooligan gangs of bolt and rivet throwers', while the unionist press were outraged by an attack on a Sunday school outing at Castledawson in Derry by AOH members.[17] The twelfth celebrations led to some disturbances in Stranorlar and Ballybofey when a party of Orangemen returning from a parade in Tyrone were attacked. Another group returning later required police protection when they were stoned but they reached their homes with the aid of the local Catholic clergy. These incidents were isolated and the following month Morrell reported that the friction had passed. He optimistically declared that political and sectarian jealousy were unknown in the county and that there was no recrimination over events in Belfast. In August an AOH-inspired campaign had begun in Donegal and other counties to boycott Belfast unionist firms in retaliation for attacks on Catholics. By September, this campaign was having an impact: lists of firms were circulated to shopkeepers by AOH headquarters, and some firms were reported to have reduced the numbers of commercial travellers they were sending out.[18]

To bring cohesion to the resistance to home rule, 'Ulster Day' was organized for Saturday 28 September when unionists could pledge their implacable opposition to home rule. An oath based loosely on the Scottish Covenants of 1580 and 1638 was drafted by Thomas Sinclair, a Belfast merchant and MP. With its strong biblical overtones, the Ulster Covenant encapsulated Protestant fears about the implications of home rule for their material well-being, their civil and religious liberties, and the unity of the Empire. The oath pledged those who took it to use all necessary means to defeat home rule.[19] The text was approved with a small amendment by the Protestant churches. When the moderator of the Presbyterian Church, Dr Henry Montgomery, endorsed it and urged that ministers make their churches available to the Ulster Day committee, his actions evoked some opposition. The *Donegal News* reported that as many as 200 of 500 ministers demanded a special assembly to reverse the decision. The extent of opposition was overstated, although some Presbyterian churches remained closed on Ulster Day.[20]

The organization of Ulster Day was undertaken by a committee headed by Dawson Bates of the UUC with representatives from the Orange Order and the unionist clubs. To raise public awareness, James Craig, the Unionist MP and leading member of the Orange Order who spearheaded the organization of resistance to home rule, arranged a series of meetings beginning in west Ulster and culminating in Belfast. None of these rallies were held in Donegal but Edward Carson, chairman of the Irish Unionist Parliamentary Party, called on Orangemen from Donegal, Cavan, Monaghan and Sligo to attend the rallies in Enniskillen on 18 September and Derry on 20 September. The turnout was smaller than anticipated. Contingents from Donegal Orange lodges and members of Donegal unionist clubs were grouped together at the meeting. In Derry, where a torchlight procession provoked some disturbances, Carson was joined on the platform by Bishop George Chadwick, himself honorary grand chaplain of the Orange Order, and local MPs.[21]

The Ulster Solemn League and Covenant and the accompanying Women's Declaration were signed on 'Ulster Day', 28 September 1912. The UUC refused to allow women to sign the covenant but, following some negotiation, a shorter Women's Declaration drafted by Thomas Sinclair was agreed. This affirmed the desire of women who signed to associate themselves with the men of Ulster in their uncompromising opposition to home rule. Arrangements locally were organized by Ulster Day committees. A total of 237,368 men signed the covenant and 234,046 women signed the declaration.[22] In Donegal, events were held in more than 100 locations and 17,985 people signed either the covenant or the accompanying declaration, which represented approximately 51 per cent of the Protestant population of the county. It is known that some Donegal people signed in Derry and Enniskillen, which would increase this figure somewhat. Of those over 16 who were eligible to sign, 73 per cent did so. This is higher than Cavan, Tyrone and Fermanagh but lower than Derry and Monaghan.[23] These figures suggest that the anti-home rule campaign was supported by a large majority of Donegal Protestants but points to the existence of a minority who demurred, either because of disinterest or support for home rule. By 1912, the liberal Protestant tradition had declined considerably in the county as in the province, but it had not vanished completely. Undoubtedly, however, the pro- and anti-home rule campaigns polarized opinion.

The stations at which the covenant was signed included churches, Masonic and Orange halls, schools and country houses. The Orange halls used were mainly in south Donegal – Ballintra, Laghey, Donegal and Darney (Dunkineely). Many of the women's declarations were signed in church porches. In Donegal town, a united service was held for Anglicans, Presbyterians and Methodists but no sermon was preached, and the signing took place at the local Orange hall. In west Donegal, where the unionist population was scattered, more private houses were used. At Ballyshannon, 379 people signed the covenant or declaration; at Ballintra Orange hall 644 signed; in nearby Laghey 440. Unsurprisingly, the largest numbers were in east Donegal with a total of 962 signing in Raphoe (485 men and 477 women) and 895 at St Johnston (490 men and 405 women). A total of 1,743 signed in Letterkenny and district (947 men and 796 women). The agents responsible for witnessing and returning the signatures were local clergymen or prominent local figures from unionist clubs or the Orange Order. Nationalists claimed that the number of signatures was exaggerated and that many children signed. A correlation of a random selection of forms returned from Donegal with the 1911 census returns has not produced any evidence to substantiate this claim; nor has it thrown up cases of fictitious names. It is not possible to rule out pressure being exerted or the possibility of people adding the names of their neighbours with or without their knowledge, but this would have required the complicity of the agents. On balance it is reasonable to conclude that the published returns of numbers signing are substantially accurate.[24]

Protestant businesses were encouraged to close for the day and most seem to have done so, despite Saturday being an important shopping day. Many of the shops in towns such as Ballyshannon and Letterkenny were owned by Protestants, even though a majority of the townspeople were Catholics. Closure would not have been without cost. In Donegal town, nationalist critics claimed that many Presbyterian and Methodist merchants stayed away from the ceremonies 'preferring to give attention to their businesses rather than to the Carson comedy' but it is not possible to establish the reliability of this claim or how widespread the practice may have been.[25]

In Donegal unionist women and men signed in roughly similar proportions to their numbers in the population at large. The indefatigable Charlotte Agnes Boyd of Ballymacool House, Letterkenny, who was vice-president of the UWUC, oversaw the organization of the signing of the covenant in her area. She acted as an agent and was responsible for a total of 326 signatories at multiple venues. Mrs Boyd also visited people in their homes to facilitate their signing. The prominence of women did not escape the notice of the nationalist press, which referred disparagingly to 'Ulsterette day'. The pun is doubly ironic as it simultaneously betrays an ambivalence on the part of some nationalists about the contemporary suffragette movement while giving the largely conservative UWUC credit it did not deserve since it was conspicuously reluctant to take any stand on suffrage.[26] One nationalist commentator did concede that the inclusion of women in public meetings at the Ulster Hall and elsewhere had been 'an instinct of genius' but having commented admiringly on the beautiful millinery and gowns, he concluded that he 'wouldn't give them the vote, though'.[27] Ulster Day passed off without incident.[28] Police suggested that nationalists took little interest in the proceedings but this is belied by coverage in the nationalist press. One letter writer to the *Donegal News* denounced the covenant as a sham and Ulster Day as an anti-Catholic farce promoted by 'drillers' and 'goose-steppers'.[29]

The nationalist response to Ulster Day tended to highlight the sectarian overtones in speeches delivered by Ulster leaders. There is evidence that some Protestants in outlying areas of Ulster were uneasy that the belligerent tone might provoke a backlash. Religious ceremonies accompanying the signing of the covenant were less frequent and more muted in Donegal than some other Ulster counties. There were fewer reports of colourful sermons whether because of the isolation of the local Protestant community or political reticence. This is not to say that the Protestant clergy did not stand four-square behind their congregations.[30] The unionist *Daily Mail* canvassed Protestant clergy for their opinions. While the survey was part of an anti-home rule propaganda campaign, the views expressed provide a snapshot of opinion among a group of leaders of the Protestant community. The dominant themes in the responses from Donegal were civil and religious liberty, economic stagnation, and social chaos. Revd William Michael, Presbyterian minister in Trenta, Letterkenny, believed that life would be intolerable in areas where Protestants were in a minority. Bishop Chadwick, without any obvious sense of irony, was concerned at the consequences of rule by 'an alien majority'. W.J. McQuade, canon of St Eunan's cathedral, feared that Ireland would be 'bankrupt financially, ruined commercially, chaotic socially, rebellious politically and riotous religiously'. Nor were such sentiments confined to the Protestant heartlands of east Donegal. Revd G.N. Trinder in Rossnowlagh pessimistically predicted that Protestants would lose their grit and emigrate or suffer absorption while Revd S.H. Orr in Dungloe pleaded that 'all we want is to be left alone and go on as we are doing'.[31]

The Ulster Covenant represented a significant symbolic step in the campaign against home rule while also bringing cohesion to a previously disparate movement. What remained unanswered was how practical effect was to be given to the pledge contained in the covenant. The upsurge in organization on the part of unionist clubs and Orange lodges was difficult to sustain once attention moved back to Westminster. No drilling was reported in Donegal in the months immediately following and there were relatively few incidents. On the night of 25 November there was a clash between unionists and nationalists in St Johnston, but it seems to have been more in the nature of a drunken brawl than a serious affray.[32] Notwithstanding the raised political temperature elsewhere in Ulster, by the end of 1912 Donegal remained relatively stable and CI Morell naively suggested that not much interest was being taken in the home rule bill. Within a matter of weeks, he was forced to record that the first clouds had begun to appear on this bucolic vista.[33]

In January 1913 the UUC approved the establishment of the Ulster Volunteer Force (UVF), comprising 100,000 recruits who had signed the covenant. The new body was to provide both a police and military force for service under a provisional government to be established in the event of home rule becoming law.[34] A military committee agreed a structure based on the existing unionist associations with divisions, regiments and battalions in each county in Ulster. Orange lodges and unionist clubs were instructed to establish district and county committees. Charles Clements, 5th earl of Leitrim, was approached to act as UVF commander in Donegal. Although lord lieutenant of Londonderry, he had a house at Mulroy in Donegal, built by his notorious grand uncle, William Sydney, 3rd earl of Leitrim, who had been assassinated in 1878. Clements advocated active resistance to home rule and his British army service during the Anglo-Boer war made him an obvious choice. He was a more enlightened landlord than his much-hated forebear, but he was involved in a long-running dispute with his tenants (and the CDB) who wished to purchase their holdings in Meevagh, Fanad, Milford, Kilmacrennan and Termon. His conspicuous involvement in the UVF inevitably engendered animosity and conflict.[35]

Parading, drilling and route marching were already well-established elements of social life in Protestant Ulster, including Donegal. Unionist clubs periodically organized drilling as a recreational activity long before the third home rule crisis. In February 1913 Inspector General Sir Neville Chamberlain sought weekly reports on resistance to home rule in Ulster. Commenting on the first of these in March, James Dougherty, the under-secretary, assured his superiors that organization of the UVF had not begun in some counties and had not assumed an established shape anywhere.[36] In May Chamberlain reported that 41,000 men in Ulster had signed a form indicating willingness to join the UVF but that its organization was still far from complete. Ominously, the Orange Order had begun to take a more active role in supporting the UVF.[37]

Activity in Donegal was haphazard, like neighbouring Derry but dissimilar to Tyrone.[38] Reflecting an impatience at the cautiousness of the existing unionist clubs and inspired by the 'forward movement' embarked on by the UUC, a new unionist club was established in Ballindrait in the Raphoe district. Its members immediately commenced drilling, albeit initially without arms.[39] Castlefinn unionist club commenced drilling in March and the following month, a group in Pettigo followed suit. The Castlefinn club was supplied with wooden guns by E.C. Herdman of Sion Mills, a leading member of the UVF in Tyrone, where the UVF was progressing rapidly and the drilling was led by ex-soldiers. By May there were six unionist clubs active, three of which were engaged in drilling. By the end of the year there were twenty unionist clubs in Donegal.[40]

The approach of the Orange marching season in July brought increased apprehension with A.A. Roberts, the newly appointed CI, anticipating 'ebullitions of political feeling' but things passed off quietly. About 3,200 Orangemen paraded at Rossnowlagh and Carrigans without incident. In Castlefinn a Union Jack was removed from the flagstaff of a Presbyterian church, allegedly by two local servant boys. The minister, Revd James Knox, seized on the incident as an illustration of religious and political intolerance.[41] Reflecting on the state of feeling in Donegal as part of a series of special police reports from Ulster, CI Roberts, with a little more perspicacity than his predecessor, identified the lack of prominent leaders as a weakness in the unionist movement locally. He considered that while most Protestants had signed the covenant, only those in east Donegal were likely to resist home rule by force. While Protestant merchants were sympathetic, their business interests made them pragmatic. Roberts suggested that many members of the UVF had no clear idea of what might be expected of them and joined only because they were told to.[42]

Roberts's observations were soon overtaken by events. The leadership vacuum was filled to some extent by Lord Leitrim. While he was 'an active spirit', Leitrim was not regarded as 'a brains-carrier' or, despite his military experience, as a good organizer. His role was that of a figure head – and even this was diminished later in the year when he suffered a severe appendicitis.[43] Hitherto, Leitrim had not been greatly involved in politics, but his new-found militancy soured his relationship with his nationalist neighbours. Drilling regularly took place at his residence in Mulroy and predictably there were periodic attacks on property. Efforts were made to prevent him motoring freely around the county.[44] There were ominous signs of friction more generally between the communities in north and east Donegal where previously friendly relations had been maintained, despite political differences. The AOH was hostile to public displays by the unionist clubs. Tensions increased when rioting broke out following the Apprentice Boys 12th August march in Derry. On

28 August, a crowd of 240 attended a protest meeting in Carndonagh. In Ramelton and other locations, AOH members jeered at unionists who were drilling publicly.[45] At Milford on 25 July, nationalists paraded outside a local hall while inside Lord Leitrim was leading drilling practice. As he departed, the glass on the windscreen of his car was shattered.[46]

A second factor that transformed the situation in the second half of 1913 was the visit of Edward Carson, who undertook a tour of Ulster in July and another in the autumn. He visited Donegal for the first time on 3 October 1913 to galvanize support for the UVF at a meeting in Raphoe. An *Irish Times* special correspondent described Raphoe as 'one of the outposts of Protestants in Ulster'.[47] Accompanied by the duke and duchess of Abercorn, Lord Rosserly and F.E. Smith, Carson travelled by train to Strabane, where he inspected a detachment of Derry members of the UVF on parade. Also in the travelling party were Sir George Richardson, the newly appointed general officer commanding the UVF, and his chief of staff, Colonel Hacket Pain. Their presence emphasized that the purpose of the visit was to promote the UVF. The party proceeded to Raphoe by motor car with a motor cycle corps of members of the UVF acting as a bodyguard. Carson inspected a parade of an estimated 1,500 members of the UVF (so described by the press; the police described them as unionist club members).[48]

At the following meeting, Lord Leitrim pledged undying allegiance to Carson's campaign and insisted that their quarrel was with the government and not with their Roman Catholic fellow countrymen. He claimed that there was no enthusiasm among Catholics in Donegal for home rule. In his speech, Carson invoked the spirit of 1798 when Donegal Protestants had routed the rebels. He stressed that they wished to live on friendly terms with their neighbours, but he did not explain how that might be possible if the armed resistance to home rule, for which they were preparing, proved necessary. As well as promoting the UVF, Carson's visit aimed to reassure Protestants in isolated areas that 'they were not alone'. Donegal unionists were alarmed at speculation of a compromise that would have excluded four or six counties from a home rule settlement and leave Protestants in Donegal high and dry. In a speech at Dungannon, the day before his visit to Donegal, Carson dismissed such speculation; he reaffirmed this position in Raphoe. Friends and comrades were all around them, he said, bound by the same covenant, 'and believe me, these friends and comrades ... will not desert you'. William Moore, MP for North Armagh, stated there would be 'no sacrificing of the outposts'.[49]

Carson's visit contributed to a boost in the number of unionist clubs and a surge in activity by the UVF. A report on the movement prepared shortly afterwards for the government estimated that there were 1,178 members of the UVF in Donegal, largely around Raphoe (890) with 206 in Ramelton and 82 in Letterkenny. Total membership in Ulster was estimated at 56,651. In

November, within weeks of Carson's visit, police estimated the number of UVF in Donegal at 2,000 with significant activity in Ballyshannon where the original club had merged with a new UVF company.[50] Two hundred volunteers took part in drilling on the outskirts of Donegal town. By the beginning of 1914, UVF numbers had risen to 2,755 with units reported in all areas of Donegal, except Moville and Dungloe, and mounted corps established in three places. Parades, manoeuvres, and field skirmishing took place widely. Only a few volunteers carried arms but most were equipped with bandoliers, haversacks and mess tins.[51] Six hundred men paraded at Rossnowlagh on 4 March 1914 under Lord Leitrim and were inspected by Sir George Richardson. The following month they mustered at Baronscourt, County Tyrone, on the estate of the duke of Abercorn.[52]

A report to UVF headquarters in Belfast at the end of 1913 indicated that the regiment had three battalions: the first was based in Ballyshannon district which included Ballintra, Donegal and Inver; the second covered Lord Leitrim's home area of Mulroy and Ramelton, Milford, Manorcunningham, Convoy, Raphoe, Lifford, Stranorlar and Ballybofey; while the third was based around St Johnston, Burt and Muff. By the summer of 1914, the number of battalions had increased to five with the redrawing of the boundaries of the second and third battalions and the creation of a new battalion based in Ramelton and Milford and a fifth in the north-eastern corner of the county adjoining Derry city. The first battalion, commanded by James Sproule Myles, claimed a strength of 818; the second led by Colonel Baillie, 751; the third under W.R. Williamson, 541; the fourth led by J. Allan Osbourne, 575; and the fifth, led by the formidable Major Pine Coffin, 675. Membership of the UVF peaked in July 1914 when the RIC estimated 3,200 members in 34 companies (the UVF's own estimate was 3,360).[53]

Who were the members of the UVF in Donegal? Previous military experience was important for leadership roles and most of the training was led by army reservists. Captain Ambrose Ricardo, formerly of the Royal Inniskilling Fusiliers and whose family had a linen business in Sion Mills, was responsible for much of the training in east Donegal.[54] The majority of the rank and file appear to have come from farming backgrounds, as evidenced by the strength of the organization in east Donegal.[55] Even in south Donegal, where the leading figure was Sproule Myles, the battalion included recruits not only from the towns but also from the agricultural hinterland. For example, the recruits from the villages of Ballintra and Laghy included many from the agricultural areas of Rossnowlagh, Ballinakillew, Moyne and Cully. Recruits came through unionist clubs, which in some cases overlapped with the UVF and from the Orange Order. CI Roberts observed that the Presbyterians were 'evidently very enthusiastic' with both Presbyterians and members of the Church of Ireland strongly represented.[56]

Women who had signed the declaration also became involved in organizing ambulance and first aid classes.⁵⁷ Their services were called on in March when Hackett Pain, UVF chief of staff, suffered a head injury after being thrown off his horse while reviewing an estimated 700 foot and 100 mounted UVF at Newtowncunningham.⁵⁸ Forty-two women were reported to have participated in an ambulance class at Ballindrait in March 1914. Donegal members of the UWUC held preparatory meetings about how to cater for the wounded in the event of conflict. Private houses rather than local hospitals were to be used for casualties and they were confident there would be an adequate supply of nurses.⁵⁹

At Raphoe, Carson promised to inspect the UVF again when he hoped to see a rifle on every man's shoulder. At the time, the RIC believed that in Donegal only a small proportion were armed, mainly gentry and large farmers who had rifles.⁶⁰ However, this was an underestimation. Systematic efforts to procure arms were already well underway. From February 1913 Lord Leitrim's family steamer SS *Ganiamore*, which plied between Glasgow and Milford, was used to import arms and ammunition. Leitrim's chauffeurs, Stephen Bullock and David McIlhenny, were tasked with procuring the arms in Birmingham and elsewhere. On one occasion in July 1913, police intercepted the boat at Portrush, but no arms were found.⁶¹ A variety of inventive routes and ruses were employed: furniture vans that travelled regularly from Glasgow to Derry were used and barrels of carbite for lamps were deployed to hide ammunition. In July 1914 customs officers and police intercepted a consignment of nearly 200 Mauser rifles and ammunition at the Apprentice Boys memorial hall in Derry just before they were to be collected by the UVF. The cargo had arrived in a furniture van. Plans by the UVF to reclaim the consignment from Victoria Street police station were thwarted when the plot was discovered, and arrangements were quickly made to transfer the arms to Dublin by train. UVF members were hastily mobilized in St Johnston to intercept the train, but this last-ditch attempt was abandoned.⁶²

This incident led to increased surveillance. A van bound for Ballybofey which had arrived on another steamer was searched but no arms were discovered. However, a box of hardware among general cargo was found to contain revolvers.⁶³ It seems certain that many more consignments were successfully delivered than were intercepted. Due to the efforts of Leitrim and others, the UVF in Donegal were claimed to be the best armed in the province at one point.⁶⁴ While this suggestion is by its nature difficult to disprove, the work of historian Timothy Bowman would indicate that it is highly unlikely.⁶⁵ In Donegal the police were initially complacent and slow to respond. County inspectors were specifically asked to report on the presence of arms. In January 1914 CI Roberts reported that an 'aiming gun of the modern type' was being passed from unit to unit and used for instruction in musketry. In March he reported that it was difficult to speak with any certainty about the importation of arms, but he believed that there were a great many rifles of various kinds stored in convenient locations in Donegal for use by the UVF. He was also certain that revolvers were largely distributed among members of the UVF.[66]

The so-called Curragh mutiny in March raised serious doubts for nationalists about the willingness and capacity of the government to confront sedition in Ulster. This incident along with the Larne gun-running the following month rang alarm bells and raised the crisis to a new level.[67] On the night of 24–5 April, 25,000 rifles were landed by the UVF at Larne, County Antrim.[68] IG Neville Chamberlain reported that nearly every unionist in Ulster who owned a motor car appeared to have placed it at the disposal of the UVF and by this means, arms and ammunition run into Larne and elsewhere had been distributed to county regiments. It was widely believed that some of these arms and ammunition found their way to Donegal. Nationalists in the Milford area attempted to block the road for a few nights after the landing at Larne in an attempt to wreck the car of Allan Osborne, the local UVF leader, who was believed to be distributing arms to UVF units. When vehicles arriving from Larne were found to be empty, it was surmised by police that the intention was to store arms at centres outside the county for later distribution to local depots such as Ballymacool.[69]

An *Irish Times* correspondent reporting on the sentiment in Ulster early in 1914 commented that it was in the north-west that opinion was most incensed, especially in Donegal and Derry, and predicted that trouble was more likely there than in the north-east. He anticipated 'fierce controversy' if Donegal were excluded from a 'new Ulster'.[70] Updating his colleagues in London in March 1914, the ever optimistic Augustine Birrell ventured that the reality of the threat of civil war was overshadowed by the general conviction among rank and file Volunteers that the occasion would never arise.[71] Others were less sanguine. Clashes had already taken place locally and the fear was that such incidents might set a match to a powder keg.[72] More serious trouble was prevented by the wise counsel of Bishop O'Donnell and the clergy and on the explicit instructions of the Unionist leadership that clashes should be avoided. In some cases, it was only with great difficulty that the clergy managed to restrain their flock from confronting their opponents.[73] After the Curragh episode and the Larne gun-running, O'Donnell became increasingly alarmed and described the situation as the worst for many years. Such was his concern about potential attacks on nationalists and Catholics in east Donegal, Fermanagh, Tyrone and north Monaghan, he suggested that strong detachments of soldiers should be deployed for their protection. However, he admitted that after the events at the Curragh, nationalists had no confidence that the army could be relied on to defend them and accepted that they might need to rely on their own efforts.[74]

The RIC described the response of nationalists in Donegal to the activities of the UVF as 'suppressed resentment'. That changed with the establishment of the Irish Volunteers on 25 November 1913 at a meeting at the Rotunda in Dublin. The initiative was a direct response to an article by Eoin MacNeill in *An Claidheamh Soluis*, the Gaelic League newspaper, calling on nationalists to arm themselves in defence of home rule as the UVF had done. Redmond was initially suspicious about this development, but the enthusiasm of the reaction was such that he could not stand aloof, and he moved belatedly to take control of the provisional committee. It is not surprising that the response to the creation of the Irish Volunteers was enthusiastic. Already there had been calls in Donegal for the AOH to commence drilling.[75] In January it was reported that the AOH in some areas were considering establishing Volunteer units but that the leadership was opposed and initially discouraged members from joining. An Irish Volunteer company was established at Burtonport in mid-January. On 1 February, following a meeting in nearby Dungloe at which Patrick Pearse delivered a fiery speech, it was claimed that a thousand men enrolled. While the police discounted the numbers, there is no doubt the response was enthusiastic.[76] By early March, six companies of Irish Volunteers had been established. Thereafter the movement grew quickly in the county aided by a visit by Colonel Maurice Moore, inspector general of the Irish Volunteers, and Captain Jack White, Ulster organizer. Numbers peaked in August when there were 77 companies and 10,781 members. At the time, the national total stood at approximately 160,000.[77]

The police suggested that the Irish Volunteers were initially drawn from 'the lower stratum' of society but that they gradually attracted support from the clergy and from Catholic magistrates. Those joining were reported to be 'the small class of farmers, labourers, artisans, shop-boys, farmers' servant-boys'. In east Donegal it was reported that farmers and their sons were drilling in unionist halls while their labourers drilled in nationalist halls close by. By May all sections of nationalism were supportive.[78] Although initially cautious, Bishop O'Donnell and the clergy warmed to the new organization and the AOH also become involved. Responding to the pattern of UVF activity, the Irish Volunteers were more active in east Donegal while the organization in the west of the county suffered from the absence of young men who were working as seasonal labourers in Scotland.

The activities of the Irish Volunteers in Donegal closely paralleled those of the UVF with drilling in public and private, route marches and mock battles. One difference is that the Irish Volunteers could mobilize larger numbers and often linked their events to large-scale public gatherings. For instance, there was a large Volunteer parade of 1,000 men in Ballyshannon on 17 March. That evening, there was a clash between nationalists and unionists in Raphoe district in which shots were fired by the UVF.[79] In June when Edward Kelly MP addressed a large meeting of Volunteers at Ballybofey, revolver shots were fired as the meeting concluded.[80]

Given their composition and the fact that they were more recently established, it is not surprising that the Irish Volunteers were less well armed and trained than the UVF. Although more numerous, by the summer of 1914 they still lacked a central organization within the county or a well-developed military structure. The police thought they possessed a small number of shotguns and some revolvers.[81] In a letter widely reported in the local press, Tom Kettle MP suggested that the moral of the Larne gun-running was that steps should immediately be taken by the Irish Volunteers to import arms on a similar scale.[82] Efforts to that end culminated in the landing of arms at Howth and Kilcoole on 26 July and 2 August. In Donegal, arrangements were made to secure arms from Scotland, particularly by Volunteers with Irish Republican Brotherhood (IRB) connections. The Cloghaneely company acquired thirty rifles. These came from James Kearns, a railway superintendent in Letterkenny who used his position to secure arms in Derry, Belfast and Scotland.[83] On 13 July the *Derry Journal* reported that 250 rifles had arrived by car in Derry while the police were preoccupied with Orange parades and had been quickly distributed and sent elsewhere.[84] By July 1914 police estimated that the Irish Volunteers in Donegal had about 500 rifles, probably an underestimate, and that small lots of arms had been sent to Raphoe, Milford and Buncrana.[85]

The emergence of the Irish Volunteers added an element of volatility to an already explosive atmosphere in Donegal. With two armed paramilitary groups in close proximity, the likelihood of serious clashes increased. There were recurring complaints from Protestant traders, particularly in east and south Donegal, that the bad feeling between the two sides was affecting trade.[86] In May there was a lull in UVF activity – nationalists attributed that to the impact of the Irish Volunteers but it may have been due to the fact that many members of the UVF were engaged in agricultural work.[87] In June a serious confrontation was averted when Captain White led a large group of 400 Irish Volunteers from Derry and Inishowen on a route march outside Carrigans, near the home of Captain Leo Moore of the St Johnston UVF. In the belief (he claimed) that a raid for arms was imminent, Moore mobilized his UVF company, many of them armed. The situation was defused when White withdrew his men.[88] By June CI Roberts reported ominously that most people in Donegal expected that civil war would ensue if there was not a peaceful settlement soon. Both sides were preparing for that eventuality.[89]

As the protracted passage of the home rule bill through parliament drew closer to a conclusion, demands for concessions for Ulster unionists were raised publicly and privately. Asquith's strategy was to defer any serious consideration of a concession until the last possible moment. By November 1913, it was clear that exclusion of Ulster, in whole or part, was the price of unionist acquiescence to home rule. Lloyd George initially proposed an approach that dominated discussions thereafter: temporary exclusion of part of Ulster for a fixed period.[90] This scheme was revived in February and serious negotiations began. The plan would have allowed individual Ulster counties to opt out of home rule for a limited period by majority vote in a plebiscite. At the end of the agreed period, the excluded counties would be automatically included, unless the imperial parliament decided otherwise. Bishop O'Donnell was apprehensive about such proposals.[91] He travelled to London to consult with Redmond who met Lloyd George and Birrell on 27 February, and again on 2 March when Asquith was present.[92] Redmond agreed to the scheme on condition that it was accepted by the Unionists and the government would seek no further concessions. Within days, the government sought and received a further concession by extending the term of exclusion from three to six years (which would allow time for two general elections). Details of the plan quickly leaked and it was rejected by the opposition in the House of Commons.

Although these proposals failed, they were acceptable as the price of peace to the nationalist leadership, including, it would appear, O'Donnell.[93] Fears about Catholic education in the four counties likely to be excluded (Antrim, Down, Derry and Armagh) were allayed by the fact they would remain subject to direct rule from Westminster, and there was the added bonus that the city of Derry was thought likely to opt for inclusion.[94] Even so, O'Donnell was fearful of the impact of concessions on the position of the IPP in Ulster.[95] It is against this backdrop that the plans for a mass gathering of nationalists in Derry on 14 March 1914 should be viewed. With rumours about partition rife, Donegal and Ulster nationalists resented the assumption that Ulster was largely unionist and feared that their interests were being ignored. The meeting was planned by Bishop Charles McHugh of Derry, following consultation with O'Donnell, but it was then called off in response to urgent appeals from Redmond who was concerned that it would play into Carson's hands at a delicate moment.[96] Viewed from London or Dublin, the cancellation was prudent; on the ground in Derry or Donegal, where the opposition to partition was growing, its wisdom was less clear. The disaffection of Bishop McHugh with the IPP can be traced back to these events; O'Donnell remained loyal at least for the moment.

On 25 May the passing of the home rule bill for the third time by the House of Commons generated rival demonstrations in Donegal and revolver shots were fired in the air in various locations. Nationalists in Donegal who had remained largely silent celebrated. Ballyshannon Town Commissioners unanimously passed a resolution congratulating Redmond on his triumph over all opposition and his dignified statesmanship in ignoring the threats and the 'hysterical and futile ravings of faction'. The commissioners protested vigorously against the suggestion of exclusion of any part of the province of Ulster, temporary or permanent, and added a ringing declaration that echoed Wolfe Tone: 'Our ideal of nationhood is an Ireland whole, indivisible, embracing all Irishmen of every creed and class in a common brotherhood.'[97]

In June the government introduced an amending bill to allow for temporary exclusion of parts of Ulster, but this was altered in turn by the House of Lords to exclude all of Ulster permanently, so it was allowed to lapse. Instead, the government agreed to a suggestion of King George V to avoid civil war by convening a tripartite conference at Buckingham Palace. At the conference, Redmond proposed 'county option' along the lines previously agreed, while Carson countered with a proposal for a block vote of six counties, an arrangement designed to exclude the majority nationalist counties of Tyrone and Fermanagh. When agreement could not be reached on other options such as poor law unions or parliamentary constituencies, the conference collapsed. The deadlock was only broken by the outbreak of the First World War on 4 August.[98] The amending bill was replaced by a Suspensory Act that postponed home rule for the duration of the war and until special provision was made for Ulster.

Writing to his wife after the collapse of the Buckingham Palace conference, Herbert Samuel, the Liberal MP and cabinet member, remarked that 'the big storm cloud of Europe makes the Irish sky seem by comparison quite bright'.[99] It is doubtful whether the sky over Donegal looked bright, but it is reasonable to assume that after such prolonged tension, there was for some a feeling of relief. However, the burning issues of the day had been temporarily shelved, not resolved. There were some farsighted observers like W.H. O'Connell, RIC deputy IG, who feared that the militarization of a great part of the male population which had occurred over the past two years was bound sooner or later to have profound consequences.[100]

3 'As much Ireland's war as England's'?: the First World War, 1914–18

> 'And ye mean to say that ye liked the Sassenach so much' said old Shan Doherty, looking intently at his son who was home on ten days leave from the trenches. 'It used to be another story at wan time,' said Shan. 'I mind hearing ye say that ye wouldn't be beholdin' to a Black Sassenach for anything.' 'But it's no harm in changing one's mind at times, is it, Shan?' said the woman [his mother]
>
> Patrick MacGill, 'Socks for the Colonel'[1]

The First World War transformed the political situation in Ireland and, despite its apparent remoteness, Donegal was no exception. The characters in Patrick MacGill's short story reflect the ambivalence towards the war of many in Donegal and shifting loyalties. On 27 September 1914 Fr James Cannon PP told a public meeting in Letterkenny that the war was 'as much Ireland's war as England's' and that this was the universal feeling in Ireland.[2] While he may have underestimated anti-war sentiment and the views of those who saw England's war as Ireland's opportunity, he reflected the outlook at that moment of the majority of both nationalists and unionists in Donegal. As the war dragged on, that position gradually changed.

In the summer of 1914, serious conflict over home rule seemed inevitable. The outbreak of war and the passing of home rule with a suspensory act lowered the temperature, at least temporarily. Getting home rule on the statute book was hailed as a significant victory for the IPP. Bishop O'Donnell issued a fulsome public statement to mark the event.[3] This was quickly followed by similar statements from the AOH county board, chaired by Fr Cannon, and a conference of the clergy of Raphoe diocese, presided over by O'Donnell. The latter described the moment as 'a turning point in our history' and so it proved, although not in the way anticipated.[4] As elsewhere in nationalist Ireland, the passing of home rule was marked by county-wide celebrations. Bonfires were lit in Letterkenny and homes were decorated with green flags. Presiding at a gathering of nationalists in Letterkenny, Fr John McCafferty, administrator of St Eunan's cathedral, declared 'the victory won and the sun of Irish freedom lighting on the hills'.[5] In a few places, such as Dunkineely and Killygordon, shots were fired but in the main the celebrations passed without serious incident.[6]

Paradoxically, the outbreak of war brought relative political calm and an almost complete cessation of political strife in the county, at least for the moment.[7] Addressing a meeting of the UWUC in Belfast on 29 September, which included delegates from Donegal, the marchioness of Londonderry declared memorably that the Ulster question was not dead but sleeping. She warned that the time might come more quickly than they expected when they would be called to devote their energies once again to the fight against home rule.[8] A few months earlier, Lady Londonderry had suffered a breakdown brought on by the stress of the situation in Donegal and Derry. She confided to a friend that her husband 'simply took his life in his hands every time he went out'.[9] Donegal nationalists, no less than unionists, were cognizant of the fact that the Ulster question had been deferred not decided.[10]

The challenges posed by the war were quickly highlighted in Donegal by an unexpected event. The battleship HMS *Audacious* was sunk by a German mine in the waters north-east of Tory on 27 October 1914.[11] The *Audacious* was the largest battleship sunk by mines.[12] An attempt by the ocean liner *Olympic*, a sister ship of *Titanic*, to tow the stricken battleship to Lough Swilly failed. The crew were rescued and the final minutes of the *Audacious* were watched by dozens of American passengers on the liner. The *Olympic* was detained in Lough Swilly for several days and its passengers were prohibited from having any contact with shore. Admiral Sir John Jellicoe, who was temporarily based at Lough Swilly, ordered that news of the sinking should be embargoed and it remained so for the duration of the war, even though it was widely known in Donegal and elsewhere.[13]

John Redmond had initially committed that the defence of Ireland could be left to the Volunteers. In a speech at Woodenbridge, County Wicklow, on 20 September, he went further and asserted that it was the duty of the Irish Volunteers 'to go wherever the fighting line extends'.[14] Four days later came the repudiation of Redmond's position by Eoin MacNeill and others, precipitating a split in the Volunteers: the majority (about 169,000) became the Redmondite National Volunteers and the minority of about 11,000 retained the title Irish Volunteers. Bishop O'Donnell was characteristically guarded in his public utterances, but it is not difficult to divine his view. Uncertainty about his position led to a mischievous version of his views that appeared in the *Gaelic American* and other Irish American journals. It was reported that he had broken with the IPP and declared that this was not Ireland's war, that Volunteers should only be used to defend Ireland and that the day was long gone when the Irish could be 'dragged along and tied at the chariot wheel of war-makers'. O'Donnell wired the editor of the New York *Freeman's Journal* that the statement was 'a concoction from beginning to end; not one syllable of it is mine. I work now, as hitherto, with the Irish leaders in their difficult task'.[15]

This affair convinced O'Donnell of the need to make a more detailed public statement. He agreed to write an article in the Volunteer journal, the *National Volunteer*.[16] Ireland, he said, was confronted with the question of what attitude to take to a conflict where the rights of small nations and

Ireland's safety depended on the outcome. He suggested that the achievement of self government mitigated the sense of joining Ireland's oppressor in the war. England was a democratic country, friendly to Ireland and with that democracy Ireland united. O'Donnell did not share Redmond's vision for a home rule Ireland within the British Empire, but he did believe that it should be the aspiration of a free Ireland to join countries such as Australia and Canada to uphold the principles of justice and nationality against aggression and tyranny. While the primary purpose of the Volunteers was the defence of Ireland and home rule, he argued that it was for the political leaders to decide how best they should be used. O'Donnell's position was nuanced and circumspect. He was clearly sympathetic to the war effort and supportive of efforts to alleviate the suffering of Catholic Belgium, but he remained reticent on the question of recruiting. He supported the National Volunteers becoming a nascent national army and accepted that they should serve wherever the fighting line extended, but without enthusiasm. On the war, he was closer to John Dillon, an old college friend, than Redmond and the shift in his attitude to the war over time followed a similar trajectory.[17]

There are no reliable figures on the impact of the Volunteer split in Donegal. The majority, if anything, may have been more decisively in Redmond's favour because of O'Donnell's influence. The bishop allowed his administrator, Fr McCafferty, to sit on the provisional committee of the Volunteers and the Volunteers formed a guard of honour for him when he was officiating at ceremonies in the diocese.[18] The nationalist press in the county unanimously supported the National Volunteers.[19] Shortly after the split, police noted the existence of a small number of Irish Volunteers mainly in the Mountcharles area.[20] By December, the number of National Volunteer companies had fallen by just six and the membership by about a thousand. Many members had stepped back from involvement lest they be conscripted.[21] The debilitating nature of the split from the minority Irish Volunteer perspective is well documented in statements to the Bureau of Military History.[22]

The war posed a dilemma for nationalist politicians in Donegal but they generally followed the leadership of Redmond and O'Donnell, and adopted positions ranging from qualified support to outright enthusiasm. All four IPP MPs for Donegal supported the war but with varying degrees of commitment. Leading members of the UIL and AOH locally fell quietly into line. Aged 31 when war broke out, Edward Kelly, MP for East Donegal, was the youngest of the Donegal MPs and most eligible for military service. He told a meeting at Letterkenny on 27 September that with self government imminent and an Irish army corps shortly to be established, Ireland was in the war just as Australia, Canada and South Africa were. He insisted that it was a matter for each individual to choose whether to enlist and there should be no compulsion, but he left no doubt as to where he thought their duty lay. Kelly's formulation that enlistment was a matter of individual choice, which fell somewhat short of Redmond's exhortation at Woodenbridge, closely echoes a phase used by the *Freeman's Journal* in an editorial the next day which suggests that it may have been an agreed formulation.[23]

Hugh Law, MP for West Donegal, repeated that message the following Sunday at a meeting in Doe when he warned that Ireland's safety was endangered and called on all young men, Protestant and Catholic, to consider enlisting in the army.[24] Law's position became less guarded over time, perhaps because his son Francis, who was in boarding school in England, enlisted.[25] He continued to support recruitment, even after the tide of public opinion had turned on the matter and ultimately split with the IPP on the subject in 1918. Swift MacNeill, MP for South Donegal and a long-time critic of Prussian militarism, wholeheartedly supported the war. But this was voiced more in London than in his constituency.[26] Finally, Philip O'Doherty, MP for North Donegal, called repeatedly during 1914 and 1915 for young men to 'do their duty' but he strongly rejected any compulsion and described as a slur the accusation that young men in Donegal were cowards or were emigrating to avoid enlisting.[27]

Recent estimates suggest that some 210,000 Irishmen served in the British armed forces during the First World War with approximately 152,000 of these enlisting between 1914 and 1918. Between 27,000 and 30,000 are thought to have died.[28] Allowing for the rural nature of the country and the absence of conscription, Keith Jeffery has argued that this compares favourably with enlistment elsewhere in the United Kingdom. Based on the number of males between 15 and 35 in the 1911 census, he calculated that between a quarter and a third of eligible young men enlisted.[29] The question of how many men from Donegal enlisted remains problematic. County estimates conceal as much as they reveal. The military practice of assuming that the recruit was from the place he enlisted bedevils attempts to calculate county figures accurately. For example, those members of the UVF from Tyrone and Fermanagh who enlisted at Finner may inflate the Donegal number while those who enlisted in Derry or Omagh or those National Volunteers who travelled south to enlist are discounted. In the case of Donegal, a county with high emigration, considerable numbers of Donegal-born enlisted in Britain, America and Australia. Some seasonable migrants from west Donegal enlisted in Scotland. Hugh Law estimated that 500 migrants from the Rosses alone enlisted in Scotland.[30]

The rate of recruitment in Donegal was below that of the neighbouring counties of Tyrone, Fermanagh and especially Derry but above that of Leitrim.[31] The *County Donegal book of honour* estimates that almost 8,000 Donegal-born men and women took part in the war and almost 1,200 died.[32]

These figures are inflated by the inclusion of world-wide enlistment among the Irish diaspora. While the figure for fatalities by its nature is firmer, the number of enlistments is difficult to validate. Given the transnational nature of the Donegal world, there is a strong case for the inclusion of at least seasonal migrants and those ordinarily resident in Donegal. Niall Mac Fhionnghaile estimates the number of Donegal-born recruits at 3,000.[33] This level of recruitment is modest but given the rural nature of the county, higher than might have been expected. Recruitment in the main towns such as Letterkenny and Ballyshannon was relatively high, but it was low in rural areas. More recent analysis of the number of those killed suggests a figure of 494 killed in action in Irish regiments or 720 in all British army regiments but this is probably an underestimation.[34] The *Book of honour* gives details of those born in Donegal who were killed in action – these confirm a pattern of stronger enlistment from the main towns and in the east of the county and somewhat less in the west. The list includes 85 fatalities from Letterkenny, 49 from Ballyshannon, 44 from Donegal town, 41 from Raphoe and 37 from Castlefinn.

Along with Derry, Tyrone and Fermanagh, Donegal was part of the recruiting district of the Royal Inniskilling Fusiliers and many local recruits joined that regiment even though it was perceived by many as largely Protestant.[35] The disbandment in the face of local opposition of the Donegal militia unit, as part of the army reforms of 1906–8, undoubtedly hindered recruitment.[36] Other Donegal men joined established Irish regiments such as the Royal Irish Rifles, the Connaught Rangers, the Munster Fusiliers and the Dublin Fusiliers. Recruits also joined three newly created divisions. The 10th (Irish) was created for new Irish recruits on 24 August. Carson persuaded the military authorities to create the 36th (Ulster) Division to facilitate the absorption of the UVF, despite the reservations of Lord Kitchener, secretary of state for war. The 3rd Brigade of the 36th (Ulster) Division which assembled at Finner camp included the Donegal and Fermanagh 11th Royal Inniskilling Fusiliers, among others.[37] Redmond's aspiration to 'put an Irish army into the field' with the creation of an Irish brigade was resisted and watered down. In October 1914 the War Office agreed to designate the 16th Division for recruits from the National Volunteers.[38] During the early months of the war, some hundreds of members of the National and Ulster Volunteers enlisted in these regiments but not in the numbers anticipated.

On 3 September 1914 CI Roberts reported that nationalists were holding back from joining the army because of uncertainty about home rule, while Donegal members of the UVF were fearful of leaving their homes unprotected and those joining up did so with misgivings.[39] The recent history of paramilitary activity was important in the decision to enlist. So too was the presence of important military and naval facilities. Ballyshannon in the south of the county had traditionally been a garrison town and in the mid-1890s a new military camp was established nearby at Finner. Many local men were already serving on the outbreak of the war or were reservists. Finner played a significant role during the war. Along with Omagh, it was the recruitment and initial training centre for Donegal and west Ulster. Both Ballyshannon and Bundoran benefitted economically. As late as March 1916, Ballyshannon Town Commissioners passed a resolution calling on the secretary of state for war to arrange for recruits from the north-west to the 16th Irish Division to be trained locally at Finner.[40]

A similar situation existed in Buncrana, where the extensive naval presence had mixed benefits. Fishing was prohibited for the duration of the war in Lough Swilly and north of Tory but the concentration of military and naval personnel benefitted local shopkeepers and farmers.[41] Control of the sea routes was vital for the war effort and Lough Swilly played an important part in that. It was temporarily the main base of the Grand Fleet while defences at Skapa Flow were being upgraded. When growing losses of merchant ships forced the adoption of the convoy system, many of the escort ships were based at Lough Swilly. Airships from Ballyliffen naval base helped defend the convoys and, late in the war, a US navy flying boat base at Ture on Lough Foyle played a similar role.[42]

Given the scale of the naval presence in Donegal during the war, the failure systematically to promote enlistment in the navy was short-sighted. Many of the ships that participated in the battle of Jutland, the largest naval engagement of the war, on 31 May 1916 were based at Lough Swilly and the casualties included several Donegal seamen. On 25 September 1917 the *Laurentic*, en route from Liverpool to Nova Scotia with a cargo of more than 3,000 gold bars, struck two mines off the north coast of Donegal and sank with the loss of 354 lives.[43] Three months later, HMS *Racoon* struck the rocks off Malin Head following a navigational error in a snowstorm while sailing to Lough Swilly to begin anti-submarine duties. All 104 hands on board were lost.[44] Early in 1915, the National Volunteers at Inishowen formally offered to assist in monitoring the coast for foreign sea and air craft and general patrolling. This was in keeping with Redmond's earlier offer of the Volunteers for home defence, but nothing came of it.[45]

Recruitment in Donegal was poorly organized. It reflected the national trend with a small surge in autumn 1914, followed by a trickle until an active campaign in spring and autumn 1915 produced modest increases. In October 1916, the Registrar General gave the official number of Donegal enlistments as 1,323 with 5,440 men of military age still available which suggests a recruitment rate by that point of approximately 1 in 5.[46] Thereafter, recruitment remained at a low level until the renewed campaign in the late summer of 1918 produced a slight increase.

Initially, it was assumed that public enthusiasm would be sufficient to generate recruits. The influence of the gentry was of limited value in Donegal beyond their own community. Enlistment in the main towns was satisfactory, as was to a lesser extent recruitment among the labouring classes and the gentry but farmers and their sons were accused of holding back.[47] Donegal farmers, like their counterparts elsewhere, were reported to be reluctant to allow their sons to enlist. They were receiving high prices for their produce and were keen to extend tillage. Higher food prices enabled them to pay better wages to their labourers, which acted as a further disincentive to enlistment.[48] The lack of patriotism among farmers remained a constant refrain in the reports on recruitment in Donegal.[49]

In January 1915, J.A.L. Montgomery, the high sheriff, wrote to the local MPs seeking their support.[50] Two months later, he wrote to Carson and others to suggest that a circular signed by the prime minister, Redmond and Carson be sent to every household to encourage enlistment.[51] The formation of the coalition government in May 1915 with Carson a member but not Redmond rendered such an initiative moot. Around the same time, the Central Council for Recruiting in Dublin requested councils to establish local recruiting committees. The response was disappointing, but Letterkenny RDC agreed unanimously that the entire council should constitute the committee and asked for a supply of posters. While the council had a nationalist majority, it was chaired by William Colhoun JP, Presbyterian farmer, county councillor and member of the board of guardians. Although sympathetic, the RDC advised the Recruiting Council that no good would result from the holding of public recruiting meetings.[52] Nonetheless, arrangements for large recruitment meetings proceeded in Donegal in the spring and summer of 1915.[53]

To engender enthusiasm, military bands paraded through the main towns in March and April.[54] In Letterkenny the band of the Irish Guards attended, and rival local bands played the recruiting party through the streets.[55] Greater care was also belatedly taken to present potential recruits with culturally sympathetic role models on the recruiting platform. In May, recruiting meetings at several locations were addressed by Lieutenant Tom Kettle MP and Henry T. Gallagher, Crown solicitor. A prominent nationalist from Strabane, Gallagher was critical of the IPP for not doing enough to promote recruitment.[56] These meetings generated public interest but not many recruits. In the following month, 110 men enlisted, a modest increase given the scale of the campaign. Despite what it termed the 'many discouragements' placed in the way of nationalists interested in joining the army, the *Derry Journal* continued to call on all able-bodied men to enlist.[57] However, meetings in Inishowen did not produce a single recruit. Inevitably, these meetings also attracted opposition in the form of anti-recruitment posters and occasional heckling as at Ballyshannon on 24 April and Kilmacrennan on 23 July.[58]

Occasionally, other disincentives to enlistment could be employed. In Gweedore, a local farmer and Sinn Féiner, Bernard Boyle, was fined 10s. for preventing two men from going to Omagh to enlist. The authorities considered this an altogether insufficient punishment and issued Boyle with an expulsion order under the Defence of the Realm Act (1914).[59]

The Ballyshannon meeting had an unusual sequel when fighting broke out between police and soldiers from Finner camp who were newly enlisted from the UVF. Ten soldiers were subsequently court-martialled. The police insisted that there was no political dimension to the incident and criticized the coverage in the *Donegal Vindicator* for scoring political points. The editor, John MacAdam, was singled out as an exception to the generally moderate tone of the local press. CI Roberts assured his superiors that the *Vindicator* was not influential, but he was ill-informed. The *Vindicator* provided a useful barometer of the shifts in nationalist sentiment during this period. MacAdam was a prominent nationalist and a friend of Bishop O'Donnell without whose goodwill any recruitment drive was likely to founder. He supported the war at the outset and his son enlisted. By the middle of 1915, his position had not changed but the *Vindicator*'s coverage reflected a growing frustration, particularly after the formation of the coalition government. After the 1916 Rising, its position moved still further under the influence of MacAdam's firebrand daughter Eily.[60] The problems caused by the presence of large numbers of UVF at Finner persisted. Following further drunken altercations in Bundoran and Ballyshannon, including verbal abuse of Catholic clergy, the military and police agreed measures to prevent further trouble.[61]

During 1915 conscription emerged as a significant issue because the need to regulate the flow and the type of recruits became more pressing. In Britain, a householder's return was completed in November 1914 and a national register the following year. Compulsory military service was introduced there in January 1916 for unmarried men between the ages of 18 and 41.[62] These developments were followed with some nervousness in Ireland where conscription was seen as likely but was widely opposed.[63] In June 1915 it was reported that young men in the west of the county were emigrating to avoid conscription but as emigration outside the United Kingdom was limited, this seems unlikely.[64] Later in the summer it was reported that 900 migratory labourers had returned from England and Scotland to avoid the operation of the Registration Act, which was seen as a prelude to conscription.[65] With conscription fears being stoked by opponents of the war, resolutions were circulated by nationalists groups for adoption by local councils. Hostility to conscription was widespread, even among Protestant farmers in east Donegal.[66]

Lieutenant Walsh, the county recruiting officer based in Letterkenny, addressed a number of councils late in 1915 and early in 1916. Members of Letterkenny RDC were recorded as being sympathetic, but they were in a minority.⁶⁷ Walsh was quick to point out that if the young men did not respond voluntarily, it would make conscription more likely. The exclusion of Ireland from the Compulsory Military Service Act in January 1916 was widely welcomed, not least by Letterkenny UDC and RDC recruiting committee who agreed that they should re-double their efforts for voluntary recruitment by holding public meetings and engaging in a house-to-house canvas. They also suggested that clergymen of all denominations in the county should call on the young men to do their duty.⁶⁸ Their efforts were to no avail.⁶⁹ The tone of the nationalist press in relation to the war, never particularly enthusiastic, had become distinctly lukewarm.⁷⁰

As casualties mounted, the human cost became even more immediate for some families. There are numerous compelling individual stories of heroism and tragedy. One of the first Donegal fatalities was Private Hugh Boyce from Ramelton on 13 September 1914. He has been working in Clydebank in Glasgow before the war but returned to enlist at Letterkenny in the Inniskilling Fusiliers and was deployed to France as part of the British Expeditionary Force in the early days of the war. Bernard Boyce, a close relative, joined the Cameron Highlanders in Scotland and was killed in July 1917.⁷¹ James Duffy from Gweedore, the only Donegal man to be awarded the Victoria Cross, was also working in the shipyards in Glasgow when the war broke out. He enlisted in the Inniskilling Fusiliers. In December 1917, while working as a stretcher bearer, he repeatedly exposed himself to heavy fire while bringing wounded men to safety. When he returned to Donegal after the war he was met with hostility and in 1921 was kidnapped for a time by the IRA.⁷² Perhaps the most tragic case among the Donegal casualties was that of the Doherty brothers from Letterkenny. Members of the Church of Ireland, the Dohertys were near neighbours of Bishop O'Donnell in Letterkenny. Daniel, James, John and William Doherty enlisted in the Ulster Division: only William survived the war.⁷³

The *Donegal book of honour* includes the names of three Donegal women who died in the war. Sisters Annie and Mary Dickson were members of the Church of Ireland from Fahan. Annie was a fellow of the Royal College of Surgeons and served as a medical officer, while Mary was a nurse with the Voluntary Aid Detachment. The third woman was Margaret Rita Watson, a Presbyterian from Letterkenny who served in motor transport with the Royal Irish Service Corps and died of war wounds in December 1919.⁷⁴ Their inclusion serves as a reminder that women played an active part in a variety of roles in the war, both at the front and at home.

Nursing was seen as 'the female version of military service'.⁷⁵ There are no figures for the number of Donegal women who served as nurses but there are some notable examples. Rosabelle Osborne from Milford became chief matron in charge of twenty-six British military hospitals in Salonika in

1917.[76] Catherine Black from Ramelton served in France and Belgium. When the war broke out in 1914, she was working at the London Hospital where she trained. As a member of the Nursing Reserve, she was assigned to the Cambridge military hospital where she worked on a ward for men with facial injuries along with Harold Gillies, the pioneering plastic surgeon. In the autumn of 1916, she was sent to France and worked in a surgical ward and casualty clearing stations on the Somme. Among the experiences that she describes with great compassion in her autobiography was working on a ward for shell-shocked officers and for soldiers with self-inflicted wounds. Her memoir provides vivid descriptions of the 'unutterable horror' of the war as well as some insight into social conditions in Ramelton. When she returned to Donegal to visit her parents, the War of Independence was at its height, and she found them barricaded in their home. She returned to work in the London Hospital and in 1928 was sent to nurse George V until his death in 1935.[77]

Newspaper coverage of the war was necessarily impersonal, belated and tightly controlled. Letters from the front provided more direct, intimate and sometimes poignant perspectives on individual soldiers and their experience and motivation. The tone of these letters tracks the changing outlook on the war as initial enthusiasm, high principles and optimism gave way to foreboding. John Doherty from Ballyshannon who joined the Medical Corps wrote home from a military hospital in Rouen on 15 December 1914. His letter tells of his first experience under fire and is imbued with a sense of adventure and patriotism, fighting Prussian militarism on the same battlefields as the wild geese. Doherty confidently predicted that they would have driven the Germans out of France before long. Writing from the trenches to his mother, on Christmas Eve 1914, Patrick McDonagh, also from Ballyshannon, echoed Doherty's confidence that the Germans would not last much longer. He had been an instructor in the Volunteers in the Ballyshannon area before the war and had answered Redmond's call to enlist. By Christmas, the novelty of the war had worn off and he asked for prayers for himself and his comrades who were 'suffering terribly to save our country from ruin'.[78] He took comfort from the companionship of friends from home, including Hugh Moan, an employee of the *Donegal Vindicator*, who died at the Somme in 1916 along with McDonagh's older brother, John, who was in the Inniskilling Fusiliers. Patrick McDonagh survived the war.[79]

Increasingly, the letters were laden with tragedy. Revd J. Jackson Wright, Presbyterian minister in Ballyshannon, was chaplain with the 36th Ulster Division and won a Military Cross at the Somme. Many of those who were killed or wounded in that battle were friends and parishioners. Captain James Sproule Myles who had enlisted initially in the Royal Inniskilling Fusiliers and later in the Royal Engineers was wounded on the first day of the battle and won a Military Cross for bravery.[80] An officer in his brigade, Lieutenant John Hamilton, a bank official in Ballyshannon, who assumed command when Myles was wounded, soon went missing himself. It fell to Wright to convey to Hamilton's family confirmation that he had been killed.[81] Not long afterwards, he wrote to another neighbour breaking the news of the death of her husband, Andrew Galbraith.[82]

Patrick McDonagh expressed his appreciation for the role played by chaplains. Redmond's strategy on the war was hampered by setbacks in relation to the use of the Volunteers as a national army but also by issues related to commissions and chaplaincy. A suspicion of institutional prejudice in the War Office and the army generally was widely shared by nationalists and by the Catholic hierarchy. Cardinal Logue confided to O'Donnell that he distrusted the *bona fides* of the government on the war.[83] There were complaints about the small number of Catholic officers and the shortage of chaplains.[84] In August 1914 there were only 17 Catholic chaplains in the British army, one of whom was Irish; by 1918, this had risen to 744.[85] In October 1914 O'Donnell was involved in drafting a strong statement on the matter from the hierarchy which bluntly stated that 'dying Catholics were entitled to the sacraments'.[86] Logue followed this with a public speech demanding the appointment of Catholic chaplains.[87] The cardinal blamed the War Office for delays in appointing chaplains but some of the responsibility lay with the individual dioceses. When, in January 1916, the assistance of the bishops was formally requested, Bishop Denis Kelly documented the numbers of Irish Catholic chaplains: there were 75 secular clergy, one of whom was from the diocese of Raphoe, and 46 regular clergy.[88] An appeal from Logue for diocesan priests to volunteer proved productive, with at least eight Raphoe priests enlisting.[89] One of the Raphoe recruits was William MacNeely from Donegal town who was a teacher at St Eunan's in Letterkenny. He later served as a chaplain in the Irish army and succeeded O'Donnell as bishop of Raphoe.[90]

First-hand accounts of the war from journalists and writers were influential in shaping opinion about the war. The work of Patrick MacGill (1890–1963) was widely circulated in his native Donegal. As a serving soldier, his writings provide insights into the experience and motivation of ordinary soldiers.[91] He had followed the established pattern of labourers from west Donegal who went tatie-hoking and navvying in Scotland. A published poet and novelist, he worked briefly as a journalist before joining the London Irish Rifles in September 1914. The following year he published *The amateur army*, a collection of articles on the life of a soldier from raw recruit to seasoned fighter. No doubt speaking of himself, he explained that the psychological process behind the decision to enlist was complex.[92] He initially considered the war a just cause but his subsequent experiences tempered that view. In *The great push*, published in 1916, he wrote that 'the justice of the cause which endeavours to achieve its object by the murdering and maiming of mankind is apt to be doubted by a man who has come through a bayonet charge'.[93]

Posted to France in the spring of 1915, MacGill's overseas service lasted 256 days. He was wounded on 28 October at the battle of Loos while working as a stretcher bearer. He returned to England and married the novelist, Margaret Gibbons, niece of the Catholic archbishop of Baltimore. The idea of boosting recruitment by engaging the services of writers to chronicle the deeds of Irish soldiers had been initially resisted by the War Office. MacGill's name was mentioned in that regard while he was still at the front.[94] After recuperation, he was transferred to a number of different regiments and eventually, following intervention by John Redmond, to the secretive propaganda branch, M7B, attached to the War Office.[95] He applied for and was provisionally granted a disability pension based on nervous disability and lung damage caused by gas. This was later disallowed following a board hearing, which found no evidence of disease and none of his having been gassed. This may be related to the fact that his gassing was probably a case of 'friendly fire' when British gas was blown back on their own troops. MacGill went on to develop a serious lung ailment and TB.[96]

Extracts from MacGill's *The great push* and *Red horizon* (1916) appeared in the *Derry Journal* and a number of stories such as 'Billet gossip' were specially commissioned. In 'A pair of spectacles' he wrote pointedly of the spirit of comradeship in France between men from Ballymena and Ballinasloe, farmers from the north and midlands, fishermen from the west and cattle dealers from the south. The unlikely hero is the Catholic chaplain who disobeyed orders and followed the men over the top. A wounded son of Ulster declares that 'bar to the church he would follow the *padre* anywhere'.[97] While such stories undoubtedly served a propagandist purpose, they do present a vivid and unglamourous picture of the war. The epigraph to *Red horizon* contains the verse: 'I wish I was back again/ in the glens of Donegal/They'll call me a coward if I return/ but a hero if I fall'.[98]

Bishop O'Donnell's sympathy for the plight of Catholic Belgium was genuine. On 13 October 1914 the Catholic bishops issued a strong statement sympathizing with the people of Belgium, lamenting the destruction of the historic city of Louvain, and calling on each diocese to organize collections to alleviate the suffering.[99] Such collections, stimulated by a letter from Cardinal Mercier, the Belgian primate, were well supported in the dioceses of Raphoe and Derry.[100] The funds collected were largely channelled via Mercier rather than through the government's official war refugees committee. By mid-October 1914, most of Belgium had fallen and thousands of refugees began arriving in England. The task of administering a scheme to support refugees in Ireland was given to the Local Government Board (LGB) led by Sir Henry Robinson.[101]

When the LGB requested DCC to provide accommodation for Belgian refugees, its initial response was unenthusiastic, even though local committees had been established to this end at the prompting of Bishops O'Donnell and McHugh.[102] An offer by Inishowen Board of Guardians to accommodate refugees was declined presumably because of the presence of naval and military facilities nearby.[103]

The first contingent of forty-eight refugees arrived in Letterkenny early in January 1915. They were welcomed by Bishop O'Donnell and housed in local council houses. The group were mainly French and Flemish speakers and included tradespeople and civil servants.[104] Further small groups were sent to Letterkenny in March and September 1915.[105] A Belgian priest was appointed by the dioceses of Raphoe and Derry to tend to their religious needs and two other Belgian priests were based at Glenveagh castle, which Cornelia Adair, the American socialite owner, had allowed to be used for recuperating Belgian soldiers.[106] Charlotte Agnes Boyd arranged for a Belgian nun to teach the refugee children in Letterkenny. The involvement of Mrs Boyd, a prominent unionist, illustrates the extent to which the effort of supporting war refugees was a shared humanitarian enterprise.[107] While fewer Belgian refugees than anticipated were sent to the north-west, Donegal was one of ten counties that took more than fifty of the 1,646 refugees who had arrived in Ireland by March 1915.[108] There was occasional signs of resentment of the favourable treatment of the refugees. When the Treasury refused to sanction a loan for marine works in Donegal, Councillor William Doherty JP complained that some of the population in the west of the county found themselves housed in conditions not greatly better than the refugee Belgians.[109]

On the home front, men but more particularly women mobilized in large numbers on a voluntary basis to make their own contribution whether through knitting socks and mufflers, organizing comfort parcels, supporting the families of enlisted men, nursing the wounded or fund-raising. A leading part was taken by groups of Protestant women in east and north Donegal but as Patrick MacGill's humorous short story, 'Socks for the Colonel', first published in the *Derry Journal* in March 1917 suggests, it was an activity not confined to one community in Donegal.[110] In the story, Doalty Doherty is home on leave and his mother is knitting socks for him. He regales her with stories of the front while she knits socks for his comrades and even his commanding officer. The Irish War Hospital Supply Committee of which Lady Londonderry was president operated under the auspices of the Red Cross and the St John's Ambulance.[111] The committee was active from early in the war in fund-raising and supplying bandages and medicines. The Red Cross had separate committees for Ulster and the rest of Ireland and Donegal fell under the former.[112] The society had a total of fourteen affiliated groups in Donegal.[113] It was seen by some as a predominantly middle-class, Protestant organization and it appears that there was a reticence to support its activities wholeheartedly. In January 1916, when DCC considered a request to support an all-Ireland Red Cross sale for wounded soldiers, it declined on the basis that there had already been several such sales locally.[114]

During 1915 developments in the medical treatment of wounded soldiers brought an unexpected and intimate connection to the realities of the war for Donegal. As the supply of dressings dwindled, sphagnum moss, found in boggy areas, began to be used as an absorbent alternative to cotton wool. The antiseptic qualities of the moss and the savings in the cost of cotton wool contributed to a growing demand that continued for the duration of the war.[115] A plethora of local and national organizations became involved in the collection and preparation of sphagnum. The creation of the Ulster Sphagnum Moss Association in October 1915 with the support of the UWUC gave a considerable boost to the activity Donegal and other northern counties.[116] The two main depots for collection and sorting of sphagnum moss in Ulster were in Belfast and Derry. There were sub-depots at the Rosapenna hotel, where classes were hosted by Lady Leitrim and Ballyshannon, Glenties, Ramelton and Buncrana.[117] Those involved were mainly but not exclusively Protestant women and those with sons or husbands at the front. Collection of the moss required a certain level of dexterity. Girl guides, boy scouts and school children were involved. Cleaning and preparation of dressings, cushions and pads was done at the sub-depots. The dressings were packed in muslin bags, which also needed to be prepared.[118] It is estimated nationally that almost one million dressings were despatched to various theatres of war between 1915 and 1919. There is no record of the number of dressings produced in Donegal but the response in the county was praised by the honorary secretary of the War Hospital Supply Committee and the founder of the Ulster Sphagnum Association.[119]

Suggestions that the relatively generous separation allowances paid to soldiers' wives (12s. 6d. per week in 1915) contributed to drunkenness and licentious behaviour were not confined to the cities.[120] The war gave strong impetus to temperance, which suited the moral climate of the time. The police who viewed the matter from a public order perspective were vigilant on illegal distillation, which was prevalent in Inishowen and west Donegal. They had a strong supporter in Bishop O'Donnell who was a consistent advocate of temperance.[121] There was also a strong Protestant temperance movement active in Donegal and this resulted at times in unlikely inter-denominational alliances. This was evident in 1915 when Lloyd George proposed the introduction of spirit and beer duties to pay for the war effort. Licensing and temperance were difficult issues for the IPP because of the political influence of the drink trade. A campaign began to resist the extension of those taxes to Ireland. Motions to that effect were enthusiastically endorsed by councils in the south of Ireland.

In Donegal there was less unanimity. At Letterkenny Board of Guardians, a motion calling on the four Donegal MPs to join Redmond and Carson in opposing the measures met with unexpected opposition and was only carried by a single vote after a stormy debate.[122]

Alongside the philanthropic effort, the war also brought commercial opportunities for some in Donegal, even among the poorest. Industrial employment was disrupted, and cottage industries suffered initially until they were able to reorient their production to meet the demands of the war.[123] The demand for blankets and other clothing resulted in lucrative contracts for suppliers that had a trickle down effect for craft workers in west Donegal and textile workers in Inishowen. In 1915 women working in relief workshops in Donegal were paid 10*d*. per piece of work plus a meal of bread and tea, at a time when rates in Dublin were a multiple of that. Demand for piecework increased considerably during the war and the most proficient knitters could earn between 30*s*. and £2 per week.[124] In Inishowen the demand for knitwear for soldiers and sailors was seen as a partial compensation for the loss of fishing in Lough Swilly, although the earnings were said to be small compared to the yield from the herring harvest.[125] Increased demand for labour in the textile factories in Derry drew many women from north Donegal. The CDB also encouraged seasonal emigration for harvest work in Scotland and to work in munitions factories, despite concerns about the working conditions.[126]

The disruption of fishing, particularly deep-sea fishing, had a considerable impact on the war economy in Donegal and helped fuel emigration. Approximately 7,000 people were employed in fishing or ancillary activities.[127] Investment in piers was immediately halted. Promised grants from the Treasury of more than £30,000 for the development of the harbours at Burtonport, Rathmullan, Burcrana and Downings were withdrawn, despite protests from DCC.[128] In contrast to fishermen further south, Donegal fishermen did not benefit from the wartime boom because of prohibitions imposed by the Admiralty owing to the presence of the British fleet and German mines and U-boats. Fishing was restricted between Tory Island and Malin head. The five steam drifters owned by the CDB were commandeered for mine-sweeping and patrol duties, and two were lost.[129] In response to the virtual collapse of the fishing industry, Councillor James O'Donnell proposed that support be given to the revival of the kelp making industry in west Donegal and on the offshore islands but investment capital was not forthcoming.[130] On Tory, where there was not previously a tradition of involvement in seasonal migration to Scotland and England for harvesting, men were forced to migrate in search of work.[131]

Recruitment, increased tillage and the collapse of fishing combined to drive an increase in the demand for seasonal labour in east Donegal and mid-Ulster and a rise in the hiring out of child labour at the hiring fairs in

Strabane and elsewhere. Low school enrolment and non-attendance at harvest time were long-standing problems but they were exacerbated by the war. Peadar O'Donnell, then principal of a small school in Aranmore Island and an activist in the Irish National Teachers' Organisation, campaigned for enforcement of compulsory school attendance legislation as a means of addressing a social problem that entrenched poverty.[132] Many children left school as soon as they were old enough for the hiring fairs. The Gweedore and Rosses Teachers' Association compiled and published data in the local press showing that in 1918, 110 children under the age of 10 had been hired out. Average school attendance in the June quarter of that year was not much more than half of the number enrolled.[133]

The number of migratory labourers going to Scotland increased at least until 1916 when it was disrupted by the fear of conscription and other wartime restrictions. Movement was controlled and generally more difficult. An order from the military authorities required passengers from Ireland to embark from one of only six designated ports that did not include Derry, the traditional point of departure for Donegal migratory labourers, or the Sligo–Glasgow route. Labourers had to travel via Belfast, which was more expensive and time-consuming.[134] Nevertheless, seasonal migration persisted largely because of the higher wages available. After conscription was introduced in Britain in 1916, the men often met with a hostile reaction in Scotland. The legal position in relation to Irish migrants was initially unclear but it was eventually confirmed that persons 'ordinarily resident' in Britain were subject to compulsory service. Seasonal workers were thus exempt but not long-term migrants. Some Donegal labourers returned from Scotland following the introduction of conscription. A number of these from south Donegal were arrested under the Military Service Act and returned to Scotland.[135] In September 1916, CI Roberts warned presciently about the potential impact of the presence of a large cohort of unemployed young men who had returned penniless from Scotland with a sense of grievance about their treatment.[136] The immediate outcome was not an upheaval of militancy but an upsurge in Gaelic football and particularly soccer in west Donegal but in the longer term Roberts's concerns about militancy were vindicated.[137]

The war had a mixed impact on agriculture with hardship and plenty cheek-by-jowl: high prices benefitted farmers but not the landless or the town population. East Donegal benefited but the west experienced significant hardship. The demand for labour generated wage inflation later in the war and contributed to unionization. Government compulsory tillage schemes had difficulty keeping pace with the demand for food and supplementary allotment schemes were adopted in towns throughout the county.[138] In 1917 the agricultural committee of DCC agreed to adopt a new tillage scheme but complained about the details and pronounced it a dead letter.[139] Perhaps the largest single impact of the war was the disruption of the work of the CDB, which had begun to improve, if not transform, social and economic life in the poorest parts of the county. That work was left largely incomplete by the time the board was abolished in 1923.[140]

4 'The squabble in Dublin': 1916 and its aftermath

> ... agus bhíothas ag caint corruair, fosta, ar na rudaí a bhí ar na páipéir: an Cogadh Mór a bhí thall sa Fhrainc, agus an iaróg a bhí i mBaile Átha Cliath eadar Éireannaigh agus Sasanaigh.
>
> Seosamh Mac Grianna, *An druma mór*[1]

Literature at its best can encapsulate a moment in history in a manner that eludes the historian. Philip O'Leary suggests there is no better way to understand the chasm between Ireland in 1914 and 1916 than to read Séamus Ó Grianna ('Máire')'s *Castar na daoine ar a chéile*, written in 1914–15, and *Mo dhá Róisín*, published in 1921 but set in 1916.[2] The main protagonists in the former are home rulers who heed the call of king and country. The latter is a patriotic love story in which the hero, Labhrás Mór from the Rosses, and heroine, Róise, from Dublin, join the Easter rebellion. Labhrás and Róise first meet at Coláiste Uladh in Donegal and the novel highlights in passing both the importance of Gaeltacht areas as inspiration for the new nationalism and the mutual misunderstandings between the metropolitan revivalists and local nationalists. Ultimately, Labhrás lays down his life for his second Róisín (Ireland), an act intended by Ó Grianna as a call to arms for Donegal and Irish youth.[3]

Mo dhá Róisín ends with the body of its fallen hero, Labhrás Ó Baoill, being returned for burial to west Donegal. In reality, the only fatality from the Rising returned for burial was 23-year-old Constable Charles McGee. A fisherman and a migrant labourer from Inishbofin Island, he had joined the RIC in November 1912 and was posted to Castlebellingham, County Louth.[4] On the evening of Easter Monday, 24 April 1916, he was taken prisoner along with two fellow policemen and Lieutenant Robert Dunville, an army officer, by a group of Irish Volunteers, including Seán MacEntee who had just returned with dispatches from Dublin. MacEntee described McGee as 'a tall, fine-looking fellow, of rather a tougher spirit than his comrades'.[5] The circumstances in which he was shot are contested. MacEntee and some of the other Irish Volunteers present claimed he was hit by accident when one of their number fired on Dunville who was attempting to draw a weapon. In his later accounts, MacEntee referred only to a single shot being fired but the inquest established that Dunville was struck with a rifle bullet and McGee had four shotgun wounds.[6] It seems certain that the fatal shot was fired by Paddy McHugh who subsequently went on the run under an assumed name and became a bomb-maker in Dublin.[7] MacEntee and three other Volunteers were charged with McGee's murder and sentenced to death but reprieved.[8]

MacEntee, who later became a senior Irish government minister, consistently expressed regret about the death of a fellow countryman and visited the McGee family in Donegal.

The long-term roots of the 1916 rebellion lie in the emergence of the new nationalism that developed in Ireland particularly after the fall of Parnell. More immediately the rebellion was a product of the efforts of the IRB, which seized the opportunity presented by the First World War and the vacuum in conventional politics to organize an uprising. Manifestations of the new nationalism were evident in Donegal during the years before the Rising. Evidence for the activities of a revitalized IRB was, of its nature, less visible but, despite police complacency, it was active behind the scenes.

Of the organizations that constituted the new nationalism, arguably the Gaelic League had the most immediate impact in Donegal. This is hardly surprising given the large number of Irish speakers.[9] The Gaelic League benefitted from the strength of the language revival movement in Ulster that sometimes crossed religious and conventional political boundaries. Branches of the Gaelic League were established throughout the county through the efforts of Seumas Mac Manus, his wife, Anna Johnston ('Ethna Carbery'), Richard Bonner and others, with the support of prominent clergy. MacManus was also a member of the IRB and SF before emigrating to the United States.[10] SF gained some traction in the county after its establishment in 1905 but it then declined. There was one branch recorded in 1910 and only a handful at the outbreak of the war with no discernible organization. The police anticipated that MacManus's return to Donegal in May 1913 would provide a new impetus, but this did not eventuate.[11] Sinn Féin's importance before 1916 was as a name to describe a distinctive outlook more than as a conventional political party. MacManus was also involved in the organization of the GAA and arranged the first meeting of the Donegal County Board.[12]

Ó Grianna's *Mo dhá Róisín* hints at the importance in the development of the new nationalism of Coláiste Uladh, which he attended. The inclusion of Irish as an extra subject in the revised primary school curriculum of 1900 generated a demand for competent teachers. Under the aegis of the Gaelic League, summer schools were established in Gaeltacht areas, including Cloghaneely.[13] Originally named Ardscoil Cholmcille, Coláiste Uladh was established in 1906 by the Ulster branch of the Gaelic League. Initially based in a private house, a purpose-built hall was later added with funding provided by Roger Casement. The college contributed to the economic development of a depressed area and was important in the attempt to revive the Donegal dialect of Irish. It attracted leading figures in the language revival movement as teachers and as students and acted as a meeting place for the exchange of ideas. As such it helped politicize and radicalize local and visiting nationalists. Eithne Coyle, who was from the locality and later became a leading figure in

Cumann na mBan, recalled that the college was an inspiration to those who attended classes there.¹⁴

Joseph Mary Plunkett attended Coláiste Uladh to learn Irish; Alice Milligan, the republican feminist writer and friend of Casement, organized dramatic entertainments there; and Patrick Pearse visited on a number of occasions. His step sister, Emily, was for some years a nurse in Fanad and his family monumental sculpture business designed the pulpit and altar rails for St Eunan's cathedral in Letterkenny.¹⁵ Pearse was also involved as a junior counsel to T.M. Healy KC in the celebrated case of Creeslough farmer and poet, Niall Mac Giolla Bhríghide, who was fined for having his name and address on his cart in Irish. At the appeal in Dublin in May 1905, Pearse pointed out that 12,000 people in Dunfanaghy Union spoke Irish, but the original verdict was upheld.¹⁶ In September 1906 Pearse lectured on bilingualism at Cloghaneely. In returning thanks, Úna Ní Fhaircheallaigh (Agnes O'Farrelly), long-time principal of the college, humorously took Pearse to task for attacking Irish girls for not wearing shawls and home-spuns.¹⁷ Pearse visited the college again in July 1907 and undertook a tour of Irish-speaking areas in west Donegal. Cloghaneely became a hub of radical activity in Donegal and it was not coincidental that the area was later a stronghold of both the Irish Volunteers and Cumann na mBan (Ní Fhaircheallaigh presided at the establishment of Cumann na mBan).¹⁸ Bishop O'Donnell, an early supporter of the Gaelic League, had originally backed the establishment of the college but the relationship soured over time.¹⁹

The home rule crisis of 1912–14 invigorated nationalism in Donegal. The establishment of the Volunteers in response to the emergence of the UVF contributed to greater politicization and militancy. Pearse visited Donegal again in February 1914 as director of organization of the Volunteers and spoke in Dungloe on the invitation of John Boyle, a county councillor, and John Sweeney, a leading Hibernian, both of whom had sons at St Enda's.²⁰ Two months later, Thomas MacDonagh spoke at a meeting in Carndonagh. In September 1914 CI Roberts reported that 'the Sinn Feiners', by which he undoubtedly meant militant nationalists generally, were 'not strong in this county and apart from sporadic anti-recruitment literature and the distributions of newspapers, did not present any cause for concern'.²¹ This is probably an accurate assessment, although the following month he added a rider that they were more effective than their numbers would indicate as 'the young men who wanted an excuse for not joining the army are only too ready to seize on the doctrine of these extremists'.²² In December 1914 the police estimated the number of Irish Volunteers in Donegal opposed to Redmond's policy on the war at about 228 with only a handful of those armed.²³

Donegal like many Irish counties had a small but committed coterie of old Fenians and Fenian sympathizers but the IRB as an organized force was neither strong nor effective. There were a few divisions of the Irish American Alliance faction, which had broken away from the AOH and which took a more radical stance on political issues. One of the most influential of the old guard republicans was former schoolteacher Richard Bonner who had been involved in the GAA and other cultural nationalist movements. Like MacManus, he had emigrated for a time, in his case to Scotland, but died at a relatively young age in January 1912.[24] Poverty and emigration made it difficult to sustain a secret oath bound society but paradoxically emigration helped bolster the republican presence such as it was. The regular movement of migrants to and from Scotland facilitated close contact with large centres in Glasgow where Irish societies flourished. Similarly, emigration to and return migration from the United States established lines of communication and finance that were invaluable to would-be insurrectionists. Daniel Kelly and James McNulty are cases in point.

Kelly was born in Killygordon in east Donegal and grew up in Derry. He was inducted into the IRB at the time of the Anglo-Boer war by Richard Bonner. When he emigrated to Scotland in 1909, he continued his IRB involvement and met leading figures such as Seán Mac Diarmada and Joe McGarrity. Kelly returned to Ireland in 1912 and secured employment on the railways, first in Derry, then in Dungloe and finally in Cashelnagore railway station. He helped establish an Irish Volunteer company at Coláiste Uladh. He was critical of the efforts of the Volunteers to secure arms and proved resourceful in sourcing thirty rifles for the Creeslough battalion commanded by James McNulty.[25] McNulty was born in Feymore, Creeslough, in 1890, the youngest of seven children. In 1909 he joined his brother Patrick in Philadelphia. He became an active member of John Devoy's Clan na Gael, the radical Irish American organization that funded the IRB and was the main financier of the Easter Rebellion. While recovering from typhoid in 1915, McNulty was sent back to Ireland and helped organize the Irish Volunteers in the Creeslough area. He became a captain in the Doe battalion, which was one of the most active in the county. Along with Daniel Kelly, he organized a rally at Doe Castle in February 1916 that Pearse was invited to but was unable to attend.[26]

The emergence of a group of more dynamic IRB leaders, such as Seán Mac Diarmada, Bulmer Hobson and Denis McCullough, contributed to increased activity in Donegal on the part of McNulty, Kelly and others.[27] During the home rule crisis, the IRB tried to use the fear of partition in Ulster to generate support for the Volunteers. Patrick McCartan and Denis McCullough visited Letterkenny early in 1914. McCullough was the Ulster representative on the supreme council of the IRB and became its president the following year. It has been claimed that the appointment of officers to positions in the Volunteers in the county was overseen by the IRB. It is impossible to verify these claims as, by definition, such activity was covert: it is likely that it did occur in some cases but on a small scale given the relatively low IRB membership in Donegal.[28]

Shortly after the outbreak of the war, Mac Diarmada sent Ernest Blythe to Donegal to form new IRB circles.[29] It was considered that it would be impossible to do anything through the Volunteers because of the split. Blythe was provided with names of people who were or used to be active in the IRB.[30] He was discouraged by what he found.[31] There was 'nothing doing' in the northern part of the county. In the west, his contacts were well disposed but pessimistic because they said 'Hibernianism was rampant and practically all the people' supported the IPP. In Gweedore 'the only advice they gave me was to get out by the first train'. That advice was prudent because the police had become aware of his presence and were on his trail. He had better luck in Ballybofey and Stranorlar where he met John Cassidy, a commercial traveller for Singer sewing machines, who was well connected through his work. They succeeded in establishing a few new circles. Similarly, in south Donegal, in Inver, Donegal town and Mountcharles, Blythe met members of moribund IRB circles who agreed to re-engage and seek new recruits. While this does seem to have borne some fruit, helped by visits to the county in 1915 and early 1916 by McCullough, Hobson and others, Blythe's impression that 'nothing would happen in Donegal for some time' was an accurate assessment.[32]

A small number of Irish Volunteers with Donegal connections participated in the Easter Rising, notably Joseph Sweeney, graduate of St Enda's and later TD for Donegal West, and Conor and Eunan McGinley who were students in UCD at the time. They were the exceptions, which is not surprising, given that the Irish Volunteers had not made great progress in Donegal. Joseph Sweeney was born in Burtonport in west Donegal in 1897. His father, Johnny Rua, was a general merchant, a local leader in the Land War, a member of the AOH and a founder of the Irish Volunteers in the area. After some time in St Eunan's in Letterkenny, Joseph was sent as a boarder to St Enda's in Rathfarnham where Pearse was a formative influence. While a student of engineering in UCD, he joined the Volunteers in Donegal but later transferred to Pearse's unit in the Dublin Brigade, which contained many current and former students of St Enda's, including Conor and Eunan McGinley from Belfast and Eamon O'Boyle from Malinmore. The McGinley brothers were the sons of the writer Peadar Toner Mac Fhionnlaoich ('Cú Uladh') from Glenswilly. Sweeney was sworn into the IRB by Pearse himself. During Easter Week 1916, he carried dispatches and fought in Liberty Hall and in the GPO. Following the surrender, he was imprisoned in Stafford Jail and later Frongoch before being released in October 1916.[33]

In the month before the Rising, Thomas J. Regan, the acting RIC CI, reported that there was only one company of Irish Volunteers in Donegal with as few as six members.³⁴ While these figures are unreliable, they do indicate the significant weakness of the radical nationalist movement in the county. A group of Donegal Volunteers did mobilize in Cloghaneely but their efforts were bedevilled by poor communication and confusion. On Easter Sunday, Daniel Kelly and six other Volunteers assembled at Cashelnagor railway station and cycled to Creeslough where they met James McNulty who led a contingent of twenty-six. They proceeded to cut telegraph wires. When they were confronted by police from the local barracks, they ordered them back inside. The Volunteers were relatively well armed with twenty-six rifles and six revolvers. Kelly and McNulty scouted the area for road and railway bridges, which they might destroy. They then awaited orders from Dublin, which never arrived, so they went home.³⁵ Next morning, Kelly and his brother Joe, still with no instructions, started off for Dublin by train. They managed to reach Portadown before being turned back and arrived home on the Tuesday. Kelly remained there unhindered by the police until Saturday, when he was arrested. Brought by train to Derry and from there to Dublin, he saw the smouldering ruins of the GPO when he was marched to Trinity College and then to Richmond Barracks. He was sent to Frongoch where he was nominated by Denis McCullough to head the reorganization of the IRB in Donegal.³⁶

Kelly was one of only two men arrested for actions related to events in Donegal – the other was John Cassidy from Ballybofey who was imprisoned in Stafford.³⁷ Their arrests passed without incident locally. CI Roberts noted complacently that neither Kelly nor Cassidy were natives of the county and that they had learned their SF doctrine elsewhere. However, he did admit that both had been assiduous in trying to spread their revolutionary doctrine and had attracted some followers.³⁸

News of the rebellion was slow to reach the north-west. On 26 April the *Derry Journal* reported rumours of 'happenings of a terrible character' in Dublin. Two locals who had just returned from there furnished 'startling details' of scenes they had witnessed. By Friday, the *Journal* was still lamenting the dearth of news and the disruption of communications that fuelled alarmist stories, but it did carry more detailed reports based on official statements from the military.³⁹ The *Donegal News* voiced similar frustration but suggested that 'great mischief' had undoubtedly been done.⁴⁰

By the following week, the scale and import of what had occurred had become clearer. In a strident editorial entitled: 'Sowers of Tares', the *Derry Journal* echoed the biblical parable to demand that the country be cleansed of 'dangerous weeds'.⁴¹ The *Donegal News* carried detailed accounts of the events of the Rising. Reporting the executions of Pearse, MacDonagh and Clarke, its tone had softened only somewhat. It attributed the rebellion to a 'conglomerate of parties … that we have come to speak of under the common denominator of Sinn Féiners'. It declared that a bitter misfortune had fallen on the land and that Dublin had been 'drowned in blood', but concluded that it demonstrated the folly of those who sought to abandon the wise leadership of the constitutional nationalist movement. John MacAdam, editor of the *Vindicator*, labelled the Rising 'fanatical criminal folly' and its leaders as 'maniacs led by raving lunatics', while in Letterkenny, the *Donegal Independent* concluded that it had 'left the country cold'.[42]

The initial response of public representatives and local authorities in Donegal closely echoed the reaction elsewhere, particularly in neighbouring counties.[43] DCC and several boards of guardians and district councils condemned the Rising.[44] At a meeting of Donegal Board of Guardians on 29 April, the clerk of the union, George Dunnion, suggested a resolution condemning 'the mad policy of a small minority'. The chairman, Patrick Gillespie, attributed the rebellion to Larkinites. A motion was then passed unanimously by the seven members present deploring the outbreak, declaring those responsible not true Irishmen, and expressing confidence in the IPP.[45] At the next meeting, Edward Melly, vice-chairman, protested vigorously against the actions of his colleagues in condemning the Rising and accused them of encouraging the British government to shoot Irish people. He pointed out that they had not demanded the arrest of Carson and his supporters when they threatened civil war.[46] Melly's patriotic zeal proved short-lived. At the following meeting, a letter was read that took issue with the impression given in the press that he supported the events in Dublin. Melly explained that he had never supported SF and that he had made his remarks on the spur of the moment.[47]

It was unusual for boards of guardians to intervene so explicitly in political issues. When the chairman of Letterkenny Board of Guardians suggested in early May that the actions of the 'soreheads' responsible for the events in Dublin should be condemned, the clerk intervened to advise guardians of the wisdom of keeping their names out of the papers. No motion was proposed.[48] At a meeting of Inishowen RDC on 8 May, a resolution was unanimously adopted 'deeply deploring … the actions of the Sinn Féin leaders in causing wanton destruction to life and property in Dublin and elsewhere'. Viewing the rebellion as a threat to the hegemony of the IPP, the resolution insisted that the nationalist population of Inishowen had 'implicit confidence' in Redmond and the IPP.[49] Perhaps the most vociferous initial response to the Rising came from the AOH in Donegal. The resolution adopted by the Ballybofey division of the AOH (Board of Erin) was notable for its alliterative terseness: 'we abhor and detest the reckless rioting of insane insurrectionists and fanatical factionists in Dublin'.[50]

In tone and content, the initial reactions in Donegal followed the lead of the public statements of Redmond and his party and they quickly evolved in a similar manner. On 6 May the *Donegal News* reported that Redmond had told the House of Commons it was right and proper that the rebellion should be dealt with firmly but had urged that the rank and file should not be severely treated.[51] On 8 May the IPP leader warned of 'rapidly increasing bitterness and exasperation in the country' at the continuing executions. Reporting these comments, the *Derry Journal* commended the speedy suppression of the rebellion but decried 'vengeful punishment' and stated that enough blood had been shed in Dublin.[52] Local councils followed suit and protested against martial law and the execution policy.

Thomas Regan initially confirmed that the rebellion had found few sympathizers in Donegal and had been denounced by all classes and creeds. He observed that even the small number of critics of the IPP refrained from exhibiting any enthusiasm for the rebellion. On 11 May the acting CI detected the beginnings of a change with some people expressing pity for the rebels whom they felt were misguided and he correctly predicted that the sentiment might become more widespread.[53] The rapidity of the change in opinion on the Rising can best be illustrated by the *Vindicator* which, as early as 19 May, commented that while 'ninety out of a hundred Irishmen' condemned it initially, 'today ... we are Sinn Féiners to the last man'. The speed of the reversal in the *Vindicator*'s position may have owed something to MacAdam's formidable daughter Eileen (Eily) Dalton MacAdam, who had been a student of Thomas MacDonagh. When she later succeeded her father as editor, the *Vindicator* moved squarely into the republican camp.[54]

On returning from leave, CI Roberts attributed the comparatively quiet state of Donegal to a number of factors, foremost of which was the influence of Bishop O'Donnell and his clergy. O'Donnell had set his face against 'Sinn Féinism' and most of the clergy followed suit. While some younger clergy were sympathetic to the revolutionary movement, they were 'held well in hand'.[55] In the immediate aftermath of the Rising, the bishop in common with most of the hierarchy remained silent. He preached at confirmation ceremonies in Convoy and elsewhere but spoke about temperance and the importance of children learning Irish.[56] At Mass in Letterkenny, the vice-president of St Eunan's College condemned the rebellion in strong terms.[57]

Roberts identified the remoteness of the county and the conservative nature of the people as factors contributing to the absence of trouble in Donegal. He confirmed that there had been a shift in opinion with many who were initially hostile expressing sympathy with the leaders who were shot and condemning the executions.[58] Roberts thought it fortunate that the rebellion had been put down quickly because if it had dragged on others in remote areas might have joined in. However, he did not think there would have been serious trouble in Donegal. Only in Dunkineely did he detect any significant change. There, a large group of Redmondite Volunteers had defected to the Irish Volunteers after the Rising. By July, the police claimed that the rebellion was little spoken of in Donegal, although church gate collections had begun for the dependants of those executed and imprisoned. In the diocese of Raphoe, it appears that Bishop O'Donnell instructed his clergy to 'exercise control and supervision' over the collections to prevent SF using them as a means of extending their influence and to ensure that money collected went for the purposes stated.[59]

O'Donnell joined the growing tide of protest against the government. In June he condemned the executions as 'an act of folly' and again in November, but less directly. He demanded an end to a system of government under which 'a band of high-minded Irishmen, however wrongfully, risk their lives and the lives of many others to overthrow the system, and gladly die amid the red ruin and carnage of a foredoomed enterprise, saying they die for Ireland'.[60] In June a sub-committee of bishops including O'Donnell was appointed to prepare a statement on the Catholic position on the rebellion.[61] O'Donnell was the most experienced member politically and it seems likely that he drafted the statement, copies of which in his notoriously impenetrable handwriting survive among his papers.[62] 'The political situation in Ireland' asserted the well-established Catholic position that rebellion against a constituted authority was illicit unless the people as a whole considered the position intolerable and not amenable to redress through normal channels. It went on to accuse the government of nursing rebellion and denied its right to execute 'rebels of its own manufacture'. The document also expressed the heartbreaking turmoil felt by all Irishmen at the events of that year and asserted that they would not forgot either those who had died at Easter week 'out of devotion to Ireland' or those who shed their blood in Gallipoli and France who also died for Ireland.[63] In the event, the statement was never issued as the bishops decided at their October meeting that the moment had passed and it would not serve any useful purpose. The secretary of the conference, Bishop Denis Kelly, prepared another statement of which O'Donnell would have approved, calling for an end to martial law and for people to rally to the IPP. However, it too was withdrawn when unanimity could not be reached.[64]

The structure of the hierarchy was not well suited to the timely issuing of statements. By mid-summer, new political challenges had emerged. The same newspaper column that reported the condemnation by Ballyshannon Guardians of wholesale executions as 'barbarous' also carried news of the deaths of local men in France and the wounding of Captain Myles, a former member of the local UDC.[65] It is striking that O'Donnell's draft statement refers to the sacrifices of those who died at Gallipoli and in France. Considerably more men from his diocese died on the Somme in 1916 than in Dublin. However, events in Dublin did highlight the question whether home rule could continue to be shelved.⁶⁶ The Rising underlined the precariousness of the situation in Ireland. Political speculation and rumours were rife among nationalist and unionist communities in Ulster to an extent not seen since 1914.

With casualties mounting at the front and the need to woo American support increasing, Prime Minister Asquith instructed Lloyd George to renew efforts to reach a political settlement. While the events that followed have tended to be dismissed by historians, it is clear that Asquith was seriously committed to reaching an agreement.⁶⁷ Inevitably, the public and private discussions focused on partition and quickly reached the questions on which the Buckingham Palace conference had broken down: the area of Ulster to be excluded and for how long. Negotiating separately with Carson and Redmond, Lloyd George produced the outlines of a home rule scheme that was to come into operation immediately but with six counties excluded for the duration of the war. On 9 June Carson persuaded the UUC to agree to further negotiations on this basis and Redmond began to consult his supporters.

Lloyd George had conveyed to Redmond that the exclusion of six counties was likely to be temporary and to Carson that it was likely to be permanent. The prospect of even temporary exclusion of six counties generated alarm among Ulster nationalists, particularly in the west of the province. The nationalist population of Tyrone, Fermanagh and Derry city was 55.4 per cent, 56.2 per cent and 56.2 respectively.⁶⁸ A hastily convened conference of nationalists in Tyrone passed a hostile resolution, which was forwarded to local authorities elsewhere in Ulster. While Donegal nationalists took some reassurance from the confirmation that they would be included in the home rule area, the prospect of being cut off from their natural hinterland through temporary or permanent partition was unpalatable. The potential impact was greater for Donegal than for Monaghan or Cavan: bordered by three of the six counties to be excluded, Donegal would be left isolated. While the police claimed that nationalists and unionists in Donegal were unperturbed, the prospect of partition generated a flurry of activity by local authorities, branches of the UIL, and especially the AOH.⁶⁹ Up to 300 members attended the June meeting of the Annagry AOH division that passed a resolution protesting strongly against the IPP's acquiescence in the exclusion of any part of Ulster.⁷⁰ The fact that the motion was directly critical of the IPP was unusual. Donegal RDC resolved to reject any settlement based on partition. Inishowen Board of Guardians declared that while they were loyal to the IPP, they would resolutely oppose a settlement based on temporary or permanent exclusion. Fr P. O'Doherty, parish priest of Carndonagh, denounced the proposals in the press as a choice between 'exclusion or manacles'.⁷¹ The *Derry People* declared that so numerous and vehement had been the protests against exclusion that it was unnecessary to hold an Ulster-wide convention of nationalists such as had been proposed.[72]

The strongest opposition to what was envisaged came from the Catholic Church in Ulster. The bishops of Derry, Raphoe, Clogher, and Down and Connor all expressed opposition. Bishops McHugh and McKenna rejected exclusion outright. O'Donnell expressed reservations but was nuanced in referring to the existing Amending Act of 1914 as his starting point and calling for a convention of nationalists from the affected areas.[73] When Joe Devlin and Jeremiah MacVeagh, MP for South Down, travelled to the north-west to sound out the bishops on behalf of Redmond, the response was extremely negative. The normally reticent Cardinal Logue ventured that it would be better to remain under English rule for fifty years than to accept Lloyd George's proposals. Logue, who was from Kilmacrennan in Donegal and was a former bishop of Raphoe, abhorred the idea of partition. McHugh denounced the proposals out of hand and refused to entertain any proposal that would lead to the exclusion of more than the four Ulster counties with unionist majorities.[74] Even O'Donnell was unwilling to endorse the proposals. He felt that it would be impossible to defend exclusion of Tyrone, Fermanagh and Derry city without a local plebiscite and that it would destroy the IPP.[75]

Faced with such concerted resistance, Redmond thought it necessary to consult the northern bishops personally and met them on 16 June in preparation for a conference of Ulster nationalists.[76] Logue and his fellow bishops advised on arrangements for the conference.[77] To the annoyance of some, it was held in Devlin's heartland of Belfast where, critics pointed out, few meetings against exclusion had been held. Devlin privately admitted that the proposals were rejected with contempt everywhere outside Belfast.[78] By any standards, the convention held on 23 June was an extraordinary gathering.[79] Redmond made it known that he would resign if the proposals were not supported. After a stormy meeting, all the wily skills of Devlin were needed to secure the passing of the resolution supporting a scheme based on temporary exclusion by 475 votes to 265. The delegates from Tyrone, Fermanagh and Derry city were opposed but their votes were outweighed by those of delegates from the eastern areas – Antrim and Belfast voted 138 to 6 in favour of the proposals, giving rise to accusations of manipulation by Devlin.[80]

The outcome was a considerable triumph for Redmond and especially Devlin. However, it proved a pyrrhic victory. The bishops remained implacably opposed, and discontent in the north-west grew rather than dissipated.[81] Bishop McHugh told the *Derry People* that the bishops from the excluded area were 'absolutely unanimous' in their opposition.[82] His diocese would have been split by exclusion of six counties, with Derry city being cut off from Inishowen and east Donegal. Philip Doherty, MP for North Donegal, had a vote at the Belfast convention as a member of Derry Corporation which he cast against the proposals. A motion was passed at the next meeting of Inishowen Board of Guardians strongly criticizing Redmond and congratulating Doherty on his 'manly action'. While the motion was passed, there was some disagreement with one senior local councillor accusing Doherty of breaching his party pledge.[83] Undeterred, at the next meeting of the IPP in Dublin on 26 June Doherty dissented from a motion welcoming the outcome of the convention.[84] In the west of the county, Glenties RDC passed a resolution opposing the exclusion of six counties by eight votes to two.[85] In July Letterkenny RDC adopted a motion from Cavan RDC expressing concern about the conflicting versions of the terms of the scheme and calling for an all-Ireland conference to be convened. An amendment for the matter to be left in the hands of the IPP was defeated, indicating a loss of faith in the leadership on the question of partition.[86]

Like Redmond, Carson also encountered difficulties in selling the Lloyd George proposals to his followers. Unionists in Donegal, Cavan and Monaghan, the three Ulster counties not excluded from the proposed settlement, were understandably disconcerted. When Carson met the UUC on 6 June to seek their approval, he was faced with resistance and heartfelt appeals from unionists from the three counties who expressed strong hostility. The proposals represented for them a betrayal of the Ulster Covenant and of the assurances given to them in 1912–14 by Carson and others that they would not be abandoned.[87] Carson accepted that their acquiescence was essential for the negotiations to proceed so he offered to meet their representatives separately. The outcome was a reluctant agreement on behalf of unionists in Donegal, Cavan and Monaghan to sacrifice themselves for the benefit of their fellow loyalists in the six excluded counties.[88] In authorizing Carson to continue with the negotiations on 12 June, the UUC pledged that in the event of a settlement being reached, they would use all their influence and power to protect unionists in Donegal, Cavan and Monaghan from injustice and oppression at the hands of an Irish parliament or government.[89]

The matter did not end there. With the detailed negotiations stalled because of opposition from southern unionists and within the Conservative Party, local discontent grew and emboldened attempts to reopen the issue. Major Somerset Saunderson and Travers Blackley from Cavan led a campaign to have the decision reversed on the basis that they had been wrongly told that a settlement was urgently necessary for the conduct of the war. Speaking for unionists in the three counties after the opening of the battle of the Somme, Saunderson complained that they were being 'sold and betrayed' by a gross breach of the pledge under which men had gone to the front.[90] The Cavan delegates met on 13 July and agreed to request an opportunity to revisit the decision but the Monaghan delegates could see no reason to change their decision and reaffirmed their confidence in Carson.[91] The Donegal delegates were also unhappy with the decision and believed it was based on a misconception that the proposals had the formal approval of the cabinet. They communicated their concern in a formal resolution symbolically adopted on 12 July 1916.[92] Carson responded to Saunderson in a letter to the press in which he denied that he had misled the delegates and accused him of a 'tissue of misapprehension'.[93]

Illness prevented Lord Leitrim, perhaps the most influential Donegal unionist, from attending the UUC meeting. He had enlisted in the Royal Inniskilling Fusiliers and was on the sick list recuperating in London.[94] He kept in close contact with Carson and events in Ulster. Disapproving of Saunderson's actions, he unsuccessfully tried to persuade him to meet Carson privately. After some prevarication, Leitrim agreed that the fateful decision of the delegates had been based on a misconception. While exculpating Carson from any blame, he concluded that unionist members from the three counties were bound in conscience to act and vote against the proposals. He suggested that the unionists in the six excluded counties should reconsider whether they had acted in accordance with the covenant and argued that it would be best to end the negotiations altogether. To Carson's retort that if unionists rejected a settlement, he was not confident that he would be able to secure exclusion of even six counties, Leitrim insisted that it was a risk worth taking.[95]

By then the likelihood of a settlement had receded because of a revolt among Tory members of the cabinet.[96] On 18 July, in an attempt to force the issue, Redmond sent a memorandum agreeing to some further concessions and insisting that matters should be finalized.[97] In response, Lloyd George presented him with revised proposals that included two changes insisted on by the cabinet: permanent exclusion of six Ulster counties and elimination of full Irish representation in the House of Commons during the transitionary period. Not unexpectedly, the document was flatly rejected by Redmond and the IPP.[98]

July 1916 marked a critical juncture for both the IPP and unionists in Donegal. The collapse of the negotiations damaged the leadership of Carson and particularly that of Redmond. Donegal nationalists and unionists were left with deep misgivings. For the former, the debacle led for the first time to serious questioning of Redmond's judgement on the issue of partition and contributed to the growth of anti-partitionism as a potent political force. In July meetings of an Anti-Partition League were held in Inishowen which were supported by local clergy.[99] Bishop McHugh emerged as an open critic of the IPP and a supporter of the growing anti-partition movement. In August it was reported that the anti-partition Irish Nation League was making progress, especially in the north of the county. A large AOH rally in Ballybofey was designed in part to stifle the growing popularity of the new organization but its impact was diminished when the military prohibited excursion trains.[100] In

November, in response to an article by Bishop O'Donnell in the *Freeman's Journal*, the *Donegal News* published an unusually virulent attack on O'Donnell, Redmond and the IPP for their willingness to compromise on the partition issue.[101] While O'Donnell remained loyal, his trust in the party was shaken. Stephen Gwynn concluded that the affair finished the IPP and weakened Redmond.[102] It also undermined the political influence of Bishop O'Donnell in Donegal. On the unionist side, already traumatized by the mounting casualties among family and friends at the Somme, the collapse of the negotiations was a relief, but it must have felt more like a stay of execution. The UUC had decided strategically to pin its hopes on a six- rather than nine-county exclusion. The promises of solidarity with their fellow covenanters had proved unreliable and for the first time the principle was conceded of six-county exclusion, with the other three Ulster counties being included within a home rule settlement. In July Edith Wheeler, president of the UWUC, wrote to Lady Londonderry to suggest that every woman and girl in the 'deserted counties' who wished to leave should be assisted in doing so.[103]

When the Lloyd George negotiations failed, Asquith appealed to Redmond to 'keep the negotiating spirit alive' but the IPP leader was dispirited and matters rested there until May 1917 when Lloyd George, by now prime minister, offered Hobson's choice – immediate home rule with exclusion of six counties, subject to review after five years, and a Council of Ireland, or a convention of Irishmen of all parties to produce an agreed scheme for self-government.[104] As Lloyd George was well aware, it was impossible for Redmond to accept the first option; the second was a long shot as substantial agreement between the parties was unlikely, but at least it put matters in Irish hands, and so Redmond accepted.

The Irish Convention, chaired by Horace Plunkett, opened on 6 July at Trinity College Dublin, but did not report until April 1918. It comprised 101 members representing a cross section of national life, including constitutional nationalists, and southern and northern unionists. SF declined to participate. The membership included four representatives of the Catholic hierarchy, including Bishop O'Donnell, as well as James Dunlevy, the chair of DCC.[105] The bishops had been divided on whether to participate but O'Donnell was strongly in favour.[106] He was doubtful about the chances of securing agreement but felt that the Convention could do some good.[107] He strongly supported Plunkett as chair.[108] Plunkett for his part commented in a confidential report to the king that O'Donnell impressed him as being eager to make a success of it.[109] Unlike Dunlevy, O'Donnell proved an assiduous member, attending all fifty-one full sessions of the Convention and voting in forty-seven of the fifty-two divisions.[110] With Redmond suffering from ill-health, he was increasingly identified as the leader of the nationalists.[111] When Redmond asked O'Donnell to act as a spokesman, he replied dutifully that, even though he did not relish the position, his maxim was to refuse no service.¹¹²

O'Donnell had two preoccupations at the Convention: avoiding partition and winning fiscal autonomy. Perhaps as a result, he focused more on the Ulster unionists (and, in turn, they on him) and tended to underestimate the concerns of their southern counterparts. He was convinced that the best way to deal with opposition in Ulster was to agree concessions such as weighted representation within a unitary state. The bishop resisted the idea of a federal solution or a state within a state. He worked hard to keep Ulster exclusion off the agenda as far as possible. Inevitably, there was some verbal sparring with the Ulster unionists, notably when Colonel Wallace, the grand master of the Orange Order, questioned him about Church teaching on mixed marriages. Wallace and his colleagues were reportedly impressed by their first close encounter with an old foe.¹¹³ Plunkett recorded in his diary that the contest between the colonel and the 'cleverest of the Irish bishops' was 'edifying'.¹¹⁴

Plunkett identified the central issue at the Convention as being fiscal autonomy versus fiscal union.¹¹⁵ O'Donnell's forceful contributions on this issue contributed to a split in the nationalist ranks and a public humiliation of Redmond. He had been involved in the discussions on the financial clauses of the third home rule bill. When he presented a draft heads-of-agreement at the Convention, its underlying principle was that financial control should reside with an Irish parliament.¹¹⁶ For O'Donnell, fiscal autonomy was the test of sovereignty in the same way as language was the test of nationhood. Control over customs and excise were central to fiscal autonomy. Despite pleas from Redmond, he tenaciously resisted Lord Midleton's counter proposals that conceded home rule (a significant step for the southern unionists) but watered down financial autonomy. For the first time, O'Donnell disagreed publicly with Redmond who was unable to deliver the unified support of the nationalist members for a compromise: Redmond withdrew, dying two months later.¹¹⁷ In exasperation, Plunkett noted in his diary that the fate of the Convention lay in the hands of the bishop of Raphoe.¹¹⁸

The outcome of the Convention was a series of reports with the majority of nationalists and southern unionists backing a modest measure of home rule. A minority of nationalists, led by O'Donnell and including Dunlevy, demanded fiscal autonomy, while Ulster unionists insisted on exclusion. The minority nationalist report, which was prepared with assistance from Erskine Childers, assistant secretary to the Convention, drew on the model of the self-governing dominions and provided for extensive protections for unionists, within an all-Ireland parliament.¹¹⁹ David Miller asserts that O'Donnell sat in the Convention as a representative of the Church not of the party and that his role was to preserve the interests of the Church, whereas Redmond's was to preserve the constitutional movement.¹²⁰ This is an over-simplification that underestimates O'Donnell's nationalism. O'Donnell has also been criticized for splitting the nationalist ranks and for passing up the opportunity to come to terms with the southern unionists. Lord Midleton described him as 'a wrecker'.[121] However, O'Donnell believed that without an assurance that the Ulster unionists would agree to or be forced to accept an all-Ireland settlement, further concessions on their part would be ruinous for constitutional nationalism.[122] In this he was proved correct. The failure of the Irish Convention opened the way for the victory of Sinn Féin.

5 'All changed': Sinn Féin, 1916–18

> New kindling was thrown on a dull fire and the kindling took flame. Public opinion was moved. The people saw their way clear to something great, and ultimate, the realization of an end, the freedom of their country.
>
> Patrick MacGill, *Maureen*[1]

Patrick MacGill's novel, *Maureen*, published in 1920 and set in Donegal, captures the transformed *zeitgeist* in his native place. In a chapter entitled 'Sein Feiners' (*sic*), the novelist describes a meeting in a cottage in west Donegal. The older members of the group are cautious about the drift of affairs and worried about pensions, but their young folk are impatient. Cornie McKelvey who had been in the British army and, like MacGill, was a victim of gas poisoning, is now an ardent republican. When 17-year-old Fergus Donnel is asked if he is one of those 'Sein Feiners', he replies: 'I am' and 'it's what everybody should be now. All the young men in the parish are Sein Feiners, every one of them'.[2]

If 1916 was the key watershed nationally, it was not until 1918 that its ramifications became clear in the north-west. The year began with the constitutional nationalist movement retaining control at least formally through its local organizations – the UIL and the AOH – and through the overt influence of clerical authorities. It ended with IPP hegemony decisively smashed and the political influence of the bishop of Raphoe significantly diminished. This transformation was hastened by the failure of the Irish Convention and the conscription crisis of the spring and summer of 1918. It was unmistakeably confirmed by the general election in December 1918.

There was nothing inevitable about the rise of SF after the 1916 Rising. With growing public sympathy for the executed leaders and a radicalization of Irish opinion, the emergence of a re-invigorated nationalist movement became likely. However, the shape that movement would take only slowly became clear. The gradual release of internees after the Rising and the national conventions of both SF and the Irish Volunteers in October 1917 were key developments. Éamon de Valera assumed the leadership of both wings of the reorganized movement. Impetus was added by a series of by-election victories, notably de Valera's in Clare in July 1917. By December, SF claimed to have 1,200 branches and 250,000 members nationwide. Police estimates of 1,039 clubs and 66,270 members may be closer to the mark. Commenting in January 1918, IG Joseph Byrne optimistically detected a flagging of enthusiasm and a tendency for 'persons of stake' to hold aloof.[3] The relative weakness of SF in the north was demonstrated by the outcome of the South Armagh by-election on 2 February 1918 when Patrick Donnelly, the IPP candidate, convincingly defeated Patrick McCartan of SF. To address the problem, the leadership in Dublin embarked on a targeted campaign, sending high-profile speakers northwards to generate enthusiasm and organizers to build the movement locally.

In Donegal, there were signs of activity during the late summer of 1917 and in the early autumn, associated with the SF and Volunteer conventions. On 29 July the O'Rahilly SF cumann was founded in Ballyshannon following an after-Mass procession to the GAA grounds. The president of the new cumann, curate Fr Cornelius Tierney, was at pains to emphasize the moderation of SF. While some people had formed the impression that it was 'a wild and revolutionary movement', he said that 'there was nothing revolutionary about it. The movement was constitutional'. He advised the young men and women who were joining it in large numbers to adhere to peaceful and orderly methods. A similar event organized by the Con Colbert SF club in Castlefinn was attended by delegates from across east Donegal. On 16 September the Jim Connolly cumann was inaugurated in Letterkenny with Dr J.P. McGinley as president and 130 members were enrolled.[4]

There were similar developments in the north and west of the county, but the pace of expansion was modest. By September 1917, there were nineteen SF cumainn in the county with a membership of 776.[5] Some of these cumainn were long established but inactive. Initially, the efforts of many clubs were concentrated on concerts and fund-raising events. On 26 December the Connolly cumann in Letterkenny organized a céilí attended by Patrick Pearse's mother and sister.[6] The first reported instance of drilling in south Donegal since 1914 took place in Bundoran.[7] On three evenings from 28 December 1917, members of SF marched in fours and engaged in rudimentary drill under the instruction of Bernard Ryan. While membership was increasing gradually, the RIC considered that it was largely confined to younger people of the 'the less responsible classes' who were attracted by the opportunity to meet and organize dances and social activities.[8] By the end of 1917, the number of cumainn had grown to 34 with a membership of 1,634. This compares with 70 branches of the AOH (Board of Erin) and 47 branches of the UIL with total memberships of 7,956 and 7,738 respectively. In contrast to the UIL and AOH, SF was said to be 'active and progressive'.[9] The number of SF clubs in Donegal was still proportionately among the smallest in the country. According to SF's own figures, the ratio of SF clubs to inhabitants in Donegal was 1 to 4,435.[10]

The burgeoning activity of the advanced nationalist movement in Donegal was evident in a series of meetings held early in 1918. Evident too was the uncertain nature and direction of that movement and the mixed public reaction. When it was announced that Arthur Griffith was to address a meeting in Bundoran, the local UDC was divided on whether to present him with an address of welcome.[11] In the event, illness prevented Griffith from attending. According to sympathetic local newspapers, more than 2,000 people from south Donegal, Fermanagh, Leitrim and north Sligo were present at the meeting on Sunday 13 January – local police estimated the attendance at less than half that number. By far the largest nationalist demonstration seen in south Donegal for some years, the meeting was chaired by H.J. Kelly and addressed *inter alia* by Seán Milroy, a veteran of the Rising, Alderman Walter Cole, one of the founders of SF, and J.N. Dolan, brother of the first SF MP. Milroy and Cole had arrived by train from Dublin the previous evening and were met by Tullaghan fife and drum band, which led a torchlight procession in the midst of a snowstorm. Next day the town was bedecked with SF banners and another procession was led by a group of women identified as the Tullaghan Ladies' SF club, carrying a large tricolour.[12] The meeting could hardly have been more colourful with the presence of bands and contingents of supporters from four counties. The platform party included clergy from surrounding districts. The strongest speech on the day was delivered by the chairman who declared that the soul of the nation had been rescued by the men of 1916. Seán Milroy's remarks encapsulated the ambiguity that surrounded the post-1916 SF movement. Echoing developments on the Western Front, he declared that SF was commencing a spring offensive in the west in preparation for routing the enemy at the polling booths.

The meeting attracted close attention from the RIC but passed off without disturbance. However, when members of the Ballyshannon pipe band were returning home afterwards, they were attacked by soldiers from Finner Camp. Stones were thrown, a drum was seized, and an unsuccessful attempt was made to seize a tricolour. In the mêlée, some soldiers and band members were injured, including a 16-year-old boy, John Teevan, who died later from his injuries. Among the Ballyshannon contingent were Margaret Kane and her 10-year-old daughter Mary who subsequently played an active role in Cumann na mBan.[13] The RIC report on the incident implicitly acknowledged that the soldiers had initiated the affray but claimed that the Sinn Féiners had fired revolver shots. In the days that followed, individual soldiers were attacked on their way to and from Finner in retaliation. As a precaution, the military authorities declared Ballyshannon and Bundoran out of bounds for soldiers to a mixed response from local traders.[14]

The Bundoran meeting was quickly followed by a tour of the north-west by de Valera, senior surviving leader of the Rising and newly elected president of both SF and the Irish Volunteers. He was accompanied by Seán MacEntee and Fionán Lynch. In a whirlwind tour between 7 and 18 February, meetings were held at Letterkenny, Milford, Carndonagh,

Creeslough, Gortahork, Dungloe, Glenties, Castlefinn, Raphoe, Ballybofey, Killybegs, Kilcar, Donegal, Ardara and Ballyshannon.[15] Police estimates of numbers attending varied from 200 at Milford in the east to 1,000 at Ardara and 1,800 at Glenties. The public meeting at the Market Square in Letterkenny was attended by contingents from all over north and east Donegal. De Valera's reception was considerably warmer in the west of the county than in the east but even in the latter, the crowds were impressive.[16]

At Raphoe, a UVF hotbed, the SF leader encountered at close quarters some of the complexities of allegiance that were part and parcel of life in Donegal. In anticipation of trouble, Irish Volunteers were summoned from Letterkenny to lend support. Under the command of James McMonagle, who carried an old Queen Anne rifle with a fixed bayonet, and armed with hurleys and improvised weapons, including bill hooks from a nearby hardware shop, the Volunteers attempted to march through the town, only to be confronted by police, soldiers home on leave and others who objected to their presence. After a stand-off, the meeting proceeded but was interrupted by intermittent heckling in which de Valera seems to have given as good as he got. His speech opened in conciliatory mode, looking forward to the time when Irishmen were not divided by sectarianism but became more strident with an attack on Orangeism and an ominous declaration: 'France was bled white', he is reported to have said, 'and please God England will soon be bled white too'. In nearby Castlefinn, later the same day, he suggested that England's critical position offered the Volunteers an opportunity to rid Ireland of English tyranny. Next day, at Ballybofey, he urged his audience to refuse to obey English laws and thereby render government impossible. This would be achieved by 'a national army of Volunteers, drilled and armed in such a manner as to be able to strike for Irish freedom when the opportunity comes, and as far as I can see, it may come very soon'.[17] In Donegal town, de Valera was met at the railway station by three bands and some 800 Volunteers, a majority carrying hurleys. In Ballyshannon, the culmination of the tour, there was a torchlight parade that included Volunteers from south Donegal, Fermanagh and Leitrim. Acknowledging the relative weakness of SF in Ulster, de Valera explained that it was because they had not yet preached its doctrine there.[18]

De Valera's visit to the north-west was a response to the weakness of the movement there and it undoubtedly succeeded in boosting radical nationalist activity. While the numbers attending the meetings were relatively large, the police felt that some attended out of curiosity rather than political commitment. De Valera's speeches were judged to be 'of the usual type' advocating independence, but CI John Hughes, who succeeded Roberts in January 1917, wondered if they would persuade 'thinking people'. IG Joseph Byrne was less sanguine and blamed such speeches addressed to 'half-educated shop assistants and excitable young rustics' for the generally turbulent demeanour of the Irish Volunteers.[19] Meetings and parades continued after de Valera's departure, culminating in a SF county meeting at Ballybofey attended by some 1,800 people according to police estimates. Contingents attended from the surrounding parts of the county and from Strabane and Killeter in Tyrone. Séamus Dawson marched a group of Volunteers from Letterkenny for the meeting for which he was later sentenced to three months in Derry Jail. The main speaker was Eoin MacNeill. Smaller parades were held elsewhere in the county, including Gortahork and Annagry.[20]

Patrick C. O'Mahony, who had accompanied de Valera on his tour, was appointed full-time SF organizer in December 1917. He worked initially in Waterford and Armagh. His immediate task was to establish branches of SF in preparation for the anticipated general election. The unit of organization was the parish cumann, which was subject to a comhairle ceanntar and a county executive.[21] By the end of March, Donegal had surpassed Cavan as the Ulster county with the largest SF membership and it retained that position thereafter. Between December 1917 and December 1918, SF membership in Donegal increased from 1,634 in thirty-four clubs to 5,491 in fifty-four.[22] O'Mahony was also tasked with assisting in the reorganization of the Volunteers and in the establishment of Cumann na mBan. Volunteers were organized in parish companies, later part of a battalion and a brigade structure. Fionán Lynch was also active in the organization of the Volunteers, as was Ernie O'Malley who arrived in the county during the general election campaign and remained for six months.[23] Though not especially accurate, police reports put Volunteer membership at 277 in five companies at the end of 1918.

Although companies of Irish Volunteers had existed in several places in Donegal since 1914, they were largely disorganized, poorly trained and leaderless. From autumn 1917 they began to be revived. In some cases this was on local initiative and in others it was prompted by Volunteer headquarters.[24] There were also numerous companies of National Volunteers notionally still in existence but they were inactive, despite attempts by Colonel Maurice Moore to reinvigorate that organization nationally.[25] Many of those who attended Moore's National Volunteer convention in August 1917 were reported to have favoured joining the Irish Volunteers and there is evidence of that occurring on a small scale in Donegal. In Letterkenny, for example, James McMonagle and some of his friends who had originally been National Volunteers helped to organize a company of Irish Volunteers. Police feared that such men would bring their arms with them. In June 1917 they estimated that there were 426 rifles in the possession of the National Volunteers in Donegal and attempts were made to seize them lest they fall into the wrong hands. In the case of McMonagle and Letterkenny, they need not have worried – the rifles possessed by the National Volunteers in that area were obsolete Italian rifles for which no suitable ammunition could be found.[26]

By December, the police were still aware of the existence of only one company of Irish Volunteers, but they had difficulty distinguishing between SF and the Volunteers. In February the IG conceded that police figures countrywide for membership of the Irish Volunteers were probably too low and that at least a percentage of SF clubs should be considered branches of the Volunteers.[27] In May he repeated that because the Volunteers were managed secretly, it was difficult to ascertain authentic numbers but advised that it should be assumed that most members of SF of military age also belonged to the Volunteers.[28] To compound an already confusing picture, in Donegal, as elsewhere, there were cases of rivalry between SF and the Irish Volunteers and a preference on the part of some local groups to call themselves SF Volunteers. It was a challenge for organizers like O'Mahony to overcome such rivalries and create a more cohesive nationalist movement. Progress in that direction was notable during the spring and summer of 1918. The establishment of a second company was noted by police in February 1918, another in March and a fourth in April with the establishment or re-establishment of companies in Letterkenny, Ardara, Donegal and Ballyshannon. Such was the progress that the first brigade area was established in Ballyshannon and officers were elected. To promote cohesion between Volunteer companies throughout the county, large military-style gatherings were organized in Ballyshannon, Bundoran, Letterkenny and Ardara.

O'Mahony's last meeting in Donegal took place in early March at Ballintra, an area with a sizeable unionist population. There was no trouble; it was even claimed that the local Orange band participated in the torchlight procession. While O'Mahony was addressing the meeting, he received news of John Redmond's death. He led the meeting in prayers and called for a minute's silence for 'a great Irishman'. He was then ordered to Waterford to assist in SF preparations for the by-election contest for Redmond's vacant seat.[29] O'Mahony was arrested in Waterford and returned to Donegal town for trial alongside James (Séamus) Dawson from Letterkenny, P.J. Brennan from Ardara, and Bernard ('Bunny') Ryan from Bundoran on charges of drilling and unlawful assembly. They refused to recognize the court as officers of the Irish Republic and declined to give bail for good behaviour. They were sentenced to three months' imprisonment. All sang the 'Soldier's Song' and threatened to begin a hunger strike if they were not treated as political prisoners. A large SF meeting was held in Donegal town to coincide with the court hearings, and it was reported that local Cumann na mBan members had purchased bandages and related medical items in anticipation of trouble. One hundred troops from the Inniskilling Regiment and seventy extra police were drafted into the town. However, the protest passed off peacefully.[30]

A number of branches of Cumann na mBan were established in Donegal in late 1917 without attracting police notice. Eithne Coyle was one of the earliest members of the organization in Donegal. She formed a branch with some friends in Falcarragh in late 1917 but it quickly fell through. Like many in west Donegal, Coyle's nationalism was shaped by a radical agrarian tradition born of poverty and hardship. Early in 1918 she set up a branch in Cloghaneely. The twenty or so women and girls who joined initially busied themselves with first aid classes and collecting funds but then became closely involved in the organization of the anti-conscription campaign in the locality. Bernard O'Donnell, captain of the local Volunteers whom Coyle later married, gave them some rudimentary military training and the branch continued to work closely with the Volunteers.[31] Alice Mary Cashel, a founding member of Cumann na mBan in Cork, was dispatched to promote the organization in early 1918. She toured the county, setting up branches as she went. Branches were established in Letterkenny in February and at Ballyshannon in March.[32] It was not until March 1918 that the police began to record Cumann na mBan numbers in the county: by the end of that month it was reckoned that the number had risen to eleven branches with 313 members.[33] Apart from Letterkenny and Gortahork, all the branches were reported to be in the south and west of the county. By the end of 1918 there were an estimated 411 members in fourteen branches.[34]

While the turning of the tide towards radical nationalism was now detectable in Donegal, the shape and nature of the movement remained uncertain. Some local voices within the UIL and especially the AOH argued for a reinvigorated constitutional movement to fight partition. As well as the growth of SF, the Irish Volunteers and Cumann na mBan, the Gaelic League remained strong and there was growing labour unrest in the north and east of the county. While the cultural nationalist cleric, Fr Cornelius Tierney, could assert in Ballyshannon that 'there was nothing revolutionary about it', de Valera's message in the same location some months later was characteristically more ambiguous: if they could win independence without physical force they should do so. It would depend on 'which method was likely to promise most success and entail the least sacrifice'.[35]

In April, when the seriousness of the Ludendorff offensive on the Western Front became known, the war cabinet hastily decided to extend conscription to Ireland. The decision had a dramatic impact in Donegal as elsewhere. The press censor reported that 'apprehension and indignation spread like wildfire'.[36] The IPP temporarily withdrew from parliament and joined a united national resistance movement in Ireland, which emerged under the aegis of the Mansion House Conference with the blessing of the Catholic bishops. The hierarchy denounced the Compulsory Military Service Act as 'an oppressive and inhuman law which the Irish people have a right to resist by all the means that are consonant with the law of God'.[37] Bishop O'Donnell described conscription as a 'galvanic shock' and 'a gross oppression' which they were bound in conscience to resist.[38] John MacAdam, editor of the *Donegal Vindicator*, colourfully predicted, 'you might as well conscript a flock of swallows or commandeer a cloud of midges on a summer day'.[39]

The conscription crisis could not have come at a worse time for the IPP. Its new leader, John Dillon, had hoped to revitalize the constitutional movement by pursuing a more radical policy. The run of SF by-election victories (South Longford in May 1917 and East Clare in July) had been halted by IPP successes in South Armagh in February, Waterford in March, and East Tyrone in April, which boosted morale. The party's inability to defeat conscription in the House of Commons seemed to demonstrate the impotency of parliamentary methods and highlighted the IPP's record on the war. Dillon bitterly complained that Lloyd George had 'let loose HELL in Ireland' and that the immediate effect was to resurrect SF.[40]

As an active supporter of recruitment, Hugh Law MP had long been conflicted on the question of conscription.[41] Unlike some of his colleagues, his opposition was based not on principle but on practicality. He supported recruitment but was convinced that conscription was impractical without general consent and would result in 'the most appalling tragedy'. He was certain there would be 'an active and desperate resistance'.[42] Law refused to join that resistance and opposed the IPP's cooperation with SF in the anti-conscription campaign, a conscientious position that did nothing for his future political prospects as MP for West Donegal.[43]

The role of the clergy was crucial in the creation of a united nationalist front to resist conscription. The bishops took a leading role because they feared that otherwise disorder and chaos would ensue. When de Valera told them the Volunteers would resist conscription by force no matter what they decided, the bishops endorsed an ambiguous pledge to resist its imposition by 'the most effective means at their disposal'. They took comfort from their conviction that physical resistance would not be practical.[44] Cardinal Logue, in particular, was suspicious of SF and insisted that 'they were pledged to do nothing in the way of violence such as shooting'.[45] Not all their clergy would have agreed: the administrator of Bishop O'Donnell's cathedral in Letterkenny, Fr John McCafferty, urged his congregation to resort to passive resistance only when every revolver was empty.[46] However, in Donegal, as elsewhere, the impact of the involvement of the clergy in the anti-conscription campaign was a moderating one. O'Donnell saw the crisis as an opportunity to recreate nationalist unity, an aspiration which appealed to constitutional nationalists who had been on the back foot for some time.

The main public focus of the campaign was on the anti-conscription pledge and the local defence committees. On 14 April alone, twenty-eight anti-conscription meetings were held in the county, most of them convened by the local clergy. The pledge adopted by the Mansion House Conference on 18 April was administered at church gates throughout the country the following Sunday. In Letterkenny it was signed at a meeting attended by approximately 2,500 people, after a procession headed by the Hibernian and SF bands, 500 SF supporters and eighty students from St Eunan's College who marched in military formation. A letter was read from Bishop O'Donnell insisting that conscription could be defeated only by a united national movement and that only such a movement could achieve political progress. Conscription, he declared, was 'an 'unwarrantable aggression' but resistance should be within the laws of God.[47]

The local defence committees established on a parish basis were predominantly controlled by the clergy, usually the parish priest. Local political organizations such as the AOH and SF were represented. The Letterkenny committee consisted of three representatives each of the UIL, the AOH, SF and the Labour Association with Fr McCafferty as chair and Fr John O'Doherty also a member.[48] At a meeting at Doe Castle presided over by Fr H. MacLoone PP, whose nephew had been killed in France some time earlier, a joint committee was established with members from both AOH and SF. A resolution was passed pledging to resist conscription 'to the death'.[49] The call of national unity could not be ignored but it was never likely that the radical nationalist movement would cede its right to independent action. Anti-conscription meetings were arranged by SF in various locations, beginning at Milford on 11 April, followed by Glenties on 12 April, and Letterkenny, Fahan, Burt and Inch on 21 April. The Glenties meeting was preceded by a march of an estimated 100 Volunteers through the town. A meeting at the Fr McFadden SF club rooms in Derrybeg on 18 April adopted a resolution to resist conscription 'to the last drop of blood'.[50]

In his April dispatch to Dublin Castle, CI Hughes reported that the people had remained calm on the advice of their clergy, but he detected a defiant spirit, particularly in SF, which was gaining ground. Six additional SF clubs were established during the month and membership in the county grew by 1,115.[51] Nationally, the police reported a 23 per cent increase in SF membership between March and May 1918 and an even greater influx of recruits into the Volunteers as young men anxious to avoid compulsory service rushed to join. This caused its own problems: in some cases, the *parvenus* were viewed with suspicion by long-serving Volunteers and many of the newcomers left again once the immediate threat of conscription passed. James McMonagle recalled that while young men were slow to join, they flocked in during the conscription crisis only to leave again afterwards. P.H. Doherty from Carndonagh, another active Volunteer who like McMonagle had originally been a Redmondite, confirmed this trend. Nonetheless, the reorganization of the Volunteers received a considerable boost from the crisis and the movement acquired a new seriousness of purpose. Whereas drilling had hitherto been more a demonstrative than a serious military activity, this changed. The number of reported cases fell noticeably during the crisis but the amount of secret night-time drilling increased. Ominously, the number of raids for arms and ammunition rose sharply.[52]

The idea of a national women's pledge, taken up by a number of suffrage and labour organizations and by Cumann na mBan, was endorsed by the Mansion House Conference.[53] The pledge, taken countrywide on *Lá na mBan* (9 June), bound those who signed it to resist conscription, to refuse to take the jobs of men displaced because of their opposition, and to assist their families. In Donegal, where it was estimated 2,700 women signed the pledge, the disparate nature of the anti-conscription alliance was manifest with clerical and radical elements vying for control. While *Lá na mBan* was formally under the aegis of a Women's Day national committee, the driving force locally was undoubtedly Cumann na mBan with its influence moderated only by the local clergy. In Letterkenny the pledge was signed after Mass by upwards of 400 women and then ceremonially conveyed to the SF club rooms where the pledges were received by Cumann na mBan.[54]

A common thread in many of the speeches about conscription was the fear that it would lead to food shortages with farmers and labourers being taken from the fields for military service. The Irish Farmers' Union passed a resolution against conscription on that basis. When DCC discussed a motion condemning the extension of conscription as unconstitutional and tyrannical, the threat to food supplies was raised as an important issue. The motion was not opposed by the unionist members of the council.[55] The high price of food during the war had contributed to a relative prosperity for the farmers, particularly in east Donegal, and the reluctance of farmers to see their sons enlist in the army was frequently noted.[56] Nationalist commentators suggested that Protestant farmers as much as Catholics were opposed to conscription. This was rejected by Hugh T. Barrie, Unionist MP for North Londonderry, and by James Craig.[57] The military intelligence officer of the northern district reported that there were some young Protestants who were opposed to conscription but that opinion on the subject was largely divided along religious lines.[58] An attempt to organize a countrywide Protestant anti-conscription pledge gained little traction in Donegal. In an editorial entitled 'nationalist treason', the *Belfast Newsletter* concluded that there were demonstrably now two Irelands: one Protestant and loyal, and one Roman Catholic and rebel.[59]

Labour made an important contribution to the anti-conscription campaign, particularly through the national strike called by the Irish Trade Union Congress for 24 April.[60] In Donegal, labour was relatively unorganized and that was reflected in the response to the general strike. The congress was reluctant to cause a major split in Ulster by insisting on an all-out strike there which contributed to patchy support. The highest density of trade union membership in Donegal was in the north and east closest to Derry and the strike was reported to have been well supported by factory workers in the city.[61] A further complication was the presence of British-based unions with mixed nationalist and unionist membership. One of the strongest unions in Derry was the Tyneside-based National Amalgamated Union of Labour which during the war had organized farm workers and labourers in east Donegal and Inishowen.[62] The union was reluctant to get involved in political affairs and concentrated on wages and conditions. In February 1918 it organized a strike at the Admiralty works in Buncrana. In August agricultural labourers in the neighbourhoods of Letterkenny, Lifford and Inishowen struck for an increase in wages.[63]

The *Derry Journal* reported that the anti-conscription strike was widely observed nationally but the police claimed that while a number of labourers in Raphoe and Buncrana districts ceased work on that day, there was no stoppage of work elsewhere in Donegal.[64] In fact, the asylum workers in Letterkenny participated in the general strike. In March, just before the conscription crisis, there had been a short-lived strike about war bonuses and union recognition in the asylum – the workers were members of the Irish Asylum Workers' Union. The management committee was chaired by Bishop O'Donnell and following meetings with William Logue, president of the Derry Trades Council, the strike was amicably resolved. The anti-conscription committee in Letterkenny included two representatives of the Labour Association, James Semple and A. McMonagle. This was certainly with the approval if not at the behest of O'Donnell.[65]

On 1 May employees on the Lough Swilly railway stopped work in protest against conscription and there were plans for further strikes on the railways in the event of an attempt to move troops and conscriptees by rail. In June eighty carpenters employed at the American sea-plane base at Ture, Inishowen, went on strike without notice. The nature of their grievances is uncertain but a growing interest in organization on the part of workers in the county was evident.[66] In September it was reported that labour in the east of the county was becoming organized to a considerable extent. An early manifestation of this was a strike of agricultural labourers on the Stewart estate at Ards which was settled for a 5*s*. per week increase; and a threatened strike in Convoy woollen mills for a wage increase resulted in the directors closing the mill for a period.[67]

Political conditions and wage militancy drove a significant growth in membership of the Irish Transport and General Workers' Union countrywide. The RIC warned the ITGWU was likely to become more powerful and troublesome. While the union professed to eschew party politics, its main organizers supported SF as did most of its members.[68] Between 1917 and 1918, membership more than quadrupled from 15,000 to 67,827 and peaked in 1920 at 120,000.[69] However, that increase was largely in the southern half of the country. In July 1918 military intelligence reported signs of increased activity on the part of the ITGWU in the northern district but at that time the only branch of the ITGWU in Donegal was in Ballyshannon. The ITGWU sent Denis Houston and Cathal O'Shannon to Derry and Donegal as organizers. Branches were formed in Burtonport, Donegal and Letterkenny in 1919 and Burt in 1922 by which time the Ballyshannon branch had become defunct.[70]

Peadar O'Donnell claimed that in Donegal conscription had a much greater impact in mobilizing people than the 1916 Rising.[71] At the time O'Donnell was still a school principal on Arranmore Island and he participated in the anti-conscription campaign on the island. Born in Meenmore, near Dungloe, O'Donnell won a scholarship to St Patrick's College, Drumcondra in 1911. He subsequently returned to the Rosses where he taught in local schools.[72] A social radical and a writer, he was county secretary of the INTO in 1917–18.[73] The INTO was affiliated to the Trade Union Congress and at O'Donnell's behest the Rosses and Gweedore branches affiliated to the Derry Trades and Labour Council. In a letter to the *Derry Journal*, he argued that politics and economics were inseparable.[74] He told INTO colleagues in Letterkenny that teachers should become rebels and schools hotbeds where working men's interests were fostered.[75] Animated by the poverty in west Donegal, O'Donnell joined a campaign on behalf of migrant workers. He travelled to Scotland during the summer to investigate conditions for himself. There he met like-minded Scottish socialists including Willie Gallacher and Manny Shinwell. On his return, he gave up his teaching job in favour of a post as full-time organizer for the ITGWU in Ulster. In that role he gained first-hand experience of an area of the country that was to be his bailiwick in the War of Independence.[76]

Despite relative prosperity due to good harvests and wartime prices for food, the growth of SF in Donegal in the first quarter of 1918 coincided with an increase in agrarian radicalism. Radical nationalism fed off agrarian discontent in the west of the county and vice versa. The anti-conscription campaign in some cases saw a fusion of agrarian and political grievances with instances of boycotting of larger farmers who did not sign the pledge. The volatility of the situation was increased by the return of migratory labourers from England and Scotland. Police reported agrarian incidents in the west and south-west. In April the renting of grasslands near Clogher precipitated a campaign for sub-division of holdings to assist small holders. Walls and fences that had been removed for grazing were rebuilt. This coincided with an anti-conscription meeting in Clogher attended by more than 300 people. In July the CDB obtained an order for the compulsory purchase of 600 acres of this grazing land for redistribution, but an appeal was lodged by the owner Major Johnston.[77]

While the anti-conscription campaign mobilized an impressive public movement, there was also a secret dimension. This became an absolute necessity after 3 July when SF, the Irish Volunteers, Cumann na mBan and the Gaelic League were proclaimed. Drilling by the Volunteers changed from demonstrative public theatre to purposeful secret activity. Such was the number of raids for arms that the UVF in the county became concerned that an attempt would be made to seize some of the arms in their dumps. Arrangements were made to have the weapons moved to Derry. This was done with the knowledge of the military but not of the police.[78] Spontaneous public confrontations with the authorities were discouraged but they could not be completely avoided. The arrest of leading members of SF and the Volunteers nationally on 18 May on the spurious basis of a German plot generated several protests. Among the 150 arrested and transported to England was Sam O'Flaherty of Castlefinn, a leading SF figure and Volunteer in east Donegal. Volunteers paraded at a protest meeting in Castlefinn. In Buncrana on 10 June a travelling cinematograph showing the funeral of Thomas Ashe led to clashes with police. The victory of the imprisoned Arthur Griffith in the East Cavan by-election on 20 June was greeted with bonfire celebrations in various parts of the county which again resulted in altercations with the police. Marching in fours was reported in Donegal, Letterkenny and Glenties. Four Volunteers were subsequently convicted in connection with the disturbance in Glenties. In a significant departure from previous practice, they agreed to enter into bail rather than accept a prison sentence.[79]

In August a serious incident occurred in Bunbeg when an army deserter was arrested and brought to the local RIC barracks. An initial rescue attempt by a group throwing stones was thwarted but a larger group returned later, and shots were exchanged. This demonstrated the vulnerability of the police in isolated areas. In reporting the incident, CI Hughes gratuitously added that 'they are a rough uncivilized people in this locality, but I doubt if they will ever face determined armed police', a comment which in the light of later events seems deeply ironic.[80]

Faced with the united nationalist opposition to conscription, the government quickly decided to defer implementation, pending a renewed recruitment drive. It was intimated that if the response was sufficient, conscription would be unnecessary. Lord French, who had been sent to Ireland essentially as military governor, announced that the number of voluntary recruits required would be 50,000. Recruitment in Donegal had fallen to a low ebb. During April, the month in which the extension of conscription was announced, there was one recruit for the army and twelve for the navy, all from Buncrana.[81] In August, when popular feeling settled down, the Irish

Recruitment Council belatedly commenced a nationwide campaign with appeals to local authorities, public meetings and new recruiting offices in different parts of the county. No public body in the county agreed to endorse the appeal for recruits and it was noted that the Catholic clergy offered no support.[82] In desperation, the campaign appealed directly to the public in newspaper advertisements. One such advertisement proclaimed the existence of a 'New Anti-Conscription League', explaining that the way to defeat conscription was to enlist. It carried the details of some of the 700 men from Donegal, Derry, Fermanagh and Tyrone who were alleged to have done so.[83] By late October, less than sixty recruits had been raised in Donegal from the new voluntary scheme.[84]

The ill-advised decision of the cabinet to extend conscription to Ireland and its humiliating inability to implement the measure fatally undermined British authority in Ireland. SF and the Irish Volunteers were the main beneficiaries; all hopes of a revival of the IPP were shattered. In his report for October, the CI referred to the conviction that there would be no conscription and that this would be exploited by SF as their doing. The truth of his words was demonstrated in the general election that followed in December 1918.[85]

6 The victory of Sinn Féin: the 1918 general election

The general election of December 1918 was the first in eight years. Important developments had taken place in the intervening years, including the home rule crisis, the emergence of paramilitary forces such as the UVF and the Irish Volunteers, the 1916 Rising and most recently the conscription crisis. All had an impact in Donegal and the election provided an opportunity to establish how far the political dial had moved. The contest took place under the terms of the Representation of the People Act (1918) that extended the franchise to virtually all men over 21 and women over 30 who were householders. This reflected a significant widening of the franchise in terms of social class and gender which, regardless of other factors, was likely to have driven change. The Irish electorate increased from less than 700,000 to almost two million. The belated extension of the franchise to women, albeit on a restricted basis, introduced an additional unknown element into the contest. The total electorate in Donegal was 69,743, of whom 23,756 or 36 per cent were women.

To outward appearances the IPP had some cards in its hand in Donegal, notably the strength of its local organization and the support of the senior clergy. According to police estimates, the number of SF cumainn in the county overtook the UIL in April, during the conscription crisis, but the UIL continued to have a larger number of members. By December, 45 branches of the UIL with 7,453 members were reported as compared to SF with 54 cumainn and 5,471 members. Even the police admitted that these figures were misleading as the SF cumainn were newly formed and active, whereas the UIL in many areas had been largely inactive because of the political monopoly they had enjoyed hitherto.[1] Of more significance in Donegal was the strength of the AOH (Board of Erin). In December 1918 there were notionally 68 divisions of the AOH with 7,351 members. While some of these may also have been inactive or merely nominal, it should be remembered that the AOH had a social and cultural role and, unlike the UIL, was not dependent on the rhythm of political life. AOH parades and festivals with bands, flags and regalia publicly asserted a Catholic nationalist identity.[2] The *Hibernian Journal* remained loyal to the IPP until the end.

A tradition of uncontested elections was a significant factor: North Donegal had not been contested since 1900 and South Donegal since 1895; West Donegal had never been contested since the constituency had been created. The most recent parliamentary election was in East Donegal in January 1910 when Edward Kelly defeated a Unionist candidate by 1,200 votes. Kelly was returned unopposed in December 1910. The more even religious split in this constituency meant that greater care was taken of political organization with registration societies ensuring that all sympathetic voters were registered.[3]

More than thirty of the outgoing IPP MPs did not seek re-election in 1918 and others stood only after persuasion from John Dillon. In Donegal the IPP campaign was hampered significantly by the withdrawal of two of its four sitting MPs, Swift MacNeill in South Donegal and Hugh Law in West Donegal. The 69-year-old MacNeill had represented the constituency since he was first elected in 1887. A liberal home ruler in the Buttite tradition, it is fair to say he was stronger on national and constitutional than local issues. His exit was hastened by Joe Devlin who engineered the selection of John Donovan, a Belfast-born barrister and the outgoing MP for West Wicklow, to replace him. As early as the end of July, Donovan was announced as the main speaker at a planned UIL rally in the constituency, which suggests that MacNeill's departure was expected.[4] A few months before the election, SF called on MacNeill to withdraw and some of his long-term supporters in the constituency defected. In explaining his decision to stand aside, MacNeill made the remarkable admission that, having been so long unopposed, he would find it difficult to solicit votes with self-respect. In departing, he left no doubt as to his views on SF, a 'revolutionary party' the success of whose programme he predicted would 'spell destruction for Ireland'.[5]

Hugh Law's decision to withdraw was in some respects more surprising. He was forty-six and had only been an MP since 1902; he had a home in Donegal, had converted to Catholicism and was a supporter of the Gaelic League, the CDB and industrial development. However, he had wanted to stand down in 1910 but had been prevailed on to continue. A strong supporter of Redmond's policy on the war, he opposed conscription but split from the IPP because of its cooperation with SF in the Mansion House Conference.[6] In response, the SF executive in the constituency called on him to resign but he refused.[7] Law did not announce his intentions until mid-November in response to a resolution from the AOH in Gweedore promising their wholehearted support if he decided to contest. Declining the offer, he pleaded ill health and family commitments. He added the caveat that he might reconsider if he thought it was necessary to win the seat for constitutional nationalism but hinted that a far stronger candidate would be forthcoming. Law's valedictory message included an attack on the SF policy as illusory and fraught with danger.[8] In the event, his retirement from politics proved temporary as he was later returned as Cumann na nGaedheal TD for Donegal in 1927.

Law's replacement as IPP candidate was Daniel McMenamin, a 36-year-old barrister and Donegal native. In East Donegal and North Donegal, the sitting MPs, Edward Kelly, a successful barrister from Ballyshannon, and Philip O'Doherty, a solicitor from Clonmany, were re-selected for the IPP.

Both were relatively young – Kelly was thirty-five and O'Doherty was forty-seven. The average age of the IPP candidates in Donegal was forty compared to twenty-six for SF, a significant generational gap, if less pronounced than elsewhere in the country.

All the SF candidates were prominent local members of SF and the Volunteers. Samuel O'Flaherty in East Donegal and Joseph O'Doherty in North Donegal had been imprisoned on foot of the alleged German plot. Joseph Sweeney, the candidate for West Donegal, had participated in the Rising. Still a student in UCD, he was at home with influenza when he was elected president of his local Volunteer company and selected to contest the election. At selection conventions on 15 September, 27-year-old P.J. Ward, a solicitor in Donegal town, was selected to contest South Donegal and 28-year-old O'Doherty for North Donegal.[9] O'Doherty was born in Derry but his father was from Inishowen. A former teacher and a contemporary of Peadar O'Donnell in St Patrick's College, Drumcondra, he later qualified as a barrister. A senior figure in the IRB and Volunteers, he participated in the Howth gun-running and was interned in Frongoch after the Rising. O'Flaherty was the son of a farmer and mill owner from Castlefinn. An Arts graduate from UCD, he was responsible for the establishment of the Con Colbert SF cumann in Castlefinn and a company of Irish Volunteers. His brothers were also involved, and his three sisters were active in Cumann na mBan. In February he introduced de Valera at a meeting in Castlefinn and in March he was the main speaker with Eoin MacNeill at a rally in Ballybofey. When he was arrested in the German plot arrests, the SF executive in East Donegal demanded that Edward Kelly MP should resign to allow O'Flaherty to contest the seat.[10]

With elections being conducted on the straight vote system, the likelihood of a split nationalist vote in some Ulster constituencies, allowing the seat to be won by a Unionist, was a cause of concern. In East Donegal, a contest between nationalists was likely to mean defeat for both. The initiative for an election pact came from the northern bishops, including Bishops O'Donnell and McHugh. The latter was disillusioned with the IPP and sympathetic to SF but he considered it necessary to ensure continued representation at Westminster for nationalists. As O'Donnell was deemed to be too close to the IPP, the pact was ultimately brokered by Cardinal Logue who was even less likely to look with favour on SF.[11] It was suggested that agreed candidates be nominated but this came to nothing. SF expressed itself open to preliminary plebiscites in closely divided constituencies, but this too was rejected.[12] It was eventually agreed to split the constituencies evenly between the parties. Logue allocated South Down, North-East Tyrone, South Armagh and East Donegal to the IPP, and Derry, East Down, North-West Tyrone and South Fermanagh to SF.[13] Given O'Donnell's status within the hierarchy and

Logue's Donegal origins, it was no surprise that East Donegal was assigned to the IPP but there was consternation within SF locally. The Unionist candidate in the constituency, Major Robert Lyon Moore, was nominated belatedly after moves to put forward a farmers' candidate came to nothing.[14]

While the pattern of older clergy supporting the IPP and the younger men supporting SF seems broadly to have applied in Donegal, the assumption that the IPP enjoyed the unambiguous support of the senior clergy requires some clarification. Bishop O'Donnell's loyalty had been sorely tested by his experience at the Irish Convention and he was relatively inactive politically for much of 1918. His belief in the need for nationalist unity was confirmed by the experience of the anti-conscription campaign and he supported the demand for an agreement to avoid a split vote. He complained to John Dillon that SF's organization in Donegal was superior to the IPP's.[15] In early December, he suggested to Dillon that the IPP should bow to the inevitable and withdraw all its candidates. Dillon refused and appealed to O'Donnell to do what he could do on the ground to shore up support.[16]

O'Donnell's backing for the party was muted. He did not attend any IPP selection conventions. It is indicative that his strongest intervention in the election took place in East Donegal where there was an agreed Nationalist candidate. A long and forceful letter from the bishop was read at election meetings, warning of the threat of partition and urging voters to support Kelly.[17] Some of his senior clergy were less restrained. In South Donegal Fr Morgan Walker chaired the selection meeting. In West Donegal Canon Scanlon, who claimed to speak with the sanction of his bishop, called for support for Daniel McMenamin. There were complaints about such interventions and of SF priests being muzzled.[18] SF responded by bringing in the indefatigable Fr Michael O'Flanagan, SF vice-president, who addressed several meetings.[19] Fr J. Ward chaired a SF meeting in Bundoran, assisted by Fr McCarville, while Fr J. Trainor delivered a rousing speech after a torchlight procession in Ballyshannon.[20]

Not all of Donegal lay within O'Donnell's Raphoe diocese. Parts of north Donegal were in the Derry diocese where the fear of partition was acute. Police reported that the clergy there were strongly pro-SF.[21] The southern area of the county, including Bundoran and the portion of Ballyshannon south of the Erne, lay within the diocese of Clogher where Bishop Patrick McKenna was reticent about active intervention in politics by the clergy. An enthusiastic Gaelic League supporter, he abhorred the prospect of partition and was involved in the arrangement of the election pact. He steered a middle course between SF and the IPP during the general election campaign.[22]

The election campaign itself was largely uneventful. The SF manifesto summoned the electorate to the flag of the Irish Republic, promised to abstain from attendance at Westminster and pledged to establish a constituent assembly in Dublin. It also committed the movement to 'any and all means available to render impotent the power of England to hold Ireland in subjection'. This sentence was deleted by the censor.[23] The campaign focused largely on the issue of self-determination. Agrarian issues in west Donegal undoubtedly contributed to support for SF but the IPP countered by claiming that it had defeated landlordism.[24] The spectre of partition was repeatedly raised by both sides while SF relentlessly exploited the IPPs support for the war and its inability to defeat conscription in parliament.[25]

SF's election machinery was more efficient, even though the AOH led by Michael Dunnion, the county chairman, had begun to make some preparations in August. AOH social gatherings were organized in Letterkenny to stem the influence of SF among younger people.[26] Serious electioneering did not commence until late November.[27] Both parties used after Mass meetings and fair days to promote their message. On 1 December the fair day at Ardara saw rival meetings and boisterous exchanges between supporters.[28] There were complaints from both sides of intimidation and some AOH halls were attacked. Charles McGinley from Creeslough described the contest in West Donegal as 'hard and bitter' while his neighbour Bernard McGinley complained that the Hibernians were quite as bitter against SF as unionists.[29] In the same constituency, it was alleged that merchants and traders were threatened with a boycott if they did not support Joseph Sweeney, the SF candidate, and an appeal was made to Bishop O'Donnell to intervene.[30] When schools were closed for an extended period from November because of the 'Spanish Flu' pandemic, Joseph Murray, a teacher in Bundoran and a Volunteer, was assigned to full-time election work as SF organizer in southwest Donegal.[31] With a death rate of 3–4 per thousand from the pandemic, Donegal was among the worst hit counties, in part, it would appear, because of the military and naval bases and returning migratory labourers.[32]

Apart from schoolteachers, SF redeployed activists from uncontested constituencies in the south of Ireland to assist in the campaign. Seán Moylan and three colleagues from Cork were assigned to North Donegal, an area he found culturally different. The young militant Volunteers he encountered had little experience of politics and he felt the need to instruct them in the ways of political campaigning.[33] In South Donegal, the SF election agent, P.M. Gallagher, a solicitor in Donegal town, arranged classes in election law and procedure for Volunteers.[34] The final SF rally of the campaign in South Donegal was organized for Donegal town. Large numbers of police and military were drafted and groups of Volunteers from around the constituency were ordered to attend in the expectation of trouble, but none ensued.[35]

The most serious event during the campaign took place in the vicinity of Glenties on 12 December, shortly before polling day. Anthony Heron, a farmer and father of six children, went to the fair in Glenties with friends and attended a Hibernian election meeting. On their way home, they encountered a group of SF supporters. Drink had been consumed and tempers were raised. A fracas developed in which Heron was reported to have brandished a stick. In the mêlée, shots were fired. Heron was struck in the throat and later died of his wounds. The cause of the affray was said to be political rivalry, but it is possible that there were previous differences between Heron and Edward Ward, a Sinn Féiner, who was charged with manslaughter. At the subsequent inquest, conflicting evidence was presented but the jury felt moved to add a rider to its verdict warning against the carrying of arms in a peaceful district.[36]

Polling day itself passed off peacefully throughout the country. With the large increase in the electorate, there was pressure on polling stations and transport was important. It was noted by the RIC that SF had most of the motor cars in West and South Donegal, but this was not the case everywhere. Thomas McShea, Irish Volunteer and SF sub-agent for Bundoran, a hotbed of SF support, complained that 'the Hibernians had all the advantages ample funds gave them in cornering all means of transport for the voters'. This was particularly important in Bundoran as there were no polling stations in the town; voters had to travel to one of the eight polling stations in Ballyshannon.[37] Notwithstanding McShea's claim about AOH funding, John Donovan's declared election expenses (£367) were considerably less than P.J. Ward's (£511). In North Donegal, Joseph O'Doherty declared £414 election expenses compared to £251 for his opponent, while in West Donegal the IPP marginally outspent SF by £418 to £412.[38]

There were some allegations of intimidation and personation on polling day. James McCaffrey from Creeslough casually admitted to the BMH that 'intimidation of voters and impersonation in those days were really looked upon by all as a patriotic duty'.[39] Potentially more serious was the alleged interference with the postal votes of soldiers by an IRB member who worked in the Post Office in Derry. It was suggested that several thousand votes were not recorded. The figure seems unlikely and only a small proportion would have related to the election in Donegal.[40] CI Hughes noted that SF members, confident of success, occupied themselves keeping order on the basis that it was in their interest for the polling to proceed expeditiously.[41] Letterkenny Volunteers were sent to Church Hill in the West Donegal constituency where it was claimed the AOH were attempting to prevent Sinn Féiners from casting their ballots.[42] Similar steps were taken elsewhere. In the interval between polling day and the count, Volunteers were assigned to 'protect the ballots' to ensure that nothing untoward took place.

The results of the election represented a decisive victory for SF. Nationally, the party won 73 seats, Unionists 26 and the IPP 6. The only two constituencies in which an IPP candidate defeated a SF opponent were

1 Casement at Cloghaneely, c.1905. (*Front row*): Séamus Ó Searcaigh, Roger Casement. (*2nd row*): Éamon Ó Tuathail, Úna Ní Fhaircheallaigh; (*3rd row*): Pádraig Carr, NT, Br Malachi.

2 Patrick O'Donnell (1856–1927), bishop of Raphoe, 1888–1922; coadjutor archbishop of Armagh, 1922–4; archbishop of Armagh, 1924–7; cardinal, 1925.
3 (*opposite*) Edward Carson addressing an anti-home rule meeting at Raphoe, 2 October 1913.

4 Charles Clements, 5th earl of Leitrim (1879–1952), commander of the UVF in Donegal.

5 A UVF training camp in Donegal, 1914.

6 Patrick MacGill (1889–1963), 'navvy poet', novelist and soldier from Glenties.

7 Joseph A. Sweeney (1897–1980), 'E' Company, 4th Battalion, Irish Volunteers, St Enda's, Holy Thursday, 1916.

8 Constable Charles McGee (1892–1916), fisherman and migrant labourer from Inishbofin island, off Donegal, who joined the RIC in 1912 and was fatally wounded by Irish Volunteers at Castlebellingham during the Easter Rising.

9 Peadar O'Donnell (1893–1986), teacher, trade unionist and IRA commander, who led an Active Service Unit in Donegal during the War of Independence. He was a leading anti-Treaty figure in the Civil War that followed.

10 Joseph Murray and members of the 1st Battalion, No. 4 Brigade (SE Donegal), IRA.

11 Alice Cashel (1878–1958), a founding member of Cumann na mBan in Cork and an organizer in Donegal. She later became a county councillor in Galway and a judge in the Dáil courts.

12 Donegal members of the Irish Republican Police, created in 1920 to supplant the RIC, protect the Dáil courts and enforce their judgments.

13 Eithne Coyle (1897–1985), Cumann na mBan organizer and republican activist, at rifle practice in 1921. She took a leading part in enforcing the Belfast boycott and in the anti-Treaty movement in Donegal.

14 Members of Cumann na mBan, Annagry, 1922. *Left to right*: Mary Phaidí Bhig, Annie William, Biddy William, Róise Jimmy Theague, Mary William.

15 The 'Drumboe Martyrs': Charlie Daly, Dan Enright, Timothy O'Sullivan, Seán Larkin, executed at Drumboe Woods, 14 March 1923.

Waterford, where Captain William Redmond prevailed in his father's old constituency, and West Belfast, where Joseph Devlin defeated de Valera. Thirty-three of the successful SF candidates were in prison, many without trial since the Germany plot arrests of May 1918. SF won a comfortable majority of seats (70 per cent) with 47 per cent of the votes cast but this underestimates its real strength.[43] Only in Ulster did SF not meet with unqualified success. Unionists won 58 per cent of the votes cast and 23 out of 38 seats (61 per cent); SF won ten seats and the IPP five. The election pact in the eight marginal Ulster constituencies facilitated the election of four IPP and three SF candidates but the arrangement broke down in East Down and the seat was won by a Unionist.

The overall turnout in Donegal was 63 per cent. Not unexpectedly, it was highest in East Donegal at 78 per cent, followed by South Donegal (62 per cent), North Donegal (57 per cent) and West Donegal (56 per cent). In East Donegal, Edward Kelly defeated the Unionist candidate, Major Robert Moore, by 7,959 votes (61.1 per cent) to 4,797 (38.6 per cent). Samuel O'Flaherty, who had withdrawn, received 46 votes. Kelly was a popular and energetic barrister and a good candidate who was likely to have performed well even against a SF opponent. This and the sizeable Unionist vote suggests that, without a pact, Moore would have won the seat. The unionist *Londonderry Sentinel* certainly thought so and bitterly attacked the role of Bishop O'Donnell and the bishops. The *Sentinel* mischievously suggested that IPP leader John Dillon, who had been defeated in Mayo, might seek a safe seat in East Donegal.[44]

Elsewhere in Donegal, SF won all three seats. In North Donegal, the largest constituency, it won its biggest vote: Joseph O'Doherty comfortably defeated the outgoing MP, Philip O'Doherty, by 69 per cent to 31 per cent. In West Donegal, 21-year-old Joseph Sweeney defeated Daniel McMenamin by 62 per cent to 38 per cent and in South Donegal, where the IPP was confident of holding on, P.J. Ward won by 55 per cent to 45 per cent.[45] This was the closest of the Donegal contests. Joe Devlin was disappointed, given the strength of the AOH there and the belated support of Bishop O'Donnell. He blamed the poor organization of the UIL for the loss.[46] Locally there was criticism of Devlin for largely confining his efforts to his own constituency. A decisive factor was that the relatively large Protestant population seemed to have stayed away. Whatever the likelihood of their supporting the widely respected Swift MacNeill, they were never likely to vote for the nominee of Joe Devlin and the AOH.[47]

To all intents and purposes, the 1918 general election brought an end to the power and influence of the IPP in Donegal. The *Donegal News*, which had called for a sweeping majority for self-determination, greeted the result as an 'unceremonious burial' for the 'backboneless Irish Party'.[48] John MacAdam of the *Donegal Vindicator*, who had been a loyal party supporter, declared in an editorial that the IPP had ceased to exist and called for SF to be given a clear run.[49] The AOH remained a significant force. The monolithic power and influence of the Catholic Church was severely dented, particularly that of Bishop O'Donnell.[50] In an ominous message to the East Donegal convention of the UIL warning of what might lie ahead, he said that a government with an army at its back cared little for the hostility of a disarmed people.[51]

While SF emerged as the victors, their victory was incomplete: the party's authority related to an assembly not yet established or recognized. Locally, political power in urban and rural councils and county councils remained for the moment in the hands of its opponents. However, while the nature of the mandate received by SF in December 1918 has been questioned, its direction was unmistakeable. Abstention from Westminster, establishment of a constituent assembly in Dublin and an appeal to the Peace Conference were repeatedly demanded at election meetings all over the county. Even in its redacted form, the commitment to the achievement of a republic was explicit. If, as SF asserted, the 1918 general election should be seen as a referendum on independence, the verdict in Donegal was clear.[52]

7 'Rendering government impossible': the political war, 1919–21

The War of Independence had both a political and a military dimension. Peadar O'Donnell described the military aspect as 'a sham war' and insisted that killing soldiers and policemen was less important than the essentially political project of destroying the machinery of government in the county.[1] Donegal remained relatively tranquil militarily, at least until the latter half of 1920 when the impact of the campaign of the Irish Volunteers, now called the IRA, began to intensify. Simultaneously, the struggle to assert practical sovereignty and to win popular allegiance proceeded locally. The aim, initially more intuited than expressly elaborated, was to paralyse and ultimately replace the existing machinery of British government. At Ballybofey in February 1918, de Valera had referred to it as rendering government impossible. What followed was a confused, sometimes chaotic, and occasionally violent period of contested authority and sovereignty, of state and counter-state. While the political dimensions will be considered in this chapter and the military in the next, they were essentially two sides of the same coin.

The three SF TDs from Donegal attended the first meeting of the Dáil in the Mansion House in Dublin on 21 January 1919, sitting together in solidarity. Having approved the Dáil constitution, the democratic programme and the declaration of independence, they turned their attention to the task of implementing the SF programme. That involved the creation of not just an alternative parliament but an alternative government, nationally and locally – what Arthur Mitchell and others have called the 'counter-state'.[2] With the Dáil government driven underground from September 1919, it was never likely that such a project could be much more than symbolic and incomplete. That was the case in Donegal, as elsewhere, but significant progress was made over the next two years, which is the main theme of this chapter.

Commenting in early January on the victory of SF, the *Donegal News* remarked perceptively that definitive as that election triumph was, it would a mistake to assume that their work was completed.[3] Just how much remained to be done was illustrated three days later at a meeting of DCC, with Francis Gallagher JP, chairman, presiding and ten other members in attendance, all JPs. A resolution from Kerry County Council, declaring Ireland a nation, one and indivisible, and entitled to the status of full nationhood was greeted with some laughter. When the secretary said he supposed they might adopt the resolution, the chairman replied that it was 'a matter of indifference'. Another councillor commented wryly that some people thought that it was as important to make democracy safe for the world as the world safe for democracy. At this point,

William Kelly, a solicitor in attendance on behalf of the road contractors of the county, interjected that they should 'start with the road contractors first. Make the roads safe for traffic.' The subject was then dropped without the resolution being adopted.⁴ Later in the year, with violent attacks on the police occurring more frequently in the south of the county and in the wake of the Rampart ambush (see next chapter), the council passed a motion received from Tipperary County Council condemning attacks on the RIC.⁵

Paradoxically, after its electoral triumph in December SF entered a period of stasis.⁶ Locally, once the excitement abated there was an anti-climax and a long period of consolidation. There was a surprisingly modest increase in the number of SF clubs and members in 1919 from fifty-six clubs and 5,363 members in January to sixty-three clubs and 5,786 members in December.⁷ The largest increase occurred in October when Sam O'Flaherty became an organizer and resumed his role as IRA commandant in east Donegal. He had been interned since the time of the German plot arrests and was recently released.⁸ There was also a surge of activity related to the Dáil loan launched in the summer to fund the operations of the Dáil government. A meeting planned for Ballybofey in October to promote the loan was proclaimed.⁹ Periodic meetings were arranged to demand the release of prisoners, but SF was generally reported not to be particularly active. There was increased activity on the part of social and cultural organizations, including the Gaelic League and especially the GAA. With public drilling being proscribed, both SF and the IRA in the county encouraged young men to become involved in Gaelic football to improve their physical fitness and as a cover for holding meetings.¹⁰

Support for the IPP did not vanish after December 1918, nor did political opposition to SF disappear. 'Divergent nationalisms' persisted. A UIL organizer was sent to the county and held a series of indoor meetings.¹¹ A new branch was formed in Carrick and increased membership was reported in Glencolumbcille. The AOH also continued its activities and efforts were made to galvanize its support. A meeting at Ballybofey in March was reported to have been poorly attended. On 17 March 1919 there were rival SF and AOH parades in Annagry but no trouble ensued.¹² As was the case in Monaghan, the rivalry between SF and the AOH continued to be intense and occasionally resulted in incidents; in contrast, SF and the AOH in Derry reached a *modus vivendi*.¹³ When three SF families in Carrowkeel were raided by the military acting on information received by military intelligence, it was rumoured that the AOH was responsible, and its local hall was burned shortly afterwards.¹⁴ Later in 1919, the AOH became more active and new divisions were formed in Kilcar and Carrick.

On the unionist side, there was little public activity and the twelfth of July parades proceeded peacefully. Peace day was celebrated in many towns and villages on 22 July to mark the formal end of the First World War: national-

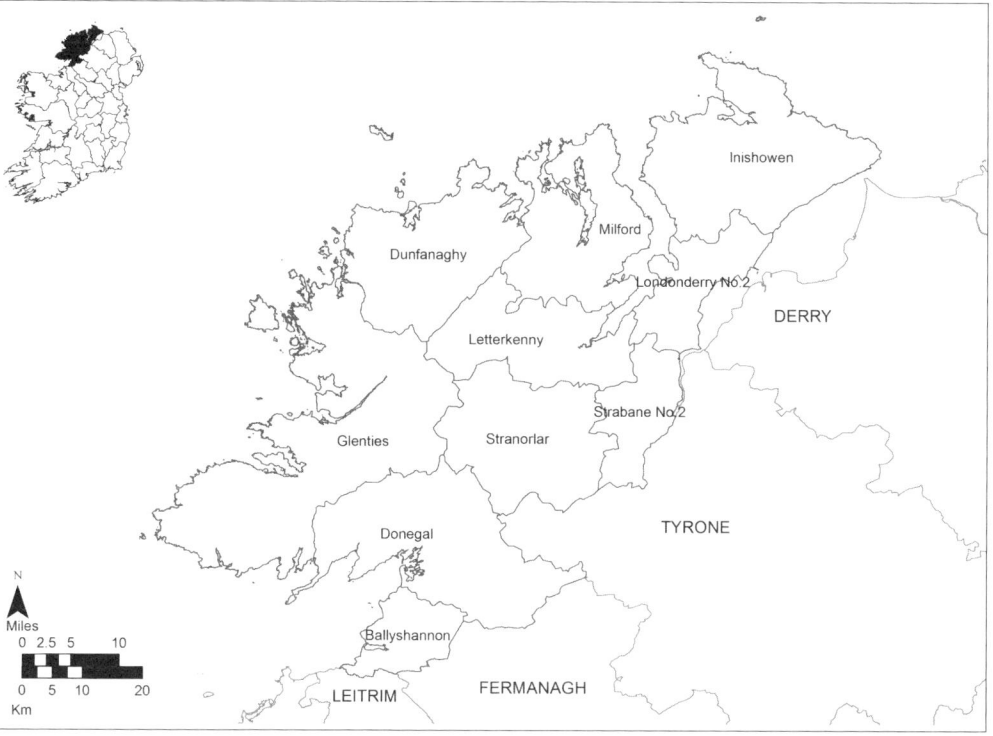

4 Local government divisions

ists held aloof but in Donegal town there was a SF counter demonstration. In the light of the poor showing in the election in East Donegal, an effort was made by unionists to encourage voter registration in preparation for forthcoming local government elections and a new unionist club was established in Muff in Inishowen.[15]

As a predominantly rural county, the municipal and urban district elections of January 1920 had a limited impact, but they provided an early opportunity for SF to extend its influence over local government. Elections were held for the urban districts of Bundoran, Buncrana and Letterkenny, and for Ballyshannon Town Commission, with forty-five seats in total to be filled.[16] For the first time, the elections were held using proportional representation, a move intended to limit SF gains. In Donegal and nationally, the outcome was a clear-cut victory for SF but a less dramatic one than in the general election. The emergence of a ratepayers' body reflected the continuing influence of a group, nationalist as well as unionist, who had dominated local government hitherto. The previous year had seen a growing labour militancy that contributed to the emergence of a labour vote, while the success of independent candidates reflected the importance of local figures and issues. SF won a large majority in Ballyshannon, enjoyed equality with the combined other parties in Bundoran and Inishowen, and were in a minority in Letterkenny.[17] Among those elected in Letterkenny was Dr J.P. McGinley, who at the time was serving a sentence in Derry Jail.

The elections for Donegal County Council and RDCs in May 1920 were of greater importance (see map 4). Because of restrictions on large public gatherings and continuing press censorship, campaigning was done mainly through personal canvassing. Some outgoing candidates appealed for support through letters to the press. Joseph MacArthur, a Presbyterian farmer from Burt who had been a member of public boards in Donegal and Derry for twenty-two years, promised that if he was elected, everything would be done in the interests of the ratepayers with due regard to economy combined with efficiency.[18] James Clarke JP, a Presbyterian farmer from Porthall, Letterkenny, who had been a member of the county council since 1913, simply stated that he had always supported the best interests of the county. He was one of two Unionists elected to the county council – a third was later nominated by Strabane No. 2 RDC.

The new political dispensation made standing on one's record problematic for some. That consideration may have inspired a proposal at Inishowen RDC prior to the local elections to rescind a motion from 1916 condemning the Easter Rising. It was passed after a bitter debate with four members dissenting.[19] SF treated the elections as an extension of the general election campaign and focused on the need to supplant foreign control at local level. Many of their candidates for the county council election were prominent members of the IRA, including P.J. Ward TD. Ward had been arrested on 30 March and was released from Wormwood Scrubs following a 17-day hunger strike shortly before polling. As a result, the legitimacy of the Dáil and the treatment of prisoners were bigger issues in the election than the routine concerns of the council.

In the elections held on 26 May, SF won fifteen seats, Nationalists (constitutionalists) three and Unionists two. The turnout was low in many areas probably because the outcome was not in much doubt. Only four of the five electoral districts were contested, and the number of candidates barely exceeded the number of seats. Pressure was exerted on outgoing members not to contest. There were several withdrawals even after nominations officially closed. In the Donegal electoral area, where there were six candidates for five seats, P.J. Ward topped the poll with a huge surplus; two other Sinn Féiners were elected along with one Nationalist and one Unionist (James Sproule Myles). In Letterkenny, there were six candidates for four seats: SF won three and the remaining seat was won by James Clarke. In Buncrana, there were seven candidates for four seats: SF won all four. The four seats in the Glenties electoral area were uncontested.[20]

The chairman or a nominee of each of the RDCs was also entitled to attend the county council. While the *Derry Journal* detected 'voter apathy', the turnout in the RDC elections was high in some areas. In the Dunfanaghy electoral area, which had 1,150 electors on the roll, 920 votes were cast (80 per cent turnout); there were 60 spoiled votes.[21] In the evenly balanced Londonderry No. 2 election, 2,172 (83 per cent) of a total electorate of 2,612 cast their votes and there were only 38 spoiled votes.[22] In all, 138 seats were available across nine rural districts. SF won a decisive victory everywhere, except in east Donegal. In the Dunfanaghy rural district, which included Gortahork, SF took all 10 seats; in Inishowen, they won 17 out of 21; in Ballyshannon, 7 out of 9 (no Nationalist stood); in Donegal 11 out of 18; in Milford 11 out of 19. Proportional representation ensured that there was a stronger unionist representation on these councils with two elected in Ballyshannon and three in Donegal. In Londonderry No. 2 district and Strabane No. 2 rural district (despite the names, these were located in County Donegal; they included Raphoe and Castlefinn), the eighteen seats were shared evenly between unionists and nationalists.

The unionist *Londonderry Sentinel* conceded that SF had 'swept the boards' and that they could 'run the councils in whatever way they wanted'.[23] What that might mean quickly became apparent. On a party vote, DCC decided not to award the contract for printing to the *Sentinel*.[24] To the victor the spoils was the understandable order of the day. The first task of the district councils, having elected a chairman, was the co-option of additional members. Eschewing any suggestion of magnanimity, SF displayed an impressive ruthlessness. In the majority of cases, those co-opted were SF members, some of them unsuccessful candidates. On a party vote, Donegal RDC rejected a proposal to co-opt a Nationalist and instead co-opted three Sinn Féiners.[25] Letterkenny was an exception – William Ward, a defeated Nationalist member of the RDC was co-opted and elected vice-chairman.[26]

In Glenties the tricolour was flown at the first meeting of the RDC. Motions were unanimously passed in favour of self-determination, recognizing Dáil Éireann, not submitting minutes to any other authority, taking no action in relation to malicious damage claims, and requesting Joe Sweeney TD to have rules drafted by the Dáil for the administration of local bodies.[27] Similar motions were passed by other councils. Those passed by Ballyshannon RDC were forwarded to the governments of Europe and the president and chairman of the Senate and Speaker of the House of Representatives in the United States. There is no record of any response.[28] At Donegal RDC, Unionist and Nationalist councillors unsuccessfully protested that a motion recognizing Dáil Éireann was out of order and the Unionists withdrew.[29] At the meeting of the board of guardians that followed, it was agreed, with two Unionist members dissenting, that any disputes between the board and officials were to be referred to courts recognized by Dáil Éireann and that no lists of ratepayers or other information should be provided to British agents. It was also resolved, with one member dissenting, that a motion passed condemning the Easter Rising should be expunged from the minute book by the chairman who proceeded to cut it out and burn it. Further resolutions were passed demanding the withdrawal of the army of occupation and pledging financial support for railwaymen who had refused to carry munitions.[30]

The even split between unionists and nationalists in Londonderry No. 2 and Strabane No. 2 created predictable ill-feeling, which was unfortunate as these were areas which proved contentious later in the context of partition and the Boundary Commission. To avoid a stalemate, Londonderry No. 2 had unsuccessfully requested the LGB to increase the number of seats from eight to nine. Unionists had held the council for nearly thirty years but, on this occasion, nationalists won a small majority of the vote, and the seats were divided evenly. The vote of the outgoing chair proved decisive in installing John Black, a unionist, as new chairman.[31] A similar stand-off occurred at the Strabane No. 2 RDC, also a long-standing unionist council, which had five nationalist and five unionist members. The nationalists proposed they should get the chair and one co-option with unionists getting two co-options. On the casting vote of the outgoing chairman, who was not a member of the new council, two unionists and one nationalist were co-opted. A unionist chairman was then elected, and the nationalists refused to accept the position of vice-chairman. The bitterness continued when the board of guardians met. Nationalists unexpectedly blocked the reappointment of Major Herdman as chair and installed a nationalist chair and vice-chair.[32]

Once the RDCs had nominated their representatives, the county council met on 18 June to inaugurate the new dispensation. P.J. Ward, the 28-year-old TD, was elected chairman. He now combined the roles of TD, senior IRA officer and chairman of a largely inexperienced council. The *Belfast Newsletter* highlighted that local government in Donegal was headed by 'a released hunger-striker'.[33] The proceedings were unexpectedly civil, at least to begin with. James Clarke, a unionist councillor, supported Ward's election as chair and wished him well. They were all there, he said, in the interests of the county. Ward responded warmly in Irish and paid tribute to his predecessors. The air of cordiality did not last long. When a motion was proposed to recognize the Dáil, Clarke and one of his two fellow unionist councillors dissented, pointing out that the previous councils had eschewed political matters and any change in that would endanger the support of large ratepayers.[34]

A particular area of concern for ratepayers was the spate of malicious damages claims arising from the activities of the IRA. SF was not inclined to entertain such claims as many of them came from their opponents. Lord Leitrim made a claim for £3,000 for damage to Doaghbeg police barracks, while the policemen involved in the Rampart ambush (discussed in the next chapter) claimed £4,000 in personal injuries.³⁵ Damages awarded by the courts were levied on the rates. It was at the discretion of the judge whether the levy should be on the relevant district or the county at large or both. In most cases, the court was responsive to a plea that the damage, at least in part, had been caused by outsiders and apportioned the damages accordingly. There is no doubt that many of the claims were inflated but the county court judge and chair of the quarter sessions, John Cooke KC, showed himself more than willing to reduce them. In June he heard a claim from Captain John Hamilton, landlord, and the RIC for £2,000 damages for the burning of Barnesmore barracks. He awarded £500 to be levied, half on the Donegal rural district and half on the county at large.³⁶ Hamilton later appealed the amount of the award but in any case, the new Donegal RDC decided to ignore the claim.³⁷ In October, Alexander Morton, farmer and industrialist, claimed £6,000 for the burning of a dwelling house, two dairies and related farm buildings at Meenavalley in south-west Donegal on 23 August. He was awarded £2,800. It was claimed that the buildings were burned to avoid the military occupying them.³⁸

In accordance with the policy of the Dáil, DCC and most district councils ignored such claims. At its first meeting, the county council resolved that no rate would be struck to meet criminal injury and malicious damage claims and that such claims would not be defended in English courts.³⁹ Ironically, some of those involved in making that decision were themselves implicated in the original damage. The group that burned the barracks at Barnesmore was led by Liam O'Duffy who was solicitor's clerk in P.J. Ward's office as well as adjutant of the South Donegal Brigade and acting O/C when Ward was in Wormwood Scrubs.⁴⁰ One landowner from Ballindrait, who had a malicious damages award in his favour which was then ignored, wrote to the county council when he received the demand for payment of rates on the same property, stating that he proposed to deduct the amount from the award. The council demanded that the rates be paid in full.⁴¹

Ignoring malicious damages claims was a stopgap while SF pursued its wider policy of removing British control of the structures of local government and justice, and creating in effect a parallel structure or counter-state. Local councils were instructed to boycott the LGB and end the practice of submitting their minutes and annual accounts. A significant complication was that substantial grants were paid by the LGB from the consolidated fund in relief of local taxation.⁴² By transferring allegiance to Dáil Éireann, county councils lost approximately 15 per cent of their income.⁴³ Little wonder that there was a transitionary period when there was a tendency to try to serve two masters. While some hoped that it might be possible to maintain a kind of dual allegiance, the issue was forced by the LGB which decided that no loans or grants would be made to councils that did not conform to orders of the board and submit their accounts for audit.⁴⁴ As an enticement, the LGB repeatedly extended the deadlines for drawing down funding under various schemes.⁴⁵ On 21 August W.T. Cosgrave wrote to local authorities promising clear guidance but indicating that they could take it that they had 'no further use for the LGB'.⁴⁶ In February 1921 a deputation of ratepayers, including members of the Donegal Farmers' Union, appealed to the DCC to take a more pragmatic approach by reversing its decision not to comply with the LGB's conditions for grants. A motion to that effect was ruled out of order.⁴⁷ As late as October 1921, a deputation from Londonderry No. 2 RDC requested that the council should do what was necessary to avail of grants in aid of the rates. Not surprisingly, Londonderry No. 2 and Strabane No. 2 were the last councils to conform. With the implementation of the Government of Ireland Act in May 1921, a reorganization of these councils was undertaken: the former was amalgamated with Inishowen and the latter with Stranorlar.⁴⁸

In the case of bodies where SF did not have a majority, republican powers of persuasion were manifest. In February 1921 armed and masked men called on a Poor Law guardian at his home near Letterkenny and informed him that if he persisted with a resolution to submit books for audit to the LGB, he would be shot. He complied.⁴⁹ The accounts of most Donegal councils were audited by the LGB for the period up to 31 March 1920 but in many cases disputes arose about the payment of the fees incurred. Thereafter, while the auditor was appointed, he found it difficult to complete his task.⁵⁰ The price of sovereignty was a considerable retrenchment in services, particularly in the area of road building and maintenance, which along with the burden of the rates became a constant bone of contention. Inishowen Board of Guardians demanded that payments should be withheld from any councils which had not cut all contact with the LGB and the money reassigned.⁵¹ In October 1921 P.J. Ward was forced to issue a long statement defending the council's record in relation to rates and services.

The collection of rates became a contentious matter in 1921 when demands were made on behalf of both the county council and the LGB. Some ratepayers chose to pay to one, some to pay to the other, and some chose to avail of the opportunity to pay to neither.⁵² The confusion and chaos that followed closely paralleled developments in neighbouring Leitrim and elsewhere.⁵³ When some rate collectors sought court orders garnisheeing the rates, P.J. Ward warned that solicitors and barristers who disobeyed the Dáil order against such practices 'would not get off without punishment'.⁵⁴ Rate collectors who worked for councils that had not yet declared loyalty to the Dáil were classed as 'enemy agents' and IRA intelligence officers were instructed to record details of their activities.⁵⁵ The position of rate collector became a more dangerous and even less popular occupation in Donegal, a fact reflected in a decision of the traditional insurers to withdraw cover.⁵⁶

The creation of an alternative court system was central to the political revolution. As well as asserting the authority of the Dáil and the counter state, the courts allowed SF to defuse some of the social and agrarian discontent growing at a time of political turmoil. Land agitation was more widespread in the west of Ireland in 1920 than for some years.[57] Donegal was no exception, but SF managed to defuse and redirect it. SF courts had begun to appear sporadically during 1919 and in May 1920 the Dáil approved a formal scheme for parish and district courts.[58] This was a pivotal moment. In July Lord Dunraven, the leading southern unionist, wrote to the *Times* that an illegal government had become the *de facto* government, its jurisdiction was recognized, and justice was being administered promptly and equably. His conclusion was that law and order was not the problem but rather the 'origin of the law', that is sovereignty.[59] In Donegal, while the militant phase was slow to appear, the political counter state was well advanced, in part due to the influence of P.J. Ward who was a solicitor. His clerk, Liam O'Duffy, who was appointed registrar by Austin Stack, minister for home affairs, was responsible for establishing parish and district courts in south Donegal.[60] Patrick Breslin, adjutant Donegal No. 1 Brigade, IRA was appointed registrar of the west Donegal district court.[61]

At its first meeting in June, DCC granted an application for the use of Ballyshannon courthouse for sittings of the republican courts.[62] An unsuccessful attempt had been made earlier that month to burn down the courthouse, presumably by the same group now claiming public ownership of the building.[63] The matter was raised in the House of Commons by Tory MPs who demanded to know what the government was going to do about barristers appearing in illegal courts in publicly owned courthouses. Hamar Greenwood, the new Irish chief secretary, denied that the courthouse was being used illegally.[64] In June and in August police seized documents relating to the establishment and operation of republican courts court in various parts of the county, including Ballyshannon.[65] Parish and district courts began to function across Donegal. A parish clerk and three justices were appointed in parish courts and district judges were also appointed.[66] The courts at Dungloe operated relatively freely and held a number of sittings from late June.[67] Courts were also reported in Bundoran, Glenties, Donegal and Letterkenny.[68] Cases ranged from drunkenness to assault and theft; more serious offences were rare. Visitors to Bundoran charged with drunkenness were ordered to leave the district immediately.[69] The court in Donegal was raided while in session but Liam O'Duffy managed to secrete all incriminating documents. He was less fortunate during a raid on 20 October 1920 and was sentenced to one year's imprisonment.[70]

The courts achieved a measure of popularity and a reputation for imposing prompt and effective sanctions, although Peadar O'Donnell claimed that the AOH resisted them.⁷¹ Some litigants chose to appear before the republican courts rather than the British alternative; those who did not were liable to persuasion. Patrick Doherty, an IRA leader in Inishowen, recalled his involvement in this activity. An elderly man who brought a case to the official court in Letterkenny was detained by Volunteers and made swear on his knees that he would desist, but he defied the threats.⁷² In some towns men wearing armlets with the letters IRP (Irish Republican Police) appeared on the streets.⁷³ In west Donegal, the successful operation of the courts required a jail in which to detain offenders and a herring station at Meenacross was pressed into service. It continued to be used until 1922 for the SF courts and for those detained by the IRA.⁷⁴

A more extreme measure in the battle for hearts and minds was the burning of courthouses to prevent British courts being held. Doherty was involved in the burning of courthouses in Malin and Carndonagh. Liam O'Duffy led a group that burned the courthouse in Donegal town, resulting in £600 compensation for the caretaker.⁷⁵ Moville courthouse was burned on 3 August and similar attempts were made elsewhere in the latter half of 1920.⁷⁶ There was also a campaign to persuade magistrates and petty sessions clerks to resign, which met with some success.⁷⁷ Such activities highlight a problematic aspect of the courts: theoretically they operated under the direct authority of the Dáil and were not subject locally to any other authority. In practice, their operation was wholly dependent on the IRA. Of necessity, their operation was haphazard, and the justice dispensed rough and ready. In some respects, their importance was symbolic.

The initial reaction of the British authorities had been to observe but not interfere with the courts, but they quickly realized their mistake as they were losing the propaganda war. By the time they began to clamp down, it was too late.⁷⁸ By the end of August 1920, DI Patrick Walsh, in a report on behalf of the CI, conceded that the vast majority of the people of Donegal were adherents of SF.⁷⁹ It later transpired that Walsh was unusually well informed as he was a SF sympathizer himself who more than once proved a useful asset to the IRA. In August 1920, when he received evidence that implicated Captain James McMonagle of the Letterkenny company, Dr J.P. McGinley and others in an attack on Drumquin RIC barracks in Tyrone in which a policeman was killed, Walsh destroyed the evidence and tipped off McGinley.⁸⁰

In the battle for hearts and minds, compliance was enforced where necessary by the traditional weapon of the boycott. Hostility to the police had resulted in a sporadic boycott from late in 1919, which spread more widely in 1920. In Dungloe tradesmen who did work for the RIC received threatening letters.⁸¹ In June the boycott was stepped up. Boycott notices appeared in Burtonport, Dungloe and Killybegs and threatening letters were sent to those supplying the police or doing business with them. The carts of two men who

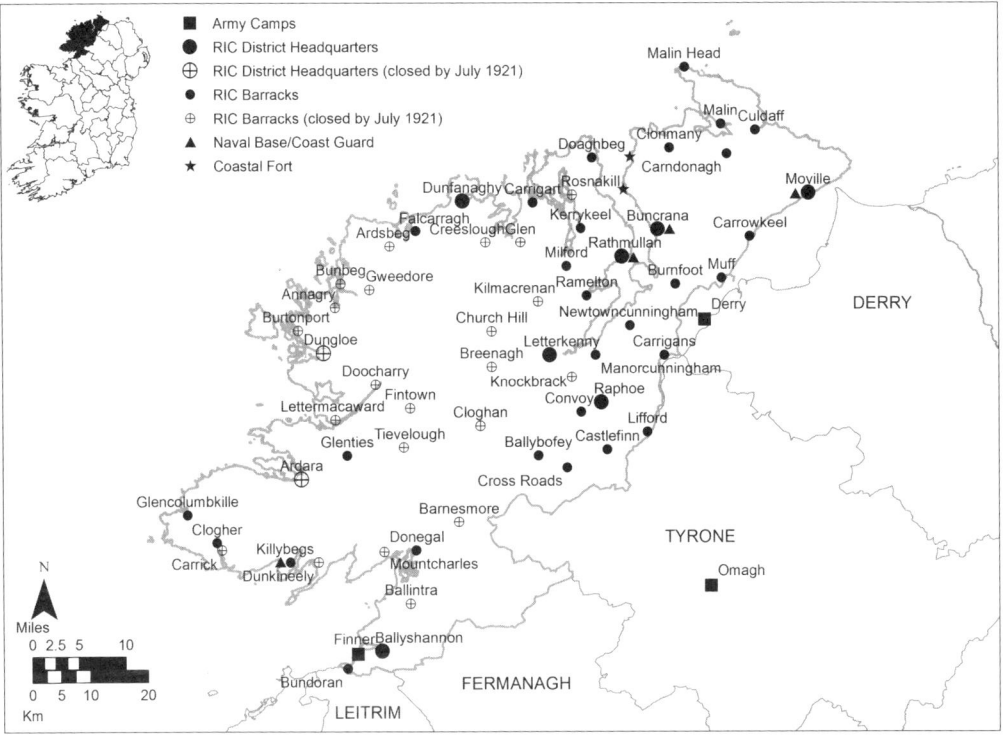

5 Distribution of Crown forces

supplied turf to the police in Creeslough were damaged. CI John Hughes, a 30-year veteran of the RIC, noted that the public attitude to the police was becoming increasingly aloof, making it difficult to do their job.[82] In July Hughes reported that 'over the whole of the county, a state of intimidation now exists'. The situation had been exacerbated by the withdrawal of the police from some areas, which left the population at large more susceptible to pressure (see map 5). The campaign extended throughout south and west Donegal and even 'people of the better class' avoided interaction with the RIC.[83]

While the aim of the boycott was the isolation of the RIC, the means to that end was surveillance and enforced community compliance. The weapon gradually extended well beyond policing to other areas of civic and social life. In reporting on 'enemy social institutions', the IRA intelligence officer of No. 3 (South Donegal) Brigade complained about the elitist Killybegs 'swank' tennis club whose 'small-minded' members were introducing 'foreign manners' into Donegal.[84] The enforcement of the authority of the new republican courts was facilitated by the persuasion of magistrates to resign and of litigants not to bring cases to the petty sessions. Establishment of the authority of the newly created Dáil department of local government was facilitated where necessary by similar methods.

Much of the attention in the writing on this period has focused on activists who constituted a small fraction of the population. Less attention has been devoted to the experience of non-combatants. As the intensity of the struggle heightened, so did the impact on the population at large. The capacity to remain neutral diminished and communal pressure to take sides grew. Anything less than wholehearted public embrace of the cause was increasingly risky, particularly with the retreat of the police from many areas. Loyalists and erstwhile constitutionalists learned to remain silent: Ernie O'Malley put it bluntly, 'people eventually learned to shut their eyes and close their mouths'.[85] In the meantime, the incipient new order enforced conformity. This was not accomplished without collateral damage to individuals and groups, not least women. The extent of intimidation and violence towards women by both sides has been highlighted by several historians. The ritual humiliation of women by forcible hair cutting was a 'symbolic and bodily violation', a traumatic punishment for the individual woman accused of fraternization or collaboration and a potent public weapon in enforcing community compliance.[86]

Such incidents were often unreported but occasionally they came to public notice. On the night of 11 September 1920, a boy called to a house on Erne Street in Ballyshannon inquiring if a female lodger was at home. The woman worked as a domestic in the RIC station around the corner. Twenty minutes later, four armed and masked men burst in, seized and gagged her and dragged her to a nearby meadow. She was beaten and her hair was closely shorn. Berated as a traitor to her country and her religion, she was forced to swear that she would not return to work in the RIC station. The victim reported the assault to the police and was given accommodation in the barracks for nine weeks for her own protection. Afterwards, she was unable to find employment locally. She lodged a compensation claim, which was heard at the next quarter sessions. Witnesses confirmed that she had suffered bruising to her face and 'continued to suffer from nervousness'. Judge Cooke commented that it was a novel claim but awarded her £40 to be levied off the ratepayers of Ballyshannon urban and rural districts.[87] It is impossible to ascertain how people locally viewed such incidents but the headline in the newly established *Donegal Democrat*, which was a pro-SF newspaper published in the town, may suggest a lack of sympathy for the victim: '£40 for shorn hair: Ballyshannon woman's claim at Quarter Sessions'.[88] Neither is it possible to estimate with any certainty how often such cases occurred in Donegal. At the quarter sessions, the police stated that the boycott of the RIC was being 'rigorously enforced' locally and there is some evidence from SF court documents that non-compliance may have been considered by the local parish or district court.[89]

As the intensity of the conflict grew and animosity towards the police escalated, more such incidents occurred. In south Donegal, two girls who had their hair shorn brought their case to a Dáil court and were awarded compensation.⁹⁰ In April 1921 three cases of hair cutting were reported and another the following month. In Middletown a party of armed men entered a house, shot the owner in the thigh and cut the hair of a woman who was present. The motive was said to be 'agrarian and family friction'. In the Falcarragh district, the house of a Mary Gallagher was raided by armed men, her hair was cut, and her dog was poisoned.⁹¹ Also in Falcarragh, on the evening of 24 April, Rose Anne Logue was abducted by armed men while walking near her home. They cut her hair and warned her that she would be shot if she remained on friendly terms with the police. It was reported that her offence was that she had placed a wreath on the grave of a constable who had been killed in the neighbourhood.⁹² The policeman in question may have been Constable James McKenna from Longford. He had been stationed in Falcarragh since 1918 and was shot near the police barracks on the night of 20 March.⁹³ Some local shopkeepers closed their shops the next day, but it was claimed that this was a result of intimidation from police and military rather than a mark of respect.⁹⁴

The boycott weapon was not only deployed against the police. When thousands of Catholic workmen were forced out of their jobs in the summer of 1920, the Dáil announced a Belfast boycott. Although this was problematic in areas with mixed populations, strenuous efforts were made to enforce it in Donegal. In Ballyshannon, Protestant shopkeepers came under considerable pressure to refuse to sell goods from Belfast and some prudently decided to publicly announce their intention to comply. This followed an incident where a car belonging to a commercial traveller from Belfast was commandeered and dumped in the River Erne.⁹⁵ At a special meeting of the Ballyshannon Town Commission in August, a strongly worded motion was passed supporting the boycott and condemning 'unionist plutocrats and profiteers'.⁹⁶

In response to increasing violence against nationalists in Belfast, the Dáil department of labour instructed local authorities that the boycott was to be 'rigidly enforced'. What the phrase rigidly enforced might mean in practice was illustrated in May 1921 when the offices of the *Donegal Vindicator* were raided by the IRA and essential parts removed from printing machines and the firm's books were seized. The North of Ireland publishing company was responsible not just for the *Vindicator* but also the *Derry Weekly News*, the *Donegal Independent* and the *Fermanagh News*. Remarkably, the firm also published *An Dáil*, a republican propaganda sheet edited by Eily MacAdam who was a member of Cumann na mBan. It had earlier been closed down by the police and MacAdam had been arrested and imprisoned in Armagh for a short time. On her release, she initially refused to believe that the IRA was responsible for the latest raid. After the truce, she wrote to Eoin O'Duffy to have the parts returned so that the firm could stay in business and recommence publication of *An Dáil*. Its offence apparently was that it had printed business cards for northern firms that were on the Belfast boycott list. She pointed out that they had received no warning and that they were 'innocently at fault'. O'Duffy ordered that the matter be investigated.[97] Activity reports for the South Donegal Brigade indicate that the boycott remained a preoccupation well into 1922.[98]

The revolutionary movement was driven by the Dáil, SF and the IRA. In Donegal, government was rendered difficult, if not impossible, in this period due in particular to the IRA, which was ultimately in the vanguard of the revolution and increasingly its most potent weapon. The seizure of control of local government in Donegal in 1920 enabled the movement to assert its sovereignty and claim popular allegiance in most of the county with the exception of parts of east Donegal. The west of the county was a particular stronghold. The authority of the British state was effectively challenged in significant areas of local administration including policing, local taxation and justice. The reluctance or inability to go further to embrace other areas and functions of the state reflected the limitations of what was possible and perhaps also the nature of the enterprise. The refusal to address land redistribution and withhold land annuities payable to the Treasury, as Peadar O'Donnell would have liked, illustrated the extent to which a narrower political ideology was uppermost.

8 The storm: the War of Independence, 1919–21

> An bhliain ina dhiaidh, ba í bliain an chogaidh í. Bhí saighdiúirí na Sasana á marú i ngach gleann sa tír, agus bhíothas ag breith ar Éireannaigh agus á gcur chun báis, agus bhíothas ag dó tithe. Ní tháinigh mórán den chogadh go Ros Cuain.
>
> Seosamh Mac Grianna, *An druma mór*[1]

On 12 November 1919 a great Atlantic gale hit the north-west coast of Ireland. The event provided Peadar O'Donnell with a title for his autobiographical first novel, *Storm: a story of the Irish war*. Written while he was still in prison after the Civil War, it features an island schoolmaster who joins the IRA. The storm of the title is a metaphor for the conflict in which O'Donnell played a leading part.[2] Seosamh Mac Grianna was also an active participant. His characteristically understated description of the War of Independence in the north-west – 'not much of the war came to Ros Cuain' – is a useful corrective to those who would overstate the scale of events in Donegal. However, there is no doubting the impact of those events on the lives of the people.

Carl Von Clausewitz's often misunderstood aphorism that war was the continuation of politics by other means accurately describes events in Donegal during 1919–21. The IRA campaign was an extension of the political struggle at a local level and was seen as such by participants. When the campaign started is a matter of debate. The Soloheadbeg ambush in Tipperary on 21 January 1919 is often seen as the opening salvo in the war nationally. In the case of Donegal, an inscription on a monument at Meenbanad in the Rosses proclaims that the first action occurred there on 4 January 1918 when Irish Volunteers held up a train and rescued two army deserters who were being taken under military escort to Derry for trial.[3] While undoubtedly a daring action, accomplished without bloodshed, it was an isolated incident that did not spark off a protracted campaign. Most local historians would point instead to the Rampart ambush outside Dungloe on 12 December 1919, in which three policemen were injured, one seriously. It was a well-planned and co-ordinated attack, and it signalled a serious escalation in the conflict.[4] On hearing of the incident, Dr J.P. McGinley, the leading SF figure in Letterkenny whose arrest had in part provoked the ambush, declared to a friend that 'Donegal is awake in earnest now'.[5]

The year saw a concerted effort to improve the organization of the IRA in Donegal, as the presence of Ernie O'Malley, P.C. O'Mahony, and Seán Milroy among others, and the emergence of a rudimentary brigade structure attest. In January 1919, police were aware of the existence of six companies with a membership of 307 men. The number remained relatively stable, rising to seven companies and 335 men in June, following the establishment of a company in Killybegs, and eight by December with a total complement of 377 men.[6] Initially, O'Malley considered that geography determined that there should be two Donegal brigades – west and east. A police report from September 1919 took a similar view, but by the end of the year the brigade structure broadly followed the four parliamentary constituencies, with the elected SF TDs and Sam O'Flaherty in command and an additional brigade in Letterkenny. Given the manner in which they emerged, it is not surprising that the brigades reflected the geographical and cultural realities rather than a strict adherence to county boundaries. Thus, East Donegal included Strabane, while the 1st Battalion of the South Donegal Brigade embraced companies in Tullaghan and Kinlough in Leitrim, Cliffoney in Sligo, and Pettigo on the Donegal–Fermanagh border.[7] Their first major engagement was an attack on the customs office in Ballyshannon on 30 May 1920 in which disaster was narrowly averted when troops from nearby Finner camp threw a cordon around the town.[8]

O'Malley had been dispatched to Donegal by Michael Collins with the cheerful words: 'You will freeze to death up there'.[9] In January 1919 he organized a meeting at Frosses which established a council for the South Donegal Brigade and appointed P.J. Ward TD as O/C and Liam O'Duffy as adjutant. O'Duffy was subsequently involved in reorganizing all the companies and battalions in the area.[10] O'Malley also presided at the reorganization of the Bundoran IRA under the command of Thomas McShea with the increasingly influential Joseph Murray as intelligence officer. Murray recalled that the IRA continued to operate predominantly on a parish basis during 1919.[11] O'Malley's first impressions were negative – he thought the officers he encountered were 'slack' and talked a lot but were disinclined to follow when called on. He devoted considerable time to re-invigorating companies, organizing training and identifying able officers.[12]

The social profile of the movement broadly follows the pattern elsewhere. The senior leadership group came from the higher and lower professional classes, with solicitors and teachers foremost. Joe Sweeney's father was a successful merchant and shopkeeper; Sam O'Flaherty's family were strong farmers. Family background and education were important: all the leadership group had secondary and higher education. The rank and file were drawn predominantly from the small farming and labouring classes. In west Donegal many were migrant labourers.[13]

During the summer of 1919, the absence of migratory labourers in Scotland contributed to a lack of political activity. Large meetings were announced for Carrick on 29 July, and Ardara and Bundoran on 31 August that were to be addressed by Seán Milroy, who had escaped from Lincoln Jail with de Valera in February. When the meetings were proclaimed, the IRA engaged in an elaborate game of bluff to enable them to proceed. A large force of Volunteers in military formation marched out in the direction of Killybegs to divert the police. As proceedings were about to begin in Ardara, police and military arrived under the command of DI Moore of Raphoe. A stand-off ensued. A serious incident was narrowly avoided when bayonets were drawn and the IRA was forced to disperse.[14] Milroy immediately made his way to Bundoran where a similar ruse was used. Police and military were successfully lured away to the east of the town, allowing the meeting to commence in the west end. Again, it was disrupted by fixed bayonets.[15]

For the most part, the IRA was preoccupied with sporadic arms raids and occasional acts of disruption such as blocking roads, cutting telegraph wires and the interception of supplies to police stations. The South Donegal Brigade benefitted from the recruitment of a number of First World War veterans who were useful for training purposes, but the lack of arms and ammunition remained a problem.[16] In 1919 that brigade had only a few old shotguns and some old revolvers. Raids on unionist farmhouses produced more of the same. Thomas McShea was sent to Dublin with funds to purchase arms from headquarters and returned with a single rifle.[17] James McNulty, O/C 3rd Battalion, was wounded in late January when leading an arms raid by Creeslough IRA on the home of Andrew Wilkinson JP. McNulty was moved to the Mater Hospital in Dublin for treatment but quickly resumed his position.[18] A planned raid on a house in Raphoe for UVF arms was thwarted by the police who seized the arms themselves.[19]

Leo Lafferty from Dublin was sent to Inishowen to organize companies. In April the IRA raided Ned's Fort, near Buncrana.[20] The only soldier present was disarmed and tied up but there were no other arms in the fort. A few nights later, shots were fired by a sentry at two men scaling the walls of Fort Dunree, which was heavily garrisoned.[21] In September, following a report that large amounts of UVF arms were stored at Baronscourt, near Sion Mills, a fruitless raid was organized. When it was reported that the arms had been moved to a house near Greencastle, owned by Sir Robert Anderson, mayor of Derry, another raid was planned but it was aborted amidst confusion.[22]

In December came the attack that marked the beginning of a new more militant phase. DI Wallace, Sergeant Farrell and two police constables were ambushed outside Dungloe in retaliation for the arrest and prosecution of two locals, Anthony McGinley and Charles McBride, and Dr J.P. McGinley from Letterkenny for soliciting for the Dáil loan.[23] The ambush forced a reassessment on the part of the police who admitted that the IRA existed in the west of the county to a much greater extent than they had believed. CI Hughes admitted for the first time that the IRA posed a serious threat.[24] Had he been aware that the arms carried by the IRA involved in the Dungloe ambush consisted only of a revolver, a shotgun, a rifle and a grenade, he might have been less concerned. It was hardly surprising that the acquisition of arms preoccupied the IRA in the following months.[25]

The organization of Cumann na mBan continued apace during 1919. Alice Cashel, who returned to Donegal in January 1919, organized a series of indoor meetings to promote Cumann na mBan.[26] New branches were established almost monthly until August by which time there were nineteen with a membership of 556. According to the RIC, there were considerably more branches and members of Cumann na mBan in Donegal than IRA. This seems implausible but it does underline the strength of the women's organization in the county. No new branches were noted by police after 1919, although membership grew marginally to a peak of 606.[27] The organization was particularly active in Gortahork in the neighbourhood of Coláiste Uladh, which contributed to the college being burned in November 1920 as a reprisal. Police denied involvement and blamed the AOH.[28]

From December 1919, the military activities of the IRA escalated. This transition from sporadic incidents and arms raids to direct attacks on police barracks and larger-scale operations reflects the first of three major evolutionary stages in the model of the war postulated by historian Charles Townshend, but with a time-lag in the case of Donegal.[29] By the summer of 1920, there was evidence that the political and military strategy was bearing fruit both in relation to the campaign against the RIC and the transfer of popular allegiance. The combination of the boycott and a growing volume of IRA actions achieved dramatic results relatively quickly. In June 1920 a policy of consolidation of police began in response to attacks on barracks in isolated areas and police resignations. A number of stations were closed (see map 5). These were then burned by the IRA – in all fourteen barracks were torched. In July CI Hughes conceded that the police were unable to deal with the situation without military support.[30]

By September the RIC had completely evacuated from Dungloe district and concentrated their forces in Falcarragh and Dunfanaghy. The police at Ardara were evacuated to Glenties and Killybegs. This decision was precipitated by the withdrawal of the British army from the west of the county. Military contingents at Killybegs, Ardara, Glenties and Dungloe were transferred to Strabane with detachments at Donegal, Ballybofey and Letterkenny; the wireless station at Bunbeg was also guarded by the army.[31] Hughes frankly admitted that this meant that there would be practically no control over the part of the county west of a line from Falcarragh to Killybegs, which would be seen as a notable victory for the IRA. This gave free rein to the West Donegal Brigade under Joe Sweeney but it also made it more difficult for the IRA to operate successfully elsewhere in the county. Control over west Donegal was never fully recovered, even with the introduction of the Black and Tans to support the police and the adoption of a more aggressive military and policing policy. Remarkably, by April 1921 the Dungloe police district (about a sixth of the county) was still unpoliced and was described as 'a miniature republic'.[32]

In south and east Donegal, much of the IRA activity focused on the border with Fermanagh (around Belleek and Pettigo) and with Tyrone (around Lifford). On 26 July, for the first time, there was a daylight raid for arms on Drumquin RIC barracks in Tyrone. Led by Sam O'Flaherty with men from four companies, the raid was well planned, but it went awry when shooting started prematurely and some of the men 'lost their heads'. One policeman was killed and another injured.[33] In another daylight raid in September led by Frank Carney of the Fermanagh Brigade, assisted by men from Ballyshannon and Bundoran, an old British army ambulance was used as a decoy to gain entry to Belleek barracks and yielded a rich harvest of weapons, including two machine guns.[34] It would be an anachronism to describe Donegal as a border county but with the spectre of partition looming, it increasingly took on some of the aspects of a frontier with notable flashpoints. This intensified from the second half of 1920 when IRA GHQ in Dublin supported a strategy of destabilizing unionist Ulster.

The uneven nature of the War of Independence geographically has been well documented with Donegal one of the less active counties.[35] The extent of guerrilla activity in the county can be tracked through the returns of indictable offences. Not all incidents were reported; of those that were, not all constituted indictable offences; and not all indictable offences were political. However, so-called ordinary crime in these years constituted a tiny fraction of the total. While agrarian crime was somewhat more frequent, it accounted for only a small proportion of indictable crime and as guerrilla activity increased that proportion diminished. In August 1920 only two of eighty-two crimes were agrarian in nature and in July 1921 only two out of seventy-four. In May 1921 Henry McGowan from Ballybofey led a raid in Ballintra on the offices of Captain Hamilton, who was reputed to be collecting rents for the trustees of the Trinity College estates. The local IRA had requested the raid but had asked that it be undertaken by outsiders to avoid recognition. Only £5 was seized as most of the rental had already been lodged. The police did not categorize this incident as agrarian.[36]

The figures for indictable crime provide an accurate measure of militant activity and when compared with the brigade activity reports, they show a similar pattern.[37] In 1918 and 1919, the average monthly number of such offences was seven in both years. The rate increased significantly in the summer of 1920 with peaks in August (82) and September (81) before falling by more than half by the end of the year. The numbers rose steeply again in the months before the truce with 79, 85 and 74 indictable offences occurring respectively in April, May and June 1921.[38] The number of indictable offences reported nationally in June 1921 was 2,256.³⁹ While the number of incidents in Donegal was similar to the summer of 1920, their seriousness had increased. Arms raids and offences against communications continued to preponderate but there were some more significant incidents. The breakdown for June is indicative: twenty cases of malicious damage to roads, railways and telegraph lines; seventeen raids for arms; fourteen malicious burnings of property; eight post office raids and raids on mail; two bank raids; three raids on railway stores; two attacks on the military, two attacks on the police, one attack on a coast guard station and a single instance of cattle maiming.⁴⁰

The increased level of activity coincided with the arrival early in 1921 of experienced fighters from the south and east who were on the run. While their number was exaggerated, their presence reflected both an impatience on the part of GHQ with progress in Donegal and a policy of stepping up the campaign in Ulster in the face of impending partition.⁴¹ A related factor was the creation of a flying column or active service unit on the instructions of GHQ. This was a strategic response to the localized nature of much of the campaign hitherto and was also necessitated by the increasing numbers of IRA who were on the run to escape arrest. It allowed the most experienced fighters to be deployed flexibly when and where they were needed to bolster local companies and lead more ambitious engagements.

The creation of the ASU marked the onset of the second transitionary stage in Townshend's typology of the war but Donegal again lagged behind other parts of the country.⁴² Commanded by Peadar O'Donnell, the ASU was formed initially in the Bogside in Derry in late December and contained members from Derry, Armagh, Monaghan, Tipperary and Cork.⁴³ It crossed into Donegal and made its way to the Dungloe area where it linked up with Joe Sweeney's brigade and was involved in a series of attacks.⁴⁴ Their first major engagement was an ambush at Meenbanad on a train carrying troops to Burtonport on 12 January. Boulders were placed on the line to stop the train and heavy fire was directed at the disembarking troops who managed to fight off the attack. At the time, it was wrongly claimed that heavy casualties were suffered by the troops.⁴⁵ Another attack on a train followed shortly afterwards at Crolly and on 23 January an unsuccessful attempt was made to blow up Falcarragh RIC barracks using guncotton. A smaller second ASU was established in the Dungloe area, led by Daniel Sweeney.⁴⁶

Attacks on trains played an important part in the IRA campaign. The Meenbanad ambush was cited by *An tÓglach* as a model.⁴⁷ The main aim of such attacks was to disrupt troop movements and supply lines. There were other advantages – mail robberies were a useful source of intelligence and helped disrupt the civil administration; and the Belfast boycott was enforced by raids on goods arriving from Belfast at train stations.⁴⁸ In July 1920 an order from the IRA to train drivers not to drive engines carrying troops or munitions was partially successful in disrupting railway traffic in many parts of the county. On 30 July the Strabane to Letterkenny line closed when drivers were suspended for refusing to carry armed troops and those who volunteered to replace them were dissuaded from doing so. Around the same time, all traffic on the Bundoran to Omagh line ceased for the same reason. The following month, railway traffic in the county was reported to be largely paralyzed.[49] The Strabane to Letterkenny line reopened in November and railway men on the Lough Swilly and Donegal Railways resumed work, having agreed to carry all traffic.[50] The dependence on the railways for troop movements was increased by the withdrawal of Crown forces from west Donegal and their concentration in the east and south. Police and troops had to be moved in and out of the west of the county repeatedly for operations against the IRA which offered a target for sniping attacks. As a result, the army began to use the sea route from Derry to Dungloe as a backdoor to west Donegal. On four occasions between 7 and 15 February, the railway line to Dungloe was torn up to prevent troop movements – in one case the train was also derailed.[51] In response, the area was saturated by police and military making it difficult for the IRA to operate.

One of the most notorious events occurred in February 1921. Mountcharles RIC barracks had been abandoned in September 1920, following a number of attacks, and the police relocated to Donegal town where they were reinforced by a contingent of Black and Tans. From there, they periodically patrolled in the Mountcharles area. A small group of IRA from the 3rd (Donegal) Brigade laid an ambush at the Glen, outside Mountcharles, on 22 February. Constable Thomas Satchwell was killed, and a soldier wounded.[52] When Satchwell's body was brought back to Donegal town, shops were ordered to close and police and Black and Tans ransacked and burned more than a dozen buildings, including the offices of P.J. Ward.[53] Later that night in Mountcharles, more houses were ransacked and burned. In the confusion, a policeman was shot by a colleague, apparently in a case of mistaken identity, and Mary Harley, a 28-year-old dressmaker who was visiting her uncle from London, was shot dead as she fled a burning building.[54] The CI attributed these events to loyalists, but they were clearly reprisals by the Crown forces. In a move that further soured local opinion, they returned to the village on the day of Mary Harley's funeral and cordoned it off. Four months after Thomas Satchell's death, his family home in Roscommon was burned by armed men.[55]

Bishop O'Donnell condemned the killing of Satchwell as a 'barbarous murder' and took comfort from the mistaken belief that no locals were involved. O'Donnell also denounced the reprisals as 'outrageous misrule'.[56] His intervention is noteworthy as he and the clergy had remained relatively quiet in the face of developments over the previous two years. Fr O'Neill, a curate in Lifford, had condemned the shooting at Dungloe in December 1919 but it was noted that the local clergy in the area had not done so. Whatever their private opinions, moderate nationalists were not inclined to draw attention to themselves by publicly criticizing disorder.[57] In a Lenten pastoral in February 1921, O'Donnell had even-handedly proclaimed that a single murder on whatever side was 'an awful crime' against God and man but, leaving no doubt as to where he felt the blame lay, he added that 'misrule always leads to crime'. O'Donnell specifically condemned the policy of reprisals, arbitrary arrest, and imprisonment without trial as 'a disgrace for any country, savage or civilised'.[58] He issued a forthright condemnation when a 20-year-old RIC man was killed in Letterkenny in May, not far from the bishop's palace. Retaliation by the Black and Tans was avoided only by the intervention of DI Walsh.[59]

Pressure from the military resulted in a hiatus in IRA activity in west Donegal. There was evidence of indiscipline and lack of commitment in some companies, which Joe Sweeney attempted to address.[60] Communications between GHQ and the local commandants, including Sweeney and Peadar O'Donnell, reveal significant problems with arms, training and morale, and an impatience on each side at what were seen as the failures of the other. In reply to criticism from Michael Collins about lack of activity in Donegal, Sweeney cited lack of arms.[61] To the annoyance of GHQ he returned some rifles that he had been lent by Henry McGowan, acting O/C 4th Brigade (South East Donegal). Richard Mulcahy, chief of staff, pointed to the incongruity of sending arms back from an area which had 'made Donegal what it is'.[62] McGowan's area also came under criticism for its inactivity, which he blamed on the strong garrison at Ballybofey and the lack of officers due to arrests.[63] Joseph Murray from the Bundoran company was appointed as adjutant with a brief to reorganize the brigade and was later appointed acting O/C when McGowan was arrested on 10 June.[64]

The arrest and imprisonment of IRA officers had a significant impact on operations. This was particularly the case after the British decision in November 1920 to adopt a policy of mass arrests and internment using the new powers granted under the Restoration of Order in Ireland regulations. On 6 December six members of the IRA were arrested in east Donegal and detained in the recently opened Ballykinlar internment camp. Between then and the truce in July, seventy-nine Donegal men were imprisoned there. The treatment of these and other prisoners became a focus of public controversy.[65]

In March 1920 Richard Mulcahy ordered a reorganization of the IRA brigades in the No. 1 Northern Division. Frank Carney from Enniskillen was appointed O/C. An ex-serviceman, he was an active member of the IRB and had been O/C Fermanagh Brigade. The four Donegal brigades were 1st West (Burtonport, Falcarragh, Gweedore and Dungloe); 2nd North-East (Stranorlar,

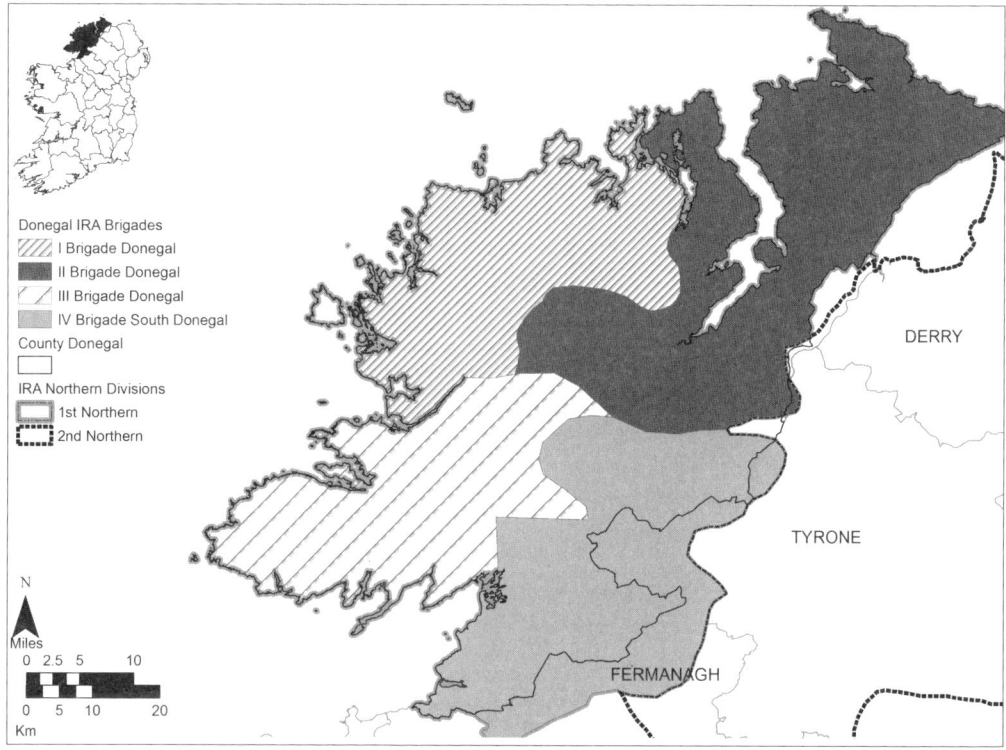

6 IRA battalion, brigade, divisional areas

Strabane, Derry, Inishowen, Letterkenny); 3rd South-West (Ardara, Killybegs, Rosses); 4th South-East (Ballyshannon including Belleek, Ederney including Pettigo, Castlederg, Ballybofey).[66] The inclusion of Belleek, Ederney, Castlederg and Derry reflected a strategic decision in the context of the evolving political situation. Peadar O'Donnell was appointed O/C 2nd Brigade.

The reorganization quickly ran into trouble because of conflict between Carney and O'Donnell. Carney was resented as an outsider and his popularity was not enhanced by his tardiness in visiting the brigades under his command. O'Donnell, who had been wounded seriously on 10 April, and Carney shared a mutual dislike that led to disagreements. Carney wanted O'Donnell to concentrate his efforts in north-east Donegal and Derry, but the demographic profile made it more difficult to operate there than on O'Donnell's home turf in west Donegal. His preference for that area also caused some friction with Joe Sweeney. O'Donnell understood that the acid test of the effectiveness of a guerrilla army was closeness to the people. However, his impetuosity brought him into conflict with IRA leaders in Derry who resented his actions in launching a series of attacks that provoked reprisals. Carney complained about him and ordered his suspension for insubordination. O'Donnell appealed his case. Liam Archer, a GHQ officer, investigated and his report was highly critical of O'Donnell, but he was left in post.[67] Joe Sweeney was appointed divisional O/C in place of Carney who had been arrested. O'Donnell was probably a better revolutionary than he was a soldier. He had a very clear view from his own perspective of the nature of the struggle and particularly of its political and social dimensions. He did not function well within a command structure but, at a time when others felt that discretion was the better part of valour, he was impatient for action. Those observing events from GHQ were aware of that.

In May 1921 two policemen, Alexander Clarke and Charles Murdoch, were ambushed and shot while walking near Clonmany barracks. Both bodies were thrown in the sea.[68] Three days later, the results of the general election to elect members to the two home rule parliaments to be created in Ireland under the Government of Ireland Act (1920) were declared. SF treated the elections as elections to the second Dáil. On this occasion the county was constituted as a single six-seat constituency. SF nominated its three outgoing TDs along with Samuel O'Flaherty (who had stood aside in 1918), Dr J.P. McGinley and P.J. McGoldrick. Edward Kelly, the outgoing IPP MP, did not seek re-election and the unionists, who would probably have won a seat, decided not to contest. The six SF candidates were duly returned unopposed.[69] In contrast, the elections for the Northern Ireland parliament were a significant setback for SF: Unionists won 40 of 52 seats with SF and the UIL winning six each.

A key factor in the political settlements, which later emerged, was that the Ulster question was dealt with before the British government seriously engaged with SF. This was a deliberate strategy on the part of Lloyd George. The Government of Ireland Act (1920) came into force on 3 May 1921. From that day, a border existed between Donegal and the six excluded counties. Donegal was isolated not alone from its Ulster neighbours but to a considerable extent from the rest of Ireland as the only land route from the county which did not cross the new border was via the bridge on the River Erne at Ballyshannon. Not surprisingly, the provisions of the act in relation to the south were largely ignored by SF but the creation of the new northern parliament went ahead. Thus, partition was an established if not widely recognized fact by May 1921. Significantly, it was at the opening of that parliament at Belfast City Hall that George V made the first overtures that led to the truce with SF and the Treaty of December 1921.

The exclusion of six counties left both unionists and nationalists in Donegal unhappy. Bishop O'Donnell had been willing to contemplate 'county option' as the only form of partition 'with any semblance of justification' but exclusion of six counties *en bloc* was anathema. In a rare interview with the *Manchester Guardian*, he spoke passionately about the abandonment of the Catholic minority. He accurately predicted that SF would hold aloof and that the bill would only strengthen the hands of the extremists.[70] On the other side of the fence, the unionist minority in Donegal were equally discommoded. In March 1920 the UUC, after a week of deliberation in committee and full conference, had decided not to oppose the government's decision to include the 'outpost counties' of Donegal, Cavan and Monaghan within the jurisdiction of the proposed southern parliament.[71] Unionists in the three counties were caught unawares. In July 1916 they had reluctantly agreed to six-county exclusion but only as a sacrifice for the Empire at a time of 'great national emergency' and on the understanding that if the concession was rejected, their demand would revert to the full nine counties of Ulster. The reaction in Donegal was hostile and was not helped by the *Derry Journal* headline: 'Unionists thrown over by their own friends'.[72] Meetings of the unionist associations in the three counties passed motions emphatically protesting against their abandonment. A campaign was hastily launched to have the decision reversed.[73] A statement by the UUC delegates from Donegal, Cavan and Monaghan was publicized stating their case.

The delegates from the 'outpost counties' met at Clones on 7 April. Those in attendance from Donegal were Mrs Agnes Boyd, Major R.L. Moore, Major Myles, Captain Wagentreiber, Captain Hamilton, Robert Neely, T.C. Wylie and J. Allen Osborne.[74] The Monaghan and Cavan delegates agreed to submit their resignations to the UUC in protest. A special meeting of the UUC was demanded to revisit the decision.[75] The meeting was held on 27 May in the Ulster Hall with Edward Carson presiding and a large crowd in attendance. A motion in favour of nine-county exclusion was proposed by General Ambrose Ricardo of Sion Mills and seconded by Colonel Perceval Maxwell from Downpatrick. The proceedings were conducted in private, but it was clearly an emotional debate. Those in favour argued that separating Donegal, Cavan and Monaghan was a breach of the Ulster Covenant and would mean an abandonment of friends and family. Those against argued that if they insisted on nine counties, the bill would fall and the default was then home rule for all of Ireland. It was also argued that, with proportional representation in operation, a nine-county unit would be inherently unstable. An amendment reaffirming the original decision was carried by a large majority.[76] The outcome, which was a source of considerable bitterness and disappointment, was described by the *Londonderry Sentinel* as deplorable. Sproule Myles did not spend long licking his wounds: within days of the decision, he took his seat on the county council and became a valuable member of its finance committee.[77]

The negotiations following the king's speech at the inauguration of the new Northern parliament in June culminated in a truce on 11 July. News of the cessation broke in the press first and brigade commanders had to contact their battalions to confirm that it was official.[78] Volunteers who had been on the run returned home and IRA companies began to parade and train publicly in a way that was previously impossible. Training camps and specialist engineering classes were organized.[79] The truce was widely welcomed by the nationalist press. The *Donegal Democrat* anticipated that it would create an atmosphere favourable to a settlement. The *Donegal News* agreed and called for the truce to be obeyed. On the other side, the speeches at the twelfth of July celebrations reflected a nervousness about what might emerge from negotiations.[80] The truce was generally observed in the county and the number of incidents fell dramatically. One ominous exception was the burning of the First Presbyterian church on Main Street, Letterkenny. The cause of the fire was unknown.[81]

CI Foster reported that the people were weary of the violence. Quoting an informant, he claimed that the IRA in Donegal were finding it difficult to carry on: they were short of funds and munitions, and Volunteers were glad of an excuse to give up the fight. The speculation about munitions and funding was accurate; the assertion about the disposition of the men may have been true for some but certainly not for all, as events were later to prove.[82] To address the shortage of funds, businesses and property owners were levied by the IRA: even Bishop O'Donnell was not exempt but the local commander helpfully added a postscript on the formal demand notice that in his case, the contribution would be voluntary.[83] In a report to IRA GHQ not long before the truce, Joe Sweeney complained about the difficulties caused by extreme poverty in west Donegal and the fact that his best officers were absent for months at a time because of seasonal migration.[84] There is evidence at least in south Donegal after the truce that some IRA had ceased attending meetings and musters and had to be called to account.[85] The police report in August written by DI Patrick Walsh – a SF spy, which may lend his views more credibility – detected a 'general and widespread desire for peace' in the county and a corresponding reluctance to contemplate a return to war. He thought that any reasonable settlement would be welcomed.[86]

A letter from Joseph Murray on 11 August to officers in Belleek who were discontented because their battalion was being divided, gives an insight into the attitude of the IRA leadership in south Donegal. Murray stressed that it was an opportune time for organization and 'knitting units together':

> We will either have to fight or we will have peace. I don't know which but in either case the IRA will require training and discipline. If we have to fight, the country will have to depend on us for protection and defence; if we have peace, it will look to us for the only available machinery for taking charge of our affairs.[87]

The War of Independence in Donegal was on a smaller scale than much of the rest of the country with the intensity of activity increasing later than elsewhere and with a preponderance of 'small jobs' rather than major incidents. Charles Townshend's comment that 'no amount of prodding from above could spur the slow-starters to make up lost ground' might reasonably be applied to the campaign in the county.[88] The IRA was most effective in the west of the county; in the east, the concentrated strength of enemy military forces constrained activity. With the implementation of the Government of Ireland Act and the creation of a border, the cold reality of partition could not be ignored for much longer.[89]

The scale of military activity is reflected in the casualty rate. During the period 1917–21, there were at least 2,356 fatalities attributable to the political violence in Ireland, of which twenty-nine were in Donegal.[90] Excluding deaths by misadventure, there were twenty-two Donegal fatalities: one in 1918, three in 1920 and eighteen in 1921, the bloodiest year of the conflict. Eight of the fatalities were policemen; four were IRA. The only British army casualty was Robert John Clout, accidentally shot at Finner in 1920. Major George Hamilton Johnston, a 70-year-old Protestant landowner and home rule supporter, was also shot in 1920, apparently accidentally during an IRA arms raid at his home in Ardara.[91] The third fatality that year was Thomas Rooney, an ex-serviceman from Ballyshannon who worked for the *Donegal Democrat*. He was shot by a member of a joint police and military patrol after he failed to stop when challenged.[92] The fatalities in 1921 included eight RIC men, two of them accidentally shot by their comrades; two coastguards, one killed by the IRA and the other a suicide; three IRA; and four civilians, all shot by the Crown forces. Mary Harley was the only female fatality. The last fatality before the Treaty was a civil bills officer who died after being assaulted and kidnapped, apparently to prevent him giving evidence at Lifford quarter sessions.[93]

The police were the main casualties of the war in Donegal. In a touching scene in Peadar O'Donnell's didactic novel, *Storm*, the schoolteacher, Éamonn Gallagher, who is about to depart the island to join the struggle, is asked by his tearful colleague Máire if he stood for murdering policemen; he replies quietly, 'I do'. Like his protagonist, O'Donnell and his colleagues wrestled with that dilemma and concluded that they should do what was necessary. Others, including it would appear O'Donnell's brother Frank, were less sure which may explain the relatively low number of fatalities.[94]

9 Cogadh na gcarad: the Civil War, 1922–3

> Rud iontach agus ábhar machnaimh dhá dhream in aghaidh a chéile, go háirid dhá dhream a bhfuil aithne mhaith acu ar a chéile. Ni bheadh gar a rá le ceachtar acu go raibh ceart, dá laghad é, ag an taobh eile. An té is fearúla a throideas ar son a thaobh féin, is é is mó a mbíonn fuath ag an taobh eile air. Agus lena chois sin, an té is fealltaí dá thaobh féin, is é is mó a mbíonn meas ag an taobh eile air.
>
> Seosamh Mac Grianna, *An druma mór*[1]

In *Green against green*, a pioneering account of the Irish Civil War, Michael Hopkinson declared that nowhere was that fraternal conflict more bitter and forlorn than in County Donegal.[2] Insofar as this is true, the reasons are not immediately obvious. Donegal came relatively late to the independence struggle and with much less intensity than elsewhere. Paradoxically, that relative freshness may have been a factor. The presence of seasoned fighters from the south and the influx of IRA men from across the newly created border with Northern Ireland were also significant in the escalation of the conflict as undoubtedly was partition and the creation of the border itself.

When it became known that the Treaty had been signed in London, the *Donegal Democrat* expressed the hope that with the national question settled, better services might be expected locally. With very few exceptions, the *Democrat* noted, councils everywhere subordinated local concerns to 'the larger and all-important national issue'.[3] The *Democrat* was to be disappointed – local politics continued to be preoccupied with the Treaty split, partition and the republic. Partition was understandably uppermost in the minds of the people of Donegal, but it was not an issue that separated the parties on the nationalist side at least in the sense that they all professed opposition to it. For Donegal unionists, partition based on exclusion of six counties was the worst possible outcome, albeit one that had been long feared.

Joe Sweeney, TD and IRA leader, was at home in Burtonport when the morning train arrived with the newspapers carrying details of the Treaty. His first reaction was that it was not what they had fought for. As an IRB member, he had scruples about reconciling his oath to fight for a republic with a settlement which fell short of that. He deferred taking a position until he returned to Dublin and sought out Michael Collins. He asked Eoin O'Duffy, another IRB member, who was with Collins at the time what the position of the IRB on the Treaty was. He was told that members could make their own minds up. With that assurance, Sweeney returned to Donegal and met with the people who 'ran the local political machine'. Having discussed the terms with them, it was decided that he should support the Treaty.[4] Two points worth noting about this account are first that other versions, including Piaras Béaslaí's, suggest that the IRB supreme council took a more directive role by informing members who were TDs that it supported the Treaty; and second that the adjournment of the Dáil over Christmas and the delay in voting on the Treaty until 7 January were significant.[5] It is widely agreed that the return of the TDs to their constituencies over Christmas, where they were exposed to the weight of public opinion, contributed to the pro-Treaty majority.[6]

News of the Treaty was initially greeted with optimism in Donegal. On 9 December the *Donegal Democrat*, echoing Griffith, declared: 'we have won liberty'. The paper maintained that the terms were more favourable than any previously proposed and met with general approval.[7] The editor confidently predicted that they would be ratified by the Dáil. John Downey, the proprietor, met regularly with local IRA leaders and was well informed – it was rumoured that he was secretly a member.[8] However, the same issue of the *Democrat* reported 'a sensational development' – a statement from de Valera that amounted to a rejection of the terms by three of the ministers of the Dáil cabinet. By 6 January, the *Democrat* conceded that there were elements in de Valera's alternative proposal that it would have liked to have seen included but it felt the die was cast when the Treaty was signed.[9]

The initial reaction of the other Ballyshannon newspaper, the *Vindicator*, was downbeat but guarded. It had resumed publication under the editorship of Eily MacAdam, after being effectively closed by the IRA for alleged breaches of the Belfast boycott. De Valera's opposition encouraged it to express reservations about the oath, but it was conflicted about opposing Griffith and Collins whom MacAdam admired. The *Vindicator* stayed on the fence for some time before finally opposing the Treaty, one of the few newspapers in the country to do so.[10] Both the *Derry Journal* and the *Donegal News* supported the Treaty, despite reservations about partition.[11]

The Catholic hierarchy discussed the Treaty on 13 December and issued a statement in favour of ratification. Cardinal Logue and most of the bishops, including O'Donnell, believed that despite its deficiencies the best course was to accept the Treaty and 'make the most of the freedom it undoubtedly brings'.[12] Given the active role he had played in earlier attempts at a settlement, O'Donnell was unusually reticent publicly. He had been involved behind the scenes in providing background information on the Ulster question to the SF delegation and could not but have been disappointed by the outcome in relation to partition. He had been willing to accept county option as the basis for exclusion (which would have meant four Ulster counties being excluded) but the Treaty effectively left the arbitrarily constructed six-county bloc unchanged, with only the vague promise of a boundary commission to make local adjustments at some point in the future. O'Donnell used his Lenten pastoral in 1922 to attack the evil of partition. He was appointed coadjutor to Cardinal Logue early in 1922 and at his installation as archbishop of Armagh in late April called for unity in the face of growing violence.[13]

The Treaty was discussed by local authorities in Donegal over the Christmas period. Inishowen RDC and Buncrana UDC led the way with motions endorsing the terms as containing 'all that was essential'.[14] Understandably, opinion in Inishowen and east Donegal was exercised by partition: some viewed the Treaty as a step forward because of the advanced status on offer to the south compared to the north. It was hoped that this might mean that the 'purgatorial existence' of nationalists in nearby Derry, Tyrone and Fermanagh would be shortened rather than extended which, it was feared, might be the outcome of rejection.[15] The *Donegal News* asserted confidently that public bodies in Donegal had made the voice of the people heard in the strongest terms in favour of the Treaty.[16] While one may question whether local newspapers reflect public opinion or merely the views of their owners, the evidence that public opinion in the county was decisively in favour of the Treaty is persuasive. That view was not disputed by most of those who were opposed to the Treaty. It is also notable that, after an extended period of violence and enforced silence, there was a new-found appetite for public debate on political matters.

A special meeting of DCC was held on 31 December to discuss the Treaty. P.J. Ward TD wrote to the secretary indicating that he was precluded from attending as there was an understanding that no member of the Dáil would participate in public discussion of the terms until the Dáil had reached a decision on them.[17] The meeting adopted a motion from Councillor Bonner that the council voice 'the opinion of 90 per cent of the electorate' that all Donegal TDs should vote for the Treaty. The motion acknowledged the limitations of the settlement but declared that the nation was bound to honour the terms agreed by the plenipotentiaries. It was agreed that copies of the motion should be sent to de Valera, Griffith and the six Donegal TDs. The minutes record only one dissentient: Hugh O'Duffy from Gortahork opposed the Treaty because it meant abandoning the republic. He admitted that the great majority of his constituents were in favour and, on the basis that he no longer represented his electoral district, he tendered his resignation. Another motion was then carried, earnestly requesting Griffith and de Valera 'to close up the ranks of the Dáil and bury their differences in the interests of the country'. At its next meeting on 24 January, a motion was unanimously passed prevailing on O'Duffy to rescind his resignation.[18]

The outcome of discussions at SF meetings in each of the four Donegal constituencies was clear. A meeting of the North Donegal comhairle ceanntair in Buncrana on 27 December heard reports of almost total support among affiliated cumainn and a motion to that effect was unanimously adopted. Two nights later, the vote at the East Donegal comhairle ceanntair meeting in Letterkenny was also unanimously in favour of supporting the Treaty. There was more opposition in West Donegal at a meeting in Dungloe the same evening, but the motion supporting the Treaty passed by sixteen to ten. In South Donegal, the vote was seventeen to three in favour.[19]

The Dáil voted by a narrow majority of 64–57 to adopt the Treaty on 7 January. Donegal TDs Joe Sweeney, J.P. McGinley, P.J. McGoldrick and P.J. Ward voted in favour, while Joseph O'Doherty and Samuel O'Flaherty voted against. According to Sweeney, O'Doherty and O'Flaherty had met with de Valera before the vote, but he declined an invitation to do so.[20] Only Ward, O'Doherty and McGinley contributed to the debate – all three speaking in succession on the final day. None of the Donegal TDs had been active contributors in the Dáil, although it should be noted that circumstances were not conducive to regular participation in what was an illegal assembly. Sweeney and O'Flaherty had never spoken and McGoldrick had interjected a few times. Ward was the most active but even he had only contributed on four occasions up to this point. In the debate on the peace negotiations in August, he had queried de Valera as to the meaning of the phrase 'a free association with the British Commonwealth group' and pointed out that the plenipotentiaries would be from the Dáil and not the cabinet.[21]

Ward's immediate reaction to the Treaty was negative: he had stood for complete separation and the Treaty did not achieve that. He then consulted his constituency: all twenty SF cumainn had debated the matter and had voted seventeen to three in favour of acceptance. Even so, he was still inclined to oppose as he considered his mandate came from his original election manifesto. However, having listened to the arguments in the Dáil, he concluded that rejection of the Treaty was feasible only if it was virtually unanimous. In the absence of unity, he argued that they should 'swallow the pill' and accept the Treaty under protest. He told the Dáil that the people were 'war-worn' and wanted peace. Echoing Collins, he felt it would be a 'stepping-stone' to full independence.[22]

Ward's contribution was cogent and reflective but no more so than Joseph O'Doherty's, which came to the opposite conclusion. He replied directly to Ward and pointedly said that he could not side with those who wanted to swallow pills. He too had contested the election unambiguously on a republican platform, even though he had been advised to play that down at the time. The Treaty would leave them further away from that goal. He admitted that his constituents would accept the settlement, but he felt that was under duress and accused those who signed the Treaty of flouting the people's will. The final Donegal contribution was from Dr J.P. McGinley who stated he would be voting according to the mandate of his constituents.

Like several other contributors, he argued that sending over the delegation meant abandonment of the republic, a point on which he was challenged by de Valera. McGinley denied that there was already a republic in existence – it was only a paper republic and 'the people of Donegal are sick of the paper republic'. 'And paper republicans too', added an unidentified TD.[23]

The Treaty split highlighted some of the existing tensions within the broader national movement between politicians and militants, the Dáil and the army, SF and the IRA, those who were in the IRB and those who were not. P.J. Ward was at pains to stress that he had made his own mind up and that no one else had influenced him. Joe Sweeney did not contribute to the debate in the Dáil but he too subsequently took care to emphasize that his decision was his own. He was criticized for not having consulted the IRA companies under his command. It is clear there was more opposition to the Treaty among rank and file IRA, including those in west Donegal. However, it is notable that a majority of the members of 1st Northern Division later declared loyalty to the Irish Free State (IFS) unlike other divisions. In its own way, this was a tribute to Sweeney's leadership.[24] One officer later recorded that but for Sweeney's influence, 'the whole division would undoubtedly have gone irregular'.[25]

Peadar O'Donnell, who attended the final debate in the Dáil, was aghast at what he saw as a betrayal of the social aspects of the revolution. He deferred to the general feeling that they should attempt to maintain the unity of the movement as far as possible, an understandable if ill-fated impulse. Strenuous efforts were made to ensure that the debate on the Treaty proceeded under the aegis of SF rather than the army. On 3 January an order was issued to Donegal brigades by Tom Glennon, divisional adjutant, that the IRA was to be kept free of politics and any man who wished to participate in the political discussion on the Treaty should do so through a SF club.[26] In response to complaints that IRA officers were standing aloof from SF, a memorandum was issued on 11 March reminding brigades that while the work of the army was the overriding concern, the ultimate objective of the army was to support the civil and social life of the country.[27]

The Treaty was ratified on 14 January and two days later a transitional Provisional government was established by pro-Treaty TDs with Collins as chairman and Griffith as president of the Dáil ministry. Preparations began immediately to establish a new National army. Opponents of the Treaty instead recognized the Dáil cabinet minority group led by de Valera. They had established an army council on 11 January and demanded the holding of an army convention to allow them to reaffirm their continued allegiance to the republic under an executive appointed by the convention. Richard Mulcahy, chief of staff, prevaricated and ultimately the holding of a convention was banned by the Dáil cabinet on the grounds that it would involve the subversion of its political authority over the army.[28]

Given the uncertainty, it became increasingly difficult to maintain discipline as some IRA men tried to sit on the fence and remain neutral while others drifted away through disillusionment or disinterest. In A company, 2nd battalion, South Donegal Brigade this had become a widespread problem in early 1922 and ten men were to be court-martialled for failing to report for duty.[29] There were many instances of men having second thoughts and changing sides from pro- to anti-Treaty and vice versa. Understandably, their intentions were distrusted. A group of IRA men who crossed the border from Tyrone and Fermanagh were suspected of declaring temporary loyalty to the pro-Treaty side to facilitate the securing of arms.[30]

Ratification of the Treaty opened the way for the release and return home of large numbers of Donegal prisoners. The case of Thomas McShea, O/C Bundoran battalion, and Captain Patrick Johnston became a *cause célèbre*. They had been arrested in April 1921 and sentenced to two years' imprisonment. They led an attempted escape from Derry Jail, with the assistance of Patrick Leonard, a prison warder. Two policemen who were chloroformed in the escape died and the three were charged with murder and sentenced to death. The IRA temporarily disrupted the trial by kidnapping the chief witness. A campaign was launched to have the death sentence commuted and the IRA made plans to rescue the three who were awaiting execution.[31] A rescue party from the 5th Northern Division was arrested by Ulster Special Constabulary (USC) when travelling to Derry with a group of Monaghan GAA players and supporters.[32] The newly created 'Northern Command' of IRA officers from the six counties approved significant retaliation. This high-risk strategy involved a series of kidnappings of prominent loyalists in border areas as a means of pressuring the British government to release the 'Monaghan footballers' as they had become known and to reprieve the prisoners awaiting execution.[33] The kidnappings inevitably provoked counter-reprisals. Most of these events occurred within the six counties but they also involved raids by republicans in Donegal, Monaghan and Cavan.[34]

On the morning of 8 February Major James Sproule Myles, Ballyshannon; Captain William Hamilton JP, Coxtown, Ballintra; and Blacker Douglass, Kinlough were kidnapped from their homes by armed men. The residence of Captain Atkinson of Cavangarden, Ballyshannon was also visited but he was not present. All those targeted came from the same general locality as McShea and Johnston and all had military backgrounds, but they had no current involvement in the conflict. Myles was a prominent businessman and county councillor and had previously been involved in the UVF, while Hamilton came from a leading landowning family and was a land agent. Blacker Douglass was a relative newcomer, having purchased the Lareen estate before the First World War. The estate included the valuable fishing rights to the Drowes on the border of Donegal and Leitrim, which may have contributed to an unpopularity locally. James Craig, prime minister of Northern Ireland, threatened vigorous action and the British government demanded an immediate response from Michael Collins.[35] In an emollient reply, Collins insisted he was doing what he could to avoid violence, neglecting to mention that he had ordered the shooting of the hangmen who were expected to execute the Derry prisoners. In the event, the three prisoners were reprieved, and the kidnapped unionists were released soon afterwards.[36] McShea, Johnston and Leonard were released in 1925.[37]

While the situation was defused, security on the northern side of the border was strengthened by the deployment of large numbers of USC and regular clashes continued. On 13 February, Captain Hugh Britton and James Gallagher were killed in Donegal town by an off-duty British soldier in an unprovoked attack. He was subsequently tried in a SF court and handed over to the British military.[38] On 21 February Captain Joseph Duffy was shot during an arms raid on a house in Ramelton.[39] Large contingents of both pro- and anti-Treaty IRA attended the funerals. Passions in east Donegal were further inflamed by an incident in late March when there was an attack on a pro-Treaty garrison in Newtowncunningham by an unidentified group of either UVF or USC from across the border in Derry. Tension was heightened by the creation in late spring of a new anti-Treaty 1st Northern Division with Corkman Seán Lehane as O/C and Peadar O'Donnell as adjutant. The officers met in Letterkenny and decided to occupy Glenveagh Castle and the Masonic hall in Raphoe. Given its location near the border, the choice of the latter location was a statement of intent.[40] Meanwhile, more than 250 members of the Tírconaill Brigade of the 1st Northern Division under the command of Joe Sweeney affirmed their loyalty to GHQ and the National army.[41] According to the *Donegal Vindicator*, a large majority of members of the Bundoran and Tullaghan companies pledged allegiance to the IRA executive.[42]

If partition played little part in the Treaty debates, the same was not true of the months that followed when the border and the plight of northern nationalists became a focus of attention in a way which brought Donegal centre-stage nationally. Collins had met James Craig in January and agreed the so-called Craig–Collins pact that ended the Belfast boycott in return for which Craig undertook to facilitate the return of Catholic workmen to the shipyards in Belfast. The failure of the pact was highlighted by the events in February described above. Collins agreed a second pact with Craig in late March, ostensibly 'to restore peace', but it too was quickly overtaken by escalating violence.[43] In response, Collins become closely involved in a plan to support IRA activity in the north and along the Donegal border.[44] This secret policy, facilitated by the IRB, was designed not to support peace but to wage war. While the apparent purpose of the campaign was to defend Catholics and undermine partition, it had the additional benefit of maintaining a precarious unity between pro- and anti-Treaty forces.⁴⁵ How well it was understood and implemented by the leadership of the National army in Donegal has remained a matter of debate.⁴⁶ The plan involved units of the anti-Treaty IRA setting up bases in Donegal from which to launch attacks across the border with arms supplied by the pro-Treaty side. They understood that they would receive co-operation from pro-Treaty forces and, for obvious reasons, would avoid clashes with them.⁴⁷

The IRA convention was finally held in Dublin on 26 March. On instructions from Richard Mulcahy, minister for defence, Commandant-General Sweeney issued an order from his headquarters at Drumboe Castle that no delegates were to be allowed to attend.⁴⁸ Among those who did attend were Peadar O'Donnell, Charlie Daly (O/C 2nd Northern Division until demoted by Eoin O'Duffy) and Seán Lehane. The convention renounced all allegiance to the Dáil, the chief of staff and the minister for defence and instead elected an executive to draft a constitution. It also agreed to intensify the Belfast boycott, which had been suspended in January. That month had seen fifty-three people killed in Belfast, more than two-thirds of them Catholics. The convention gave a further impetus to plans for a renewed northern offensive.⁴⁹ Lehane enlisted veterans from his own command in Cork and Daly, his second in command, did likewise in Kerry. They then travelled to Donegal as the first step in a campaign against the six counties organized with at least the tacit support of Collins.

The new National army outnumbered the anti-Treaty IRA in Donegal and held most of the evacuated military and police barracks. The anti-Treaty side held the RIC barracks in Ballyshannon, Carndonagh and Castelfinn, and Finner Camp.⁵⁰ The handover of Finner by British troops on 17 February was an important symbolic moment.⁵¹ Celebratory social events were organized in the camp for the locals. On 14 April the first group of reinforcements from the Southern Division IRA arrived in preparation for a northern offensive and occupied Finner. Transport was commandeered locally for their use as well as beds and bedding from the Great Northern hotel Bundoran and the Sheil Hospital in Ballyshannon.⁵²

Whatever the original intentions of the northern offensive, in practice the presence of two rival forces in close proximity to each other added an element of danger to an already volatile situation. On 30 April National army troops arrested seven members of the anti-Treaty 4th Brigade, 1st Northern Division near Ballybofey and seized their arms and ammunition. It was alleged that they were roughly treated. Their O/C immediately wrote to Brigadier Joseph Murray from Finner demanding their immediate release and an apology, failing which he would take direct action.⁵³ To defuse the situation, Joe Sweeney met with Lehane and Daly at Drumboe Castle, but the meeting was inconclusive. Lehane insisted that he would continue to engage in cross-border raids, which was the mission he had been entrusted with. Large quantities of arms had been shipped from Dublin to the north via Donegal. A new 'rising' was agreed between divisional commanders for early May but while units in Derry and Tyrone were active, there was little sign of joint activity from Donegal.

Lehane's men launched an attack on Derry from Buncrana that led to harsh reprisals by the USC in Derry. A large force of anti-Treaty IRA from Donegal, supported by Derry IRA, attacked the border posts at Derry and Elagh and the home at Molenan of Major Moore, an Orangeman and member of the UUC. Sweeney's forces did not participate.[54] To finance their activities, men from Lehane's division robbed a number of banks and post offices. One such raid in Buncrana ended in a shoot-out with National army troops in which a woman and a girl were killed. On 4 May four soldiers under the command of Tom Glennon, three of them from Donegal, were killed in disputed circumstances by Lehane's troops in an ambush at Newtowncunningham. These killings, which pre-dated the formal commencement of the Civil War by almost two months, greatly increased the animosity between the two sides.[55]

Despite the friction, plans to escalate activity in the north continued. General Tom Barry, IRA director of operations, visited Donegal in mid-May bringing news of a short ceasefire to allow detailed preparations for a full-scale offensive. Presumably to this end, senior officers returned to Dublin with Barry.[56] Charlie Daly wrote to his brother Tom of his concern that they were losing ground in Donegal and his hopes of getting additional recruits from the south.[57] Members of the division were given a week's leave and some of those from the south commandeered motor cars from loyalists and went home to Munster. Discipline among those who remained in Donegal then appears to have collapsed with allegations of dereliction of duty, black-marketeering in seized goods, and drunkenness. Stern action was taken, including court martials.[58]

Reinforced by IRA who had fled across the border, anti-Treaty forces became increasingly active with raids for arms, seizures of cars, motorcycles and other items and a stricter enforcement of the Belfast boycott. Seán Mac Cumhail, adjutant 4th Brigade, ordered that vehicles be returned, except those owned by 'Belfast people'.[59] A threat from the British military in Derry to retaliate if cross-border activity from Donegal did not cease was dismissed by Charlie Daly but troops along the border were reinforced, particularly at Lifford.[60] A British army armoured car was destroyed by a landmine at a spot known as the Camel's hump between Lifford and Strabane.[61]

While the Belfast boycott had limited impact on that city's major industries, which were its main target, it was a source of considerable disruption in Donegal.[62] In April Craig singled out the ruthless destruction of goods in Donegal in his complaints to Collins about the boycott.[63] It was enforced with the assistance of members of Cumann na mBan which, at a national convention in the Mansion House on 5 February, had voted decisively to reject the Treaty.[64] A majority of Cumann na mBan in Donegal took the anti-Treaty side. Eithne Coyle later claimed that there were 63 branches of the organization in Donegal at the time with 1,200 members.[65] She was appointed organizer in the north-west and led an extensive campaign by Cumann na mBan members in Donegal in support of the boycott. She was indefatigable in enforcing it with raids on trains and train stations. On 18 April the *Londonderry Sentinel* described one daring raid on a train on the Lough Swilly line where Coyle issued instructions for the removal and burning of Belfast newspapers in a 'cool, decided tone', revolver in hand.[66] In June she established a headquarters for Cumann na mBan in Glenveagh Castle and set up first aid posts at various locations along the border.[67] Peadar O'Donnell recalled that the National army 'regarded her as an IRA officer more than a Cumann na mBan organiser which indeed she was'.[68]

Towards the end of May 1922, the phrase Belleek salient began to appear in the British press.[69] James Craig in the Northern Ireland parliament referred to the area 'which has come to be known as the Belleek salient'.[70] A salient in military terms is a portion of a battlefield that protrudes into enemy territory: the Ypres salient, which was the site of intense fighting in the First World War, would have been familiar to contemporaries. Its usage in describing events in the triangle of land to the north of Lough Erne between Belleek and Pettigo undoubtedly reflects the way in which the events that took place there in late May and early June were viewed. For a brief period, a remote stretch of land on the border of Fermanagh and Donegal became the focus of national and international attention.[71]

The events in the Belleek–Pettigo triangle were a microcosm of the Ulster question in all its complexity and involved high politics and local bother in equal measure. Viewed from London, it was a familiar border dispute on a remote frontier and an opportunity to teach the IRA and Michael Collins a lesson. For Collins and for the leadership of the IRA, it was a proxy war, the longed for implementation of the secret northern offensive policy. Activists on both sides welcomed the opportunity to face the enemy in a less surreptitious manner than had been the custom. Those who had recently fled across the border from Tyrone and Fermanagh relished the chance to fight back. Locally, the area had seen sporadic UVF and Irish Volunteer activity before 1914 and IRA activity, particularly since 1920. Even so, little could have prepared the local inhabitants for what was to transpire when they found themselves in the middle of a full-scale war zone.

Partition and the consequences of an arbitrary border were the main causes of the Belleek–Pettigo battle. Under the Government of Ireland Act (1920), the border with Northern Ireland ran along the existing county boundary, even though Fermanagh had a nationalist majority. An immediate problem arose because the part of Fermanagh north-west of Lough Erne was landlocked and could only be accessed by road through Donegal or by water across Lough Erne. The border villages of Belleek and Pettigo stood 20 km apart at the south-west and north-east points of the triangle. The former, which was predominantly in Fermanagh, was largely nationalist while the latter which was in Donegal had a large unionist population. Belleek fort (the Battery) on raised ground overlooking the town of Belleek was in Donegal as partially was the bridge across the Erne into the village. The problem was later resolved by the building of a bridge further east at Roscor and two others at Boa Island but at the time access was restricted.

By late May, trouble had been brewing for some time. Nicholas Smyth, who had fled Tyrone, made his way to Pettigo where he joined thirty or more IRA from the six counties who occupied the old RIC barracks. An intelligence dispatch on 26 May reported that police on the northern side of the Termon river had a machine-gun trained on the barracks.[72] Smyth was made welcome by Danny Gallagher, O/C of the local battalion who had his headquarters in the village. He also attempted to make contact with Charlie Daly; many of the Tyrone men were sympathetic to the republican side. Near Belleek, anti-Treaty troops occupied Cliff house which was owned by Major Moore, a leading Orangeman and a member of the USC in Derry. National army troops were in position at Belleek fort.

On 27 May, following rumours of kidnappings in Pettigo, a force of around sixty USC from Enniskillen led by Captain Basil Brooke, future prime minister of Northern Ireland, crossed Lough Erne in an appropriately named steamer HMS *Pandora*, towing a flotilla of small boats. The raiding party took possession of Magherameenagh Castle.[73] They fired on a pro-Treaty patrol guarding the bridge at Belleek and at the troops on the Battery who returned fire. The IRA group from Cliff house advanced along the railway line from Belleek and exchanged fire with them. The USC withdrew to Buck Island where they were reinforced. By now, the people of Belleek were reported to be 'clearing out'.[74] Some stayed with relatives in the countryside while others crossed the border. The Great Northern hotel in Bundoran was requisitioned for the refugees by the National army.[75]

The local National army battalions were mobilized and the troops at Belleek and Pettigo were reinforced. Michael O'Farrell, divisional adjutant, took over command in Pettigo from Danny Gallagher. A trench was dug at the bridge, which marked the border, to prevent an attempt to advance through the village to relieve the group stranded at Lough Erne. A large force of USC took up positions across the river and a two-hour gun-battle ensued after which the USC withdrew. The USC later attempted to outflank the Pettigo troops by crossing a narrow isthmus at Waterfoot but were prevented by a group led by John Travers and Jim Scallan.[76] Sporadic firing continued at Belleek for most of Sunday 28 May. In the afternoon, a force of USC in Crossley tenders and a Lancia armoured car approached from Garrison direction and came under fire. The driver was killed and the USC were forced to withdraw. The Lancia was brought to Ballyshannon for repair. Both National army and anti-Treaty IRA were involved in this action.[77]

As luck would have it, Michael Collins and Arthur Griffith were in London for a meeting at Downing Street on 31 May and faced angry questions from Lloyd George and Churchill. Collins was not well informed about events but denied involvement. Churchill informed the House of Commons that he had received 'the most unqualified assurances' from the Provisional government that they were in no way responsible and that they 'repudiated the actions in the strongest possible terms'.[78] This was not accurate. Sweeney was reluctant to engage in cross-border activities and his troops largely followed his instructions on that matter. However, from their own accounts, it was clear that the National army engaged in cross-border gun-battles at both Belleek and Pettigo in which at least four USC were killed, and undoubtedly individual groups of soldiers were less scrupulous about moving in and out of Fermanagh.[79] Sweeney did privately admit that his troops engaged in some limited cross-border arms raids. In the case of Pettigo, which was invaded by British forces, the distinction between anti-Treaty IRA and National army forces was blurred and confused.[80] Collins blamed the USC for the crisis and demanded an inquiry. While Lloyd George was inclined to play the crisis down, Churchill, never a man to miss an opportunity to add fuel to a fire, took a different view. Under pressure from Craig, Churchill ordered military reinforcements be sent to the area, including artillery, which risked a significant escalation. He communicated to Collins that if they were fired on from across the border, they would respond.[81]

Amid rumours of impending cross-border attacks by USC, raids were ordered by Joseph Murray, O/C 4th Brigade, on houses in Ballintra and nearby districts. This area had been a UVF stronghold before the war and more recently has seen some activity on the part of a shadowy paramilitary group called the 'Red Hand'. Some arms were seized but they were not thought to have been used recently. On the night of 1 June Murray's troops were patrolling the streets of Ballyshannon when shooting took place from the vicinity of St Anne's church above the town in the direction of pro-Treaty troops based at the Barracks across the river and republican troops on the Mall. The latter returned fire, but there were no casualties.

The following day, large numbers of police and British troops equipped with artillery advanced towards Pettigo.[82] They were supported by spotter aircraft from Aldergrove airport. Artillery was also reported to be advancing along the southern shore of Lough Erne towards Belleek. On 3 June soldiers from the Lincolnshire Regiment landed at Boa Island from across Lough Erne. There followed a pincer attack on the IRA forces in Pettigo. Hugely outnumbered and outgunned, they resisted for a time before being forced to evacuate on 4 June but not before sustained artillery fire had been directed at them and at the village. Three IRA members were killed in the fighting: William Kearney and Bernard McCanny (aka McKenna) from Drumquin in County Tyrone, and Patrick Flood from Pettigo.[83] Flood, who was nineteen, had joined the IRA in 1919 and appears to have joined the National army in March 1922, although this was denied by his father who was a republican. Flood's uncle Daniel, who was a hotelier, merchant and county councillor, supported the Free State.[84] Kearney and McKenna belonged to the 2nd Northern Division in Tyrone: they were not attested members of the National army as they were expected to return to active service across the border but they were described as 'attached to National forces'.[85] Joseph Murray later stated than all the men killed were 'our men', while Joe Sweeney referred to Flood, Kearney and McCanny as 'three of my men'.[86] British troops continued to occupy Pettigo in County Donegal until 1923 and this gave rise to claims of mistreatment of local nationalist families.[87]

Attention then turned to Belleek and the same military strategy was adopted. On 8 June, troops advanced on the village from the Pettigo road to the north and the shore road to the south of the lake and were met with some desultory resistance. Shots were fired from Belleek fort and from another location. P.H. McDermott reported to his O/C that it was rumoured that anti-Treaty forces were involved and added, somewhat implausibly, that 'none of our men were engaged as far as I know'. British artillery then shelled the fort, and the garrison was forced to withdraw to Ballyshannon. The tricolour was lowered and the Union Jack was flown over Belleek fort in County Donegal until August 1924.[88]

The people of Belleek and Pettigo slowly began to return to their homes, in some cases to find that they had been looted.[89] Although the issues that had led to it remained unresolved, the battle for the salient ended with a decisive victory for the Crown forces. That was always likely, given the huge disparity in numbers and equipment committed by both sides. In particular, the large-scale deployment of British troops and the lack of any cohesive and fully committed leadership on the nationalist side determined the outcome. It was a significant encounter for several reasons: it was the largest engagement by the IRA since the beginning of the War of Independence and the first use of heavy artillery by Crown forces since 1916. Collins was publicly uncomfortable at suggestions of duplicity and critical of Joe Sweeney for allowing his men to get involved. However, as Mossy Donegan, one of the veterans from Cork, later pointed out, the incident was precisely the kind of engagement that the secret northern policy was intended to provoke.[90]

While Collins continued to send arms northwards for use by the IRA in the six-county area, he stepped back from a joint northern offensive. A decision by the Provisional government on 3 June reflected the change of emphasis: it was agreed that a policy of 'peaceful obstruction' should be adopted towards the Belfast government and that no troops, either National army or republican, should be allowed to invade Northern Ireland.[91] Churchill's unconditional backing ensured that the Northern Ireland government was the main beneficiary of the affair. Even Lloyd George was uneasy about the drift of events, pointing out in a rebuke to Churchill that despite the presence of 9,000 British troops and 48,000 USC, 400 Catholics had been killed in two years without anyone being brought to justice.[92]

In an attempt to heal the Treaty split, Collins produced a draft constitution that did not contain an oath of allegiance but this was rejected by the British. A revised version was more consistent with the terms of the Treaty and therefore less palatable for republicans.[93] The election pact between Collins and de Valera in the Dáil elections of June 1922 was another attempt to avert further division. Avoiding a bitter election campaign was seen as a means of maintaining the precarious unity that existed. It could equally be argued that contested elections offered a democratic means of deciding contentious issues and that the pact simply perpetuated the split. Donegal in 1922 had able military commanders but a deficit of political leadership. The pro-Treaty side had already selected its six candidates for the election by the time the pact was agreed but two stood aside to allow a clear run for the six existing TDs, four pro-Treaty and two anti-Treaty. No other candidates were nominated, even though with proportional representation a unionist candidate would have stood a good chance of election. Nationally, pro-Treaty SF TDs won 58 seats and anti-Treaty SF won 36.

The assassination of Sir Henry Wilson, Unionist MP for North Down and security adviser to the Northern Ireland government, on 22 June finally precipitated the events that led to outright Civil War in Ireland. Faced with an ultimatum from the British, Collins launched an attack on the IRA executive headquarters at the Four Courts in Dublin. The building had been occupied on 14 April by a large force of IRA, led by Rory O'Connor. Paradoxically, Collins's men were responsible for Wilson's killing but, with the British threatening to intervene militarily themselves, Collins acted on the morning of 28 June. When the garrison ignored an order to vacate the building, it was shelled using field guns borrowed from the British army. 'The fateful day has come', declared a statement from the executive in the Four Courts, including Peadar O'Donnell. O'Donnell immediately ordered some of the 1st Northern Division who were in Dublin to return to Donegal.[94] He was arrested after the fall of the Four Courts and spent the duration of the Civil War in prison.

The anti-Treaty IRA persisted with its plans for a renewed border campaign and a party of Cumann na mBan, including Sheila Humphreys and Úna O'Connor, travelled to Ballybofey via Finner to establish a field hospital. It quickly became apparent that the situation had changed, and the pro-Treaty side was quicker to react.[95] Seán Lehane reported to Ernie O'Malley that his division had been 'altogether unprepared for hostilities'. He clung to the hope that a joint border campaign could avert civil war in Donegal at least.[96] On the National army side, Commandant Joe Sweeney was taken unawares by the attack on the Four Courts but immediately took the initiative.[97] On 29 June, the National army attacked and captured Ballymacool house near Letterkenny. Finner was taken next day.[98] Captain James Connolly from Kinlough was killed while retreating. His father had been killed by the British army in 1920 and Commandant Murray, who now led the National army forces locally, had given the oration at the funeral.[99] Sweeney, whose headquarters were at Drumboe, then seized the barracks at Ballyshannon, Buncrana and Bridgend, giving him control of the spine of the county.

Because of their engagement in the northern offensive, republican forces had located themselves close to the border in east Donegal, which now left them hemmed in between Sweeney's men and the USC. In the absence of Seán Lehane, Charlie Daly acted as O/C and Michael O'Donoghue was his second-in-command. They evacuated Lifford and Castlefinn with the intention of consolidating in Raphoe but were quickly forced to withdraw from there. Inch fort, which had been seized by Derry IRA, was later taken by pro-Treaty troops using artillery. The retreating anti-Treaty forces made their headquarters at Glenveagh Castle and sought to regroup but it quickly became evident that they were fighting an uphill battle.[100] Their campaign in Donegal was hampered by divisions among the leadership at national level as how best to proceed and by a lack of local leadership figures of sufficient status. Whatever his eccentricities as a soldier, the absence of Peadar O'Donnell was a significant loss. Frank O'Donnell, his brother, was O/C Rosses Brigade based at Gortahork.

A further problem was the indiscipline and disaffection that had set in from June and which was increased by the quick sweep of pro-Treaty forces through the county. Michael O'Donoghue recalled that there was an atmosphere of chaos, demoralization and corruption.[101] Eithne Coyle attributed much of the misbehaviour and indiscipline to a 'ragbag and bobtail' of adventurers who had joined after the truce, some from the northern counties. She blamed the burning of Protestant houses in Raphoe on the latter group and admitted that some raids on houses, commandeering of vehicles and seizure of good on the pretext of enforcing the Belfast boycott were spurious. She exempted the main body of the anti-Treaty forces from this criticism but admitted that it ultimately led to demoralization in their ranks.[102]

On 5 July Joe Sweeney made one last attempt to avoid further conflict. At his request, he met Charlie Daly and his senior officers at Daly's headquarters in Church Hill. A generally friendly conversation ensued: tea was taken but no agreement emerged. Sweeney offered to allow the local anti-Treaty IRA return to their homes and the southerners to leave Donegal with their arms and transport. A refugee centre had already been established at the Great Northern hotel in Bundoran and safe passage was available for any IRA men from the six counties who wished to avail of it, on condition that they surrendered their arms. Daly refused Sweeney's offer and suggested instead an agreement that each side would refrain from attacking the other. He insisted they would continue with their border campaign. Sweeney declined on the basis that the Provisional government could be the only authority in Donegal. It was later claimed that Daly prevented a possible ambush of Sweeney by some of the northerners, by ordering that all his men should remain until Sweeney and Glennon had left the village.[103]

Of necessity, the anti-Treaty side in Donegal was forced to resort to a guerrilla campaign along the lines of the War of Independence. A column of about thirty men was dispatched to the Finn Valley to harry pro-Treaty forces and launch cross-border raids but within a few days they were surrounded near Ballybofey and surrendered. Another unit headed towards Dungloe before returning to Glenveagh. They had plentiful supplies raided from shops, ostensibly as part of the Belfast boycott. In the summer weather, they found diversions away from the toils of war. They boated, swam and fished in the nearby lakes. A hotel beside Lake Gartan was used as a field hospital managed by members of Cumann na mBan. It appears that some of the young IRA men were adept at finding reasons to spend time at the hospital to such an extent that Seán Lehane felt it necessary to deliver a stern lecture to his troops and to the nurses.[104] But the realities of Civil War were never far away: on 10 July, in an ambush at Drumkeen, two National army soldiers, Jack Sweeney and Charlie McGinley, were killed. The deaths were widely condemned by the local clergy and the press and resulted in some local IRA members leaving the fight.[105]

In the latter half of July, the main body of IRA withdrew from Glenveagh and began a peripatetic campaign, criss-crossing the county. Because of the dangers in travelling in large groups, their forces were subdivided which generated considerable logistical problems in terms of supplies and communications. Eithne Coyle carried dispatches between the different groups and between 1st Northern Division and the Western Division, which attempted to take the pressure off the men in Donegal. Communications were difficult because the bridge at Ballyshannon was permanently manned by National army troops. When it was decided to merge the two divisions, Con Lehane remarked wryly that 'it wouldn't make the bridge at Ballyshannon any wider'.[106] On 15 August men from the Western Division moved north through Sligo and Leitrim and attacked National army troops in Bundoran. A revised structure was also implemented on the National army side with

Seán Mac Eoin, head of the Western command, and Sweeney in command of 1st Northern Division at Drumboe. The Rock barracks in Ballyshannon was the headquarters for south Donegal. In response to continued republican activity, a night-time curfew was imposed from the beginning of August on the area between the Drowes at Tullaghan and the Bradogue at Bundoran. Curfews were also imposed in Letterkenny, Buncrana, Raphoe and other areas. In mid-September, Mac Eoin and Sweeney led a systematic sweep of north Sligo and Leitrim. Kinlough and Tullaghan were cleared of anti-Treaty IRA and prisoners were taken to Finner.[107]

Republican activity in the area was clearly causing concern as the offices of the anti-Treaty *Donegal Vindicator* were raided yet again on the night of 23 September and its printing presses destroyed, despite the efforts of Eily MacAdam.[108] Eithne Coyle was arrested on 25 September 1922 and held for six weeks in the Rock barracks before being transferred to Mountjoy. Coyle found the garrison indisciplined and the conditions 'awful'. She complained to the O/C who told her that she had been doing a man's job and should not object to being treated like a man. When her mother wrote to the parish priest complaining that she was not being allowed to attend Mass, which had been permitted by the British when she was in Mountjoy, he replied unsympathetically that if half of what he heard about her daughter was true, his congregation was a lot better off without her.[109] Such comments were not isolated: the militancy of Cumann na mBan attracted some hostility from clerical quarters, so much so that it prompted formal complaints to Bishop O'Donnell from a republican convention in Letterkenny.[110]

The death of Michael Collins on 22 August was a shock to both sides but it brought a renewed commitment on the part of the government to prosecute the war. Commandant Sweeney narrowly escaped death in late September when a car in which he was travelling near his home in Burtonport was fired on in what appears to have been an opportunistic rather than a planned attack. Sweeney returned fire and wounded one of the assailants who escaped.[111] The emergency powers legislation introduced on 27 September, which established military courts with sweeping powers, added greatly to the pressure on the anti-Treaty side. The offer of an amnesty was availed of by several leading Donegal republicans, further depleting their numbers.[112]

The decline in morale on the republican side can be tracked through the letters and dispatches of Charlie Daly and Seán Lehane to Ernie O'Malley and others over the summer and autumn of 1922. Following an army convention in Dublin on 18 June, Daly confided his doubts about their presence in Donegal – he did not see that they had 'any business being there'. In July O'Malley urgently reported to Liam Lynch, chief of staff, that the men in Donegal were starving.[113] On 8 September, Daly reported that they had had 'a pretty rough' time, were 'greatly outnumbered' and had been 'almost smashed from the start'. The county was 'not very sympathetic' for flying columns. He was surprised by the level of poverty and disliked having to billet with the people for that reason. An element of bitterness was evident in his comment that 'he could not think of firing a shot against an "Orange Special" or any English man, while a Free Stater remains'.[114] On 17 September Daly complained of 'a hostile civil population and a hostile clergy', adding forlornly that Liam Lynch 'sent us up here and then seems to have forgotten all about us.'[115] Lynch, for his part, was impatient, and felt that instances of hostility from the local population should be 'dealt with sternly'. He found it difficult to believe that things could be as bad as claimed but ordered that they should be sent assistance.[116]

Lehane's communications struck a similar note. While committed to fighting on, he complained in September that the local population was for the most part hostile, adding that 'it couldn't be much worse in the six counties'. In October he reported bluntly that 'we are only furking [sic] fight here and stealing about the place like criminals'. In exasperation, he complained that the local people were not interested in the republic but 'in money and ease'.[117] At the outset, Lehane's forces numbered approximately 115 men on active service but by September this had been reduced to 25 armed men, mostly from outside the county. At that point, the strength of National army forces in barracks in the area was estimated to be 2,700.[118]

In late October Lehane was instructed to withdraw from Donegal. He ordered the remnants of the column led by Charlie Daly in west Donegal to rendezvous with his section, which was based in the east. However, Daly's men were surprised by National army troops near Dunlewey and arrested. Lehane and his group made their escape from the county by way of a boat commandeered at Donegal town, which brought them to Sligo, where men from the Western Division escorted them to a camp in Arigna. The war in Donegal had fizzled out by November 1922, notwithstanding attempts to revive it early in 1923.

Daly and the seven men arrested with him were tried by court martial on 30 November for possession of arms and sentenced to death in January 1923. Protests were made locally, including at a meeting of DCC, but it was widely assumed that the sentences were simply a means of guaranteeing good behaviour by others. That optimism dissipated when Captain Bernard Gannon of the National army was killed in an apparent attack on a barracks at Creeslough. The source of the attack is disputed but not the outcome. Joe Sweeney was instructed by GHQ that Charlie Daly, Daniel Enright, Seán Larkin and Timothy O'Sullivan were to be executed by firing squad. Sweeney was surprised that someone from the north would be included so he sought and received confirmation that Larkin from south Derry was to be included. A last-minute appeal for clemency by Archbishop O'Donnell was unsuccessful. The executions were carried out at Drumboe early on the morning of 14 March.[119]

The executions were immediately followed by anti-Treaty IRA reprisals locally that included the burning of the family home of Archbishop O'Donnell at Kilraine. The insult to a man who had been a champion of the nationalist cause throughout his life was all the more unfortunate as he had privately attempted to secure a reprieve. The executions marked a sad dénouement to the Civil War in Donegal. Three of the four men executed were from Kerry. In truth, their fate may owe more to the gruesome tit-for-tat atrocities in Kerry earlier in March and the wider policy of execution and reprisal that was such a grim feature of the conflict. The Civil War in Donegal had largely petered out and the ruthless reprisal policy of the government served little purpose other than to prolong the legacy of bitterness on the republican side. The formal cessation of hostilities was announced in May 1923.

The most recent estimate of National army casualties in the Civil War is approximately 780, with 488 killed in action; on the anti-Treaty side, the equivalent figure was at least 426.[120] James Langton in *The forgotten fallen of the Civil War* lists fourteen National army fatalities in Donegal in the period from the Treaty to the end of the Civil War – he includes all three fatalities at Pettigo. The National Graves Association has identified nine republican deaths: four of these were executions and two were caused by the British army. This suggests an overall total of at least twenty-four military deaths in the period.[121] However, as six were directly or indirectly related to the border war of which five were caused by the British army, it would be misleading to consider them Civil War fatalities. The total of eighteen military fatalities remaining is still much higher than the figure for IRA dead in the War of Independence (four) but well below some other parts of the country, including nearby Sligo. There are no reliable figures for civilian casualties.[122]

After the fatal ambush at Newtowncunningham in May 1922, Charlie Daly wrote to his mother that he would prefer to cross the border and be killed by B Specials than fire a shot against 'our own fellows'.[123] While the Civil War had diminished that reluctance on all sides, Joe Sweeney, Daly's former friend and comrade, would probably have shared his sentiments. Reflecting on his own role in the executions at Drumboe, he expressed his discomfort:

> it is an awful thing to kill a man you know in cold blood ... Trading shots with a man in a battle is one thing, but an execution is something else altogether ... I didn't agree with it, but they were orders and you had to do it. It is very hard to describe war among brothers. It was fierce and it was atrocious.[124]

10 Donegal and the Irish Revolution

In 1587 the 14-year-old Red Hugh O'Donnell was kidnapped in Tírconaill and held hostage in Dublin Castle for the good behaviour of his father and the rebellious septs of the O'Donnell clan. More than three hundred years later, in the dying days of the Irish Civil War, a similar incident occurred. In March 1923, after the Drumboe executions, Peadar O'Donnell was taken from the Curragh to Finner camp and held to ransom for the good behaviour of republicans in Donegal. It was widely understood that he would be the next 'for the sandbags' (execution by firing squad) in the event of further National army casualties. Such an extreme measure was obviated by the ending of the war a short time later. While the circumstances of these incidents were different, they share common elements: the tension between centre and periphery, sovereign and subject, compliance and rebellion. However, despite the coincidence of surnames, Peadar O'Donnell would not have welcomed the comparison with his namesake. He was a critic of the strain of largely Catholic nostalgic nationalism in Donegal that harkened back to an imagined golden age. His view of the Irish Revolution embraced a more radical republicanism. Red Hugh and Red Peadar derived their soubriquets from very different sources.

The order to dump arms on 24 May 1923, which formally ended the Civil War, represented a setback for O'Donnell, but he spent much of the rest of his life fighting for the completion of his version of the Irish Revolution. Defeated militarily, republicanism regained political momentum in the 1920s, an early indication of which was the election O'Donnell to the Dáil in August 1923 while still in prison. In an unexpected outbreak of conventional politics, there were nineteen candidates for eight seats in Donegal. Former unionist, James Sproule Myles topped the poll; four Cumann na nGaedheal candidates were elected, one Farmers' Party candidate and two republicans (O'Donnell and Joseph O'Doherty).[1] Nationally, republicans won 44 seats to 63 for Cumann na nGaedheal. The result confirmed the victory of the pro-Treaty side but offered republicans an incentive to pursue their ends by other means. This ultimately resulted in the creation of de Valera's Fianna Fáil party, which entered the Dáil in 1927 and government in 1932. Its success owed something to the social radicalism espoused by Peadar O'Donnell and others but, for his part, O'Donnell continued to pursue his radical agenda in the IRA, the Republican Congress and other organizations.

The Irish Revolution in Donegal was inextricably linked to partition. To break the deadlock on the subject during the Treaty negotiations, Lloyd George suggested a Boundary Commission.[2] Article 12 of the Treaty provided for a commission to determine the border 'in accordance with the wishes of the inhabitants, so far as may be compatible with economic and geographic conditions'. The deliberately ambiguous nature of the clause bedevilled subsequent discussions. The abortive Craig–Collins agreement of March 1922 sought to expedite matters which were further delayed by the Civil War and by the refusal of the Northern Ireland government to appoint a representative. Archbishop O'Donnell's name was freely mentioned as a possible Free State commissioner.[3] When the commission was eventually established, it comprised Justice Richard Feetham from South Africa, Eoin MacNeill, representing the IFS and J.R. Fisher, nominated by the British government to represent Northern Ireland.

The commission began its work in November 1924 and conducted its business mainly in private.[4] Public submissions were invited, the members toured the border area and later met groups and individuals who had made submissions. Among these was a committee of nationalist businessmen from Donegal who argued for the inclusion of the city of Derry in the IFS or, if not, that the border should coincide with the River Foyle.[5] Conversely, the Donegal Protestant Registration Association (DPRA) proposed that all of Donegal should be included within Northern Ireland for cultural and economic reasons. In the knowledge that this was highly unlikely, it suggested that Inishowen should be transferred or at a minimum the border should be redrawn to transfer unionist majority areas in the former Londonderry No. 2 and Strabane No. 2 rural districts to Northern Ireland. Both nationalists and unionists argued the importance of Derry to its Donegal hinterland, but they reached opposite conclusions.[6] Feetham took an approach of minimizing disruption of the existing borders and avoiding large-scale transfers either way. The commission recommended adjustments on the border in east Donegal that would have transferred several areas to Northern Ireland, including St Johnston, Bridgend, Muff, Carrigans and Killea. The transfer of Derry the other way was rejected on the basis that its nationalist majority was not large enough to justify the economic dislocation. The same rationale was used to justify leaving Strabane in Northern Ireland. On the Fermanagh border, the commission recommended transfer of Pettigo to Northern Ireland and Belleek to the Free State.[7]

When the report of the commission was leaked in the *Morning Post* newspaper, a wave of protest followed, especially from nationalists.[8] The absence of large transfers from Northern Ireland and the losses in east Donegal were the most contentious.[9] Eoin MacNeill resigned, and it was hastily agreed to set aside the report and confirm the existing boundaries. That outcome was a disappointment for both nationalists and unionists. For the former, it confirmed their fears that partition was more than a temporary arrangement; for the latter, it compounded the dislocation caused by the settlement of 1920–2.

While complaints of a 'reign of terror' were overstated, their experience in the conflict had been undeniably difficult.[10] Violent attacks on persons as opposed to property were relatively rare but raids on houses, harassment, commandeering of vehicles and seizure of goods under the aegis of the Belfast boycott were commonplace. The focus of the IRA on the border in 1922–3 intensified the pressure on unionists in east Donegal. During the period eleven big houses were burnt.[11] The records of the Irish Distress Committee (later the Irish Grants Committee), established by the British government to compensate those who were most affected, contain a large number of applications, especially from east Donegal.[12]

Viewed from a long-term perspective, the decline in the fortunes of Donegal Protestants began in the late nineteenth century with disestablishment, the large-scale transfer of land ownership and the revolution in local government. The process was hastened by the social, demographic and political changes wrought by the First World War and completed by the War of Independence and partition. Partition represented a serious blow. It separated Donegal Protestants (as well as Catholics) from their near neighbours and co-religionists across the border. Even after the disappointment of the Boundary Commission, some in east Donegal clung to the hope that the border would be redrawn in a manner that ameliorated some of the more arbitrary dividing lines within local communities but that hope proved illusory. A petition organised by east Donegal Unionists in 1934 in favour of moving the border to incorporate them within Northern Ireland came to nothing.[13]

Given the circumstances, it is not surprising that the Protestant community in Donegal did not thrive after partition. David Fitzpatrick's pithy summary captures the options open to Protestants in the border counties: 'co-existence with nationalists, emigration or die-hard resistance'.[14] By 1922, the option of die-hard resistance was gone. Some chose or felt obliged to leave. Given the close ties culturally with Protestants in Northern Ireland, there was some movement eastwards across the border but the evidence for any large-scale movement is at best inconclusive.[15] A private census of movement from the Free State across the new border into Fermanagh between 1920 and 1925 submitted to the Boundary Commission included the names of more than 250 Donegal Protestants.[16] Those who stayed adjusted to the new dispensation and 'kept their heads down'. Donegal, like other IFS counties, was increasingly Catholic. The Protestant population in the county declined but, apart from being an 'unfriendly house', there is no evidence of pogroms or forced removal. At the 1926 census, the total population of Donegal was 152,508, down 9.5 per cent from 1911; the Catholic population fell by 6.1 per cent; and the non-Catholic population fell by 22.4 per cent to 27,567. The non-Catholic population was 18.1 per cent of the total (down from 21.1 in 1911).[17] It is misleading to aggregate all Protestant denominations together. In 1926, the

Episcopalian population of Donegal was 13,774 (down 23.6 per cent), the Presbyterian population was 12,162 (down 19 per cent) and the Methodist population was 1,202 (down 29.2 per cent). The explanation for the relatively larger decrease in Methodist numbers is not clear.[18]

Although the decline in the Protestant population in Donegal began before 1911, the events of the following decade undoubtedly hastened it.[19] David Fitzpatrick suggests that an ageing population, combined with low nuptiality and fertility, were contributory factors in the decline, regardless of the Irish Revolution.[20] Some of the decline may be explained by the First World War and by the departure of military personnel and their dependants after 1921; some may be attributed to general migration or emigration after 1918. The rate of decline in the Protestant population in the larger towns in Donegal such as Letterkenny (37.7 per cent) and Ballyshannon (34.6 per cent) was higher than the county average, but the proximity of military barracks may skew the picture. The decline in the Protestant population in Ballyshannon and Letterkenny rural districts and especially in east Donegal was noticeably lower. The decline in the Protestant population in west Donegal was above average for the county – in Glenties rural district it was 29.1 per cent. Presumably this reflects the isolated nature of the population in an area from which the police had been driven during the War of Independence.[21] It is notable that the decrease in the non-Catholic population in Donegal, Monaghan and Cavan was well below the average for the IFS (32.5 per cent). This may reflect the strength and cultural resilience of the Protestant communities in the border counties.[22] Notwithstanding the political and economic dislocation caused by partition, much of the social and cultural life for both communities continued as before and transcended the border: the churches, Protestant and Catholic, the Orange Order and the AOH, and some (but not all) sporting organizations continued to operate to a large extent on a cross-border basis.

The demographic figures mask the lived experiences of individual families. Colonel John Vaughan Hart of Kilderry is an example of a major landowner (the family owned more than 6,000 acres in the late nineteenth century and a number of properties, including Doe Castle) who chose to leave his ancestral home and the IFS. In 1928 he moved his family across the border to County Derry where he owned property. He had been fearful about their safety in the period between 1918 and 1923, although he did not experience personal attacks and was generally uncomfortable with life under the IFS. He was closely involved with the DPRA and made submissions to the Boundary Commission. He was insistent that his concerns were political and cultural rather than religious and argued that DPRA should seek minimal changes to the border in individual localities, including his own. The outcome sealed his decision to leave.[23]

In contrast, Lord Leitrim chose to maintain his connections with Donegal. His house had been subject to a number of attacks during the War of Independence and there was a bitter no-rent campaign on his estates in 1922. However, the Rosapenna hotel reopened in 1924 and remained under his management until 1940. He spent much of his later years at Mulroy until his death in 1952.[24] James Sproule Myles (1877–1956) is probably a better exemplar of what one geographer has called 'adaptive co-existence'.[25] His family was closely involved in the business and community life of south Donegal and west Ulster. Partition presented a significant economic and cultural challenge. A successful businessman, with a thriving timberyard and hardware shop in Ballyshannon, Myles had close family connections in Northern Ireland. Despite the turning of the tide in favour of SF in Donegal from 1918, the introduction of proportional representation for local elections presented an opportunity to seek a platform, which he seized. He was elected to DCC in 1920 and pursued a constructive role, particularly on local issues. After partition, which he had opposed but now acquiesced in, Myles successfully contested the 1923 general election as an independent candidate. In his election address, he stated that on general principle he was a supporter of the Treaty and of the policy of the IFS government but reserved the right to act and vote as he thought fit in the interests of the country and of the 'the county of Tirconaill', in particular.[26] Myles was subsequently re-elected six times, always on the first count. He lost his seat in 1943.[27]

The Irish Revolution was not a single uniform phenomenon. A major theme in this volume has been spatial, religious and political diversity. Nationalism and unionism became increasingly polarized, but both covered a wide spectrum. Accordingly, the study of the revolution requires multiple lenses. The events of the revolutionary decade were experienced differently by different individuals and groups; their perspective on the nature and meaning of the revolution varied accordingly. For Peadar O'Donnell, revolutions are made by 'driving the non-propertied to revolt' but they are then betrayed by the middle classes who are 'the nervous peace-makers'. He espoused an alliance of workers, small farmers and peasants that would seize control of the revolution.[28] In spite of his efforts there is not much evidence of social revolution in Donegal during the period. There were occasional agrarian incidents driven by landlessness and the demand to break up estates. No doubt, there were often ulterior motives for IRA activity such as arms raids on the homes of large farmers. If, as some theorists argue, radical nationalism was a 'disease of development' with areas of intermediate development more prone, Donegal, or at least west Donegal, was not fertile territory because of the level of poverty.[29]

Endemic poverty remained a feature of life throughout the period and, if anything, was exacerbated. The CDB's attempt to address the underlying causes was disrupted by the First World War and the following conflict. While high wartime prices brought windfall profits for some, the benefit was less evident in the west of the county. Concern about unemployment and emigration was regularly expressed but it reached a crescendo in 1922. Widespread distress and even starvation were reported in west Donegal. Maud Gonne and Charlotte Despard visited the county and launched an appeal through the nationalist White Cross.[30] Grants to ease distress were made but not fully expended. During the Civil War, a constant refrain from the IRA men from the south was the shocking poverty of the people. Far from generating social revolution, the condition of the people made the IRA campaign more difficult to sustain.

There may be some validity in the interpretation that the split in the nationalist movement leading to the Civil War was between Wolfe Tone's 'men of no property' and those with a stake in society, but that view has clear limitations in the context of Donegal. The IRA leadership group fell into both categories and there was no clear pattern in how they sided. Personal loyalty was a bigger factor than property in how the rank and file divided. It is true that within the wider community, business, commerce, the Church and the press almost unanimously supported the Treaty. The county was strongly pro-Treaty which reflected a pragmatic choice and the predominance of an inherent conservatism not unusual in a peasant society in transition.

The Church and religion were important but not decisive factors. The rise of nationalism coincided with an extension of the power and influence of the Catholic Church and for much of the period one reinforced the other. Bishop O'Donnell was a dominant figure as a churchman and a nationalist, but his influence declined after 1918. While some, particularly younger, clergy threw their weight behind SF, that movement swept to power in spite of the Church. The Civil War coincided with (if it did not facilitate) the re-engagement of the senior clergy and the reassertion of their power. O'Donnell became coadjutor archbishop of Armagh in January 1922 and later succeeded Michael Logue. He played a less public political role in his new position: while supporting the Free State, he was privately bitterly critical of its policy of executions.[31] The church's influence in the social and cultural life of the IFS is unquestionable. One can only speculate how different that might have been if Ireland had not been partitioned into two 'states', one predominantly Catholic and the other predominantly Protestant. It is one of the many ironies of the settlements and divisions of 1920–2 that partition which Bishop O'Donnell personally abhorred enhanced the power of his church after independence.

Donegal in 1923 presented strong elements of continuity and discontinuity. The achievement of an extensive measure of self-government, though not full independence, represented a significant change. Locally, political power was held by Cumann na nGaedheal. Significantly, Joe Sweeney decided to step away from politics and devoted himself to a military career in the National army. The 1923 elections were marked by greater diversity and a reappearance of familiar faces, sometimes in new guises. This development was not uncommon in other counties but in the case of Donegal it was not quite a 'return to Redmondite roots'.[32] John White of the Farmers' Party won a seat and Hugh Law re-entered the political arena, standing unsuccessfully for that party. Four years later, he was elected as a Cumann na nGaedheal TD and held the seat until 1932. Daniel McMenamin, who had contested Donegal West for the IPP in 1918, stood unsuccessfully as an independent in 1923 but was elected for the National League in June 1927 and served as a Cumann na nGaedheal and later Fine Gael TD until 1957. The Redmondite National League established in 1926 won a respectable 11.3 per cent of the first preference vote in Donegal in 1927. The re-emergence of erstwhile home rulers was facilitated by the AOH, which regained some of its power and influence in the county. The AOH had more divisions in Donegal during the 1920s than in any other county in the IFS.[33] Michael Óg McFadden, a leading AOH member in the county, was elected as a Cumann na nGaedheal TD in 1927 and held the seat, with one short break, until 1951.[34]

The active part played by women, particularly in Cumann na mBan, was not reflected in an enhanced status in the life of the county after 1923. The social conservatism of the new state guaranteed that in this area as so many others nothing much had changed. Eithne Coyle remained a life-long activist in republican causes. After her release from prison, she became president of Cumann na mBan. Like many of her colleagues, she had to fight another prolonged battle to be awarded a pension for her activities in the War of Independence. She was granted a partial pension in 1945 but was refused recognition of service between April 1918 and March 1919.[35] With economic recession, employment opportunities had, if anything, diminished and emigration was the only alternative for many. An examination of the nominal rolls of Cumann na mBan members in Donegal indicates that by the 1930s large numbers had taken that route. Of the twenty-three members of the Meenacross company in west Donegal, thirteen had emigrated to the United States by the time the rolls were compiled. The number of emigrants from other companies was smaller but still sufficient to confirm the resumption of a familiar pattern.[36]

The rate of emigration among IRA members was also high. At the end of the Civil War, the intelligence officer of the 1st Northern Division reported that in some areas, the most reliable Volunteers were emigrating as were practically all the ex-prisoners.[37] Of the thirty-seven members of the Bundoran 'B' company, six, including Captain Patrick Johnston, moved to the United States.[38] Some of those on the losing side might have considered themselves political exiles as well as economic migrants. That was certainly the case with many of the republican prisoners when they were released. James McNulty who had returned from the United States before 1916 was wounded in 1919 and imprisoned in Derry in February 1921 where he was part of the failed escape attempt later in the year. When he was finally released in 1924, he returned to the United States with his young family, disappointed and disillusioned. Those who were on the Free State side had at least the possibility of employment in the new Garda Síochána or the army – Joseph Murray had a distinguished career in the former and Joe Sweeney in the latter.

The War of Independence in Donegal was marked more by its level of popular mobilization than by the level of violence. Paradoxically, the opposite is true of the Civil War when the casualties were higher and the level of mobilization arguably less. In contrast to the decade that followed, the revolutionary period saw a short-lived blossoming of creativity, which was reflected in the work of Patrick MacGill, the Mac Griannas and Peadar O'Donnell. While their writings document the decade of revolution from very different perspectives, they shared much in common. All three were from west Donegal; they were all in their own way idealistic social radicals; and, ultimately, they were all disappointed in the outcome of the revolution they helped to create.

Notes

CHAPTER ONE *'Seod glas san fharraige mór': Donegal in 1912*

1 The quotation that opens this chapter, 'A green jewel in the great sea' is a translation of a line from the 1902 song 'Sean Dún na nGall' by John Clinton O'Boyce, a Portsalon schoolteacher and friend of Casement.
2 Roger Casement (Pentonville Prison) to Fr Eamon Murnane, 3 July 1916 (NLI, Casement papers, MS 17,044/1); Cecil A. King, 'Some Casement associations with Donegal', *DA*, 8:1 (1966), 59–66; Michael Laffan, 'Casement, Sir Roger David', *DIB*.
3 A.G. Lecky, *In the days of the Laggan presbytery* (Belfast, 1908), p. 1.
4 *Commission on emigration and other population problems, 1948–54* (Dublin, 1954), p. 20.
5 Buncrana had a population of 1,848 in 1911.
6 Frank Sweeney, 'Donegal railways' in Jim MacLaughlin and Seán Beattie (eds), *Atlas of County Donegal* (Cork, 2013), pp 4, 5, 9; Frank Sweeney, 'Letterkenny and Burtonport extension railway; its social context and environment' (PhD, NUIM, 2004), pp 34–6.
7 John Cunningham, 'The port of Ballyshannon', *DA*, 52 (2000), 36.
8 *Commission on emigration and other population problems, 1948–54* (Dublin, 1955), p. 282.
9 *Census of Ireland, 1911, Province of Ulster, Donegal* [Cd. 6051 IV], p. viii.
10 Roger Casement to Gertrude Bannister, 12 Aug. 1912 (NLI, Casement papers, MS 13,074/7ii/12); Casement to Bannister, 10 Sept. 1912 (NLI, Casement papers, MS 13,074/iii/1); Casement to Blanche Constance Casement, 16 Oct. 1912 (NLI, MS 22,317/2).
11 *Census of Ireland, 1911, Donegal*, pp vii, 163.
12 Pádraig Ó Baoighill, *Cardinal Patrick O'Donnell, 1856–1927* (Letterkenny, 2008); Patrick Maume, 'O'Donnell, Patrick', *DIB*.
13 Plunkett diary, 11 Sept. 1917 (NLI, Horace Plunkett papers, MS 42,222/37).
14 Pat Bolger, 'The Congested Districts Board and the cooperatives in Donegal' in William Nolan, Liam Ronayne and Mairéad Dunlevy (eds), *Donegal history & society* (Dublin, 1995), p. 611.
15 Augustine Birrell, *Things past redress* (London, 1937), p. 209.
16 Birrell to O'Donnell, 21 Aug. 1911, quoted in Leon Ó Broin, *Augustine Birrell in Ireland* (London, 1969), pp 44–5.
17 *LS*, 29 Dec. 1923; 23 Mar. 1946. Chadwick resigned in 1916 due to ill-health and died in Dublin in 1923.
18 CDB, *20th report for the year ending 31 March 1912* (1912), [Cd. 6553], appendix xix, p. 53.
19 DCC, 16 Jan. 1912 (DCA, CC 1/1/5/58).
20 Martina O'Donnell, 'The role of the Congested Districts Board in estate purchase and improvement in Donegal, 1891–1923', *DA*, 50 (1998), 121.
21 DATI, *Agricultural statistics Ireland, 1910*, 56 [Cd. 5964], 1911, p. 22.
22 CDB, *20th report*, appendix xxi, pp 55–9.
23 CDB, *24th report* (Dublin, 1916), appendix viii.
24 CDB *30th report* (Dublin, 1923), pp 7–12.   25 Ibid., p. 87.
26 DATI, *Agricultural statistics Ireland, 1910*, 56 [Cd. 5964], pp 33–7; Department of Industry and Commerce, *Agricultural statistics Ireland, 1847–1926* (Dublin, 1928), p. xxxv.
27 Ibid., p. lvi; DATI, *Agricultural statistics, Ireland*, 56 [Cd. 5964], pp 99, 106.
28 For its impact, see Seán Beattie, *Donegal in transition: the impact of the Congested Districts Board* (Dublin, 2013).
29 William L. Micks, *An account of the constitution, administration and dissolution of the Congested Districts Board for Ireland from 1891 to 1923* (London, 1925), pp 35–47.

30 Ibid., pp 48–9.   31 CDB, *16th report* (1907), pp 17–23.
32 CDB, *20th report* (1912), pp 22–3.
33 CDB, *16th report* (1907), p. 64; *20th report*, p. 27.
34 Ibid., p. 81.   35 Ibid., pp 73–4.
36 Micks, *Congested Districts Board*, pp 60–1.
37 Ibid., pp 51–4, 61–4; CDB, *20th report* (1912), pp 26–7.
38 *Census of Ireland, 1911, County of Donegal*, table xix, pp 82–3.
39 Beattie, *Donegal in transition*, p. 71.
40 Desmond Murphy, *Derry, Donegal and modern Ulster, 1790–1921* (Omagh, 1981), pp 224–7; Micks, *Congested Districts Board*, pp 71–2; Judith Hoad, *This is Donegal tweed* (Inver, 1987), p. 103.
41 Beattie, *Donegal in transition*, pp 76–9; Murphy, *Derry, Donegal and modern Ulster*, pp 225–6.
42 Micks, *Congested Districts Board*, pp 68–74; Beattie, *Donegal in transition*, pp 70–4; Seán Beattie, 'The lace schools of County Donegal, 1880–1920' in MacLaughlin & Beattie (eds), *Atlas of County Donegal*, pp 417–23.
43 Lavinia Edna Walter, *The fascination of Donegal* (London, 1913), cited in Jim MacLoughlin, *Donegal: the making of a northern county* (Dublin, 2007), pp 318–22.
44 Walter, *Fascination of Donegal*, pp 318–19.
45 CDB, *30th report* (1922), p. 21; Hoad, *Donegal tweed*, p. 103.
46 Bolger, 'The Congested Districts Board and the cooperatives in Donegal', p. 658.
47 Patrick Gallagher, *My story* (London, 1939); Diarmaid Ferriter, 'Gallagher, Patrick', *DIB*.
48 On the labour movement in Derry see Emmet O'Connor, *Derry labour in the age of agitation, 1889–1906* (Dublin, 2014); Adrian Grant, *Derry: the Irish Revolution, 1912–23* (Dublin, 2018), pp 18–19.
49 *Commission on emigration*, p. 325; Census of Ireland, 1911, Donegal, p. 168; MacLaughlin (ed.), *Donegal*, pp 4–5.
50 *Census of Ireland, 1911, Donegal*, p. viii.
51 John Coolahan, *Irish education: history and structure* (Dublin, 1981), p. 55; *Census of Ireland, 1911, Donegal*, table xxxviii, p. 167.
52 DCC, 25 Aug. 1914 (DCA, CC 1/1/6/104); CDB, *20th report* (1912), pp 29–30; Kieran Kelly, *Letterkenny: where the winding Swilly flows* (Letterkenny, 2014), pp 54–5.
53 Anthony Begley, *Ballyshannon: genealogy and history* (Ballyshannon, 2011), p. 236.
54 *Census of Ireland, 1911*; Jim Mac Laughlin, 'The politics of nation-building in post-famine Donegal' in Nolan et al. (eds), *Donegal history & society*, p. 610.
55 DCC, 16 Apr. 1912 (DCA, CC 1/1/5/97).
56 *DN*, 15 June 1918. Dunlevy remained chairman until 1920. He was a member of the Irish Convention and supported Bishop O'Donnell's minority report.
57 *IT*, 6 Jan. 1912; *County of Donegal, Lennon Wylie Street Directory, 1912*.
58 DCC, 27 Aug. 1912 (DCA, CC 1/1/5/123).
59 Diarmaid Ferriter, *'Lovers of liberty'?: local government in 20th century Ireland* (Dublin, 2001), p. 11.
60 Helen Meehan, 'The Hamiltons of Brownhall', *DA*, 60 (2008), 55–6.
61 *County of Donegal: Lennon Wylie Street Directory, 1912*; *Royal Irish Constabulary Lists, 1911*.
62 *Royal Irish Constabulary and Dublin Metropolitan Police. Appendix to the report of the committee of inquiry, 1914, containing minutes of evidence with appendices*, HC, 1914 [Cd. 7637], appendix vii; John D. Brewer, *The Royal Irish Constabulary: an oral history* (Belfast, 1990), p. 7; *IT*, 16 Jan. 1912. The number of police rose to almost 500 in 1920.
63 In 1921 Donegal again became a single constituency but with six seats. Two additional seats were added in 1923.

64 Patrick Maume, *The long gestation: Irish nationalist life, 1891–1918* (Dublin, 1999), pp 32–3.
65 DI John Shankey (for CI), Jan. 1912 (TNA, CO 904/96).
66 Séamus McPhillips, 'The AOH in County Monaghan' (MA, NUIM, 1999), pp 8–9.
67 Maume, 'O'Donnell, Patrick', *DIB*.
68 Seán Beattie, 'The Ancient Order of Hibernians in Donegal, 1904–1927', *DA*, 70 (2018), 109–11.
69 DI Shankey, Mar. 1912 (TNA, CO 904/86).
70 IG May, July, Sept. 1912 (TNA, CO 904/87, 88).
71 Beattie, 'The AOH in Donegal', p. 112.
72 IG report, Jan. 1912; DI Shankey, Jan. 1912 (TNA, CO 904/86); *IT*, 18 Jan. 1912.
73 David Fitzpatrick, 'The Orange Order and the border', *IHS*, 33:129 (May 2002), 66.
74 Grand Lodge of Freemasons of Ireland: membership registers, 1733–1923, iii, p. 321 (GLI, Dublin: accessed online 10 Mar. 2021). Myles first joined the Freemasons in 1904 when he was twenty-six.
75 *IT*, 13 July 1912; Diane Urquhart, '"An articulate and definite cry for political freedom": the Ulster suffrage movement', *Women's History Review*, 11:2 (2002), 277–9.
76 DI John Shankey, Jan. 1912 (TNA, CO 904/86).
77 *DJ*, 3 Mar. 1937; Ian Kenneally and James T. O'Donnell (eds), *The Irish regional press, 1892–2018: revival, revolution and republic* (Dublin, 2018), p. 111.
78 The *Vindicator* Story, website http://www.vindicator.ca/history/vinStory/index.html (accessed June 2019); Cecil A. King, *Memorabilia: musings on sixty-odd years as a newspaper man* (Ballyshannon, 1989), pp 124–5.
79 Conor Curran, *The development of sport in Donegal, 1880–1935* (Cork, 2015), pp 5–6, 18.
80 Conor Curran, *Sport in Donegal* (Dublin, 2010), pp 69–70.
81 On modernization and Miroslav Hroch's model of the link between nationalism and intermediate development, see Tom Garvin, *Nationalist revolutionaries, 1858–1928* (Oxford, 1987), pp 1–8.

CHAPTER TWO *The home rule crisis, 1912–14: promised land or Armageddon?*

1 Pauric Travers, *Settlements and divisions: Ireland, 1870–1922* (Dublin, 1988), pp 81–3; Patricia Jalland, *The Liberals and Ireland: the Ulster question in British politics to 1914* (Brighton, 1980), pp 126–8.
2 Daithí Ó Corráin, 'Resigned to take the bill with its defects: the Catholic Church and the third home rule bill' in Gabriel Doherty (ed.), *The home rule crisis, 1912–14* (Cork, 2014), pp 197, 200–202.
3 Dillon to Redmond, 14 Jan. 1912 (NLI, Redmond papers, MS 15,182/19); Ó Corráin, 'Resigned to take the bill', pp 198–200.
4 *IT*, 18 Jan. 1912; IG Jan. 1912, DI John Shankey Donegal, Jan. 1912 (TNA, CO 904/86).
5 DI Shankey, Mar. 1912 (TNA, CO 904/86).
6 *Freeman's Journal* (hereafter *FJ*), 24 Apr. 1912; Ó Baoighill, *O'Donnell*, pp 129–30.
7 CI Donegal, Nov., Dec. 1912 (TNA, CO 904/88), Jan. 1913 (TNA, CO 904/89).
8 Grant, *Derry*, p. 38; Fergal McCluskey, *Tyrone: the Irish Revolution, 1912–23* (Dublin, 2014), pp 37–43.
9 CI Donegal, May 1913 (TNA, CO 904/90).   10 IG, June 1913 (ibid.).
11 Memorandum on drilling in Ulster, 23 Feb. 1912 (TNA, CO 904/86).
12 DI Shankey, Feb. 1912 (TNA, CO 904/86).   13 DI Shankey, Mar. 1912 (ibid.).
14 *IT*, 11 Mar. 1912.
15 IG, Apr. 1912; CI Donegal, Apr. 1912 (TNA, CO 904/86).

16 CI Donegal, May 1912 (TNA, CO 904/87).
17 *DN*, 14 Sept. 1912; *BN*, 1 July 1912; CI Donegal, June 1912 (TNA, CO 904/87).
18 CI Donegal, July, Aug. 1912 (ibid.); IG, Sept. 1912 (TNA, CO 904/88).
19 A.T.Q. Stewart, *The Ulster crisis: resistance to home rule, 1912–14* (London, 1969), pp 61–3.
20 *DN*, 14 Sept., 28 Sept. 1912; *IT*, 31 Aug., 12 Sept. 1912; *Ulster Herald*, 28 Sept. 1912.
21 *Ulster Herald*, 21 Sept. 1912; *IT*, 18 Sept. 1912; *Weekly Irish Times*, 28 Sept. 1912; *LS*, 21 Sept. 1912.
22 On the Covenant, see Aidan O'Connell, 'The Ulster Covenant in Donegal, 1912', *DA*, 63 (2011), 45–58.
23 Ibid., p. 50.   24 *DN*, 5 Oct. 1912.   25 Ibid.
26 *Ulster Guardian*, cited in *DN*, 28 Sept. 1912.
27 *Ulster Herald*, 5 Oct. 1912.
28 CI Donegal, Aug., Sept. 1912 (TNA, CO 904/88).
29 *DN*, 14 Sept., 5 Oct. 1912.
30 R.W. Wilson, letter to *Irish Times*, cited in *DN*, 7 Sept. 1012; *DN*, 5 Oct. 1912.
31 *DN*, 5 Oct. 1912.
32 CI Donegal, Nov. 1912 (TNA, CO 904/88).
33 CI Donegal, Dec. 1912 (ibid.).
34 IG, Jan. 1913 (TNA, CO 904/89); *BN*, 20 Jan. 1913.
35 *DN*, 6 Apr. 1912, 22 Nov. 1913; *II*, 17 Oct. 1912, 25 Feb. 1914.
36 Unionist movement in Ulster: memorandum by J.B. Dougherty, 10 Mar. 1913 (TNA, CO 904/27/3).
37 IG, Apr., May 1913 (TNA, CO 904/89, 90).
38 Grant, *Derry*, p. 31; McCluskey, *Tyrone*, p. 27.
39 CI Donegal, Jan., Feb. 1913 (TNA, CO 904/89); County reports synopsis, Jan. 1913 (TNA, CO 904/89).
40 CI Donegal, June–Sept., Nov. 1913 (TNA, CO 904/90, 91).
41 County reports synopsis, Mar., Apr. 1913 (TNA, CO 904/89); CI Donegal, Mar., May 1913 (TNA, CO 904/89, 90).
42 CI Donegal, July 1913 (TNA, CO 904/90); Report on condition of Ulster: County of Donegal, July 1913 (TNA, CO 904/27/3).
43 CI Donegal, Dec. 1913 (TNA, CO 904/91).
44 *Strabane Chronicle*, 18 July 1914; *IT*, 18 July 1914; CI Donegal, June 1914 (TNA, CO 904/93).
45 Ibid.   46 CI Donegal, Oct. 1913 (TNA, CO 904/91).
47 *IT*, 3 Oct. 1913; *FJ*, 3 Oct. 1913.
48 *IT*, 3 Oct. 1913; *FJ*, 3 Oct. 1913; CI Donegal, Oct. 1913 (TNA, CO 904/91).
49 *IT*, 3 Oct. 1913; *II*, 3 Oct. 1913.
50 Further notes on the movement in Ulster, Nov. 1913 (TNA, CAB 37/117/83); CI Donegal, Nov. 1913 (TNA, CO 904/91).
51 CI Donegal, Feb., Mar., Apr. 1914 (TNA, CO 904/92, 93); County reports synopsis (TNA, CO 904/92).
52 CI Donegal, Jan. 1914 (TNA, CO 904/92).
53 Quincy Dougan, 'Donegal's Ulster Volunteers', www.bygonedays.net (accessed June 2019); CI Donegal, Feb., Mar., May, July 1914 (TNA CO 904/92, 93, 94).
54 Timothy Bowman, *Carson's army: the Ulster Volunteer Force, 1910–1922* (Manchester, 2007), p. 57.
55 CI Donegal, Nov. 1913 (TNA, CO 904/91).
56 Ibid.   57 CI Donegal, Mar. 1914 (TNA, CO 904/92).
58 *Cork Examiner*, 4 Mar. 1914; *FJ*, 5 Mar. 1914.

59 Unionist movement against home rule, Mar. 1914 (TNA CO 904/27/3); CI Donegal, June 1914 (TNA, CO 904/93).
60 Report on the condition of Ulster, July 1913 (TNA, CO 904/27/3).
61 *FJ*, 7 July 1913; Stewart, *Ulster crisis*, pp 93–4; CI Donegal, July 1913 (TNA, CO 904/90).
62 *DJ*, 10, 13 July 1914; CI Donegal, July 1914 (TNA, CO 904/94); St Johston UVF alleged plot to hold up train on 11 July 1914, Deputy IG to Major-Gen. L.B. Friend, 18 Dec. 1914 (TNA, CO 904/28).
63 *DJ*, 10, 13 July 1914.   64 Stewart, *Ulster crisis*, p. 94.
65 Bowman, *Carson's army*, pp 135–45.
66 CI Donegal, Mar. 1914 (TNA, CO 904/92).
67 *DN*, 1, 4 Apr. 1914; *DJ*, 29 Apr. 1914.
68 Deputy IG, May 1914 (TNA, CO 904/93).
69 CI Donegal, Apr., May 1914 (TNA, CO 904/93).
70 *IT*, 6 Jan. 1914; *Irish Daily Telegraph*, 6 Jan. 1914.
71 Augustine Birrell, 'Ulster', 5 Mar. 1914 (TNA, CAB 37/119/36).
72 CI Donegal, Oct., Dec. 1914 (TNA, CO 904/91).
73 CI Donegal, Jan. 1914 (TNA, CO 904/92); Denis Gwynn, *The life of John Redmond* (London, 1932), p. 249.
74 O'Donnell to Redmond, 9 May 1914 (NLI, Redmond papers, MS 15,217/4).
75 CI Donegal, Nov. 1918 (TNA, CO 904/91).
76 CI Donegal, Jan. 1914 (TNA, CO 904/92); *DJ*, 2 Feb. 1914.
77 Conflated from CI Donegal, Feb.–Aug. 1914 (TNA, CO 904/92–94).
78 CI Donegal, May, June 1914 (TNA, CO 904/93).
79 CI Donegal, Mar. 1914 (TNA, CO 904/92).
80 Ibid.; CI Donegal, June 1914 (TNA, CO 904/93).
81 CI Donegal, Mar. 1914 (TNA, CO 904/92).
82 *DJ*, 29 Apr. 1914.   83 Daniel Kelly (BMH WS 1004, pp 7–9).
84 *DJ*, 13 July 1914.   85 CI Donegal, July 1914 (TNA, CO 904/94)
86 CI Donegal, May 1914 (TNA, CO 904/93).
87 Ibid.   88 CI Donegal, June 1914 (ibid.).
89 Ibid.
90 Asquith to King, 14 Nov. 1913 (TNA, CAB 41/34/34); Jalland, *Liberals and Ireland*, pp 166–75, 196–206.
91 O'Donnell to Redmond, 9 Oct. 1913 (NLI, Redmond papers, MS 15,217/4).
92 Jalland, *Liberals and Ireland*, pp 197–200; Roy Jenkins, *Asquith* (London, 1967), pp 335–8; Ó Baoighill, *O'Donnell*, pp 130–1.
93 Redmond memorandum to Asquith, 2 Mar. 1914 (NLI, Redmond papers, MS 15,181/3).
94 Grant, *Derry*, p. 48; John Simon, 'Effects of optional exclusion by counties on Irish representation', 10 Mar. 1914 (TNA, CAB 37/119/40); Jalland, *Liberals and Ireland*, p. 203.
95 O'Donnell to Redmond, 25 Feb. 1914 (NLI, Redmond papers, MS 15,217/4).
96 Redmond to McHugh, 26 Feb. 1914 (CÓFLA, O'Donnell papers, Arch/10/5/15); McHugh to Redmond, 28 Feb. 1914 (NLI, Redmond papers, MS 15,203/5); Eamon Phoenix, *Northern nationalism: nationalist politics, partition and the Catholic minority in Northern Ireland, 1890–1940* (Belfast, 1994), pp 11–13.
97 Ballyshannon Town Commission, 1 June 1914 (DCA BTC/1/1, p. 411).
98 Ronan Fanning, *Fatal path: British government and Irish revolution, 1910–1922* (London, 2013), pp 126–8; Jenkins, *Asquith*, pp 357–60.
99 Jalland, *Liberals and Ireland*, p. 259.
100 Deputy IG report, May 1912 (TNA, CO 904/93).

CHAPTER THREE *'As much Ireland's war as England's'?: the First World War, 1914–18*

1 *DJ*, 16 Mar. 1917.   2 *DJ*, 30 Sept. 1914.   3 Ibid., 23 Sept. 1914.
4 Statement for Letterkenny conference, 23 Sept. 1917 (CÓFLA, O'Donnell papers, Arch/10/4/25); *DJ*, 28, 30 Sept. 1914.
5 Ibid., 30 Sept. 1914.
6 CI Donegal, Sept. 1914 (TNA, CO 904/94); *DJ*, 23 Sept. 1914.
7 CI Donegal, Aug. 1914 (TNA, CO 904/94).   8 *DJ*, 30 Sept. 1914.
9 Personal diary of Lady Lillian Spender, Jan.–Sept. 1915 (PRONI, D1633/2/20).
10 *DJ*, 28 Sept. 1914.   11 *The Times*, 14 Nov. 1918.
12 Helmut Pensel, *A history of the war at sea* (Annapolis, 1977), p. 160.
13 John Jellicoe, *The grand fleet, 1914–1916: its creation, development and work* (New York, 1919), p. 135.
14 *FJ*, 21 Sept. 1914; Stephen Gwynn, *John Redmond's last years* (London, 1919), pp 154–5.
15 *Strabane Chronicle*, 24 Oct. 1914.
16 *National Volunteer*, 24 Oct. 1914; *Kerry Press*, 24 Oct. 1914.
17 *National Volunteer*, 24 Oct. 1914.   18 Ó Baoighill, *O'Donnell*, pp 138–40.
19 See, for example, *DN*, 31 Oct. 1914.
20 CI Donegal, Sept. 1914 (TNA, CO 904/94).
21 CI Donegal, Dec. 1914 (TNA, CO 904/95).
22 Thomas McShea (BMH WS 782, pp 1–2); Patrick Breslin (BMH WS 1448, p. 2).
23 *FJ*, 28 Sept. 1914; James McConnel, 'Recruiting sergeants for John Bull? Irish nationalist MPs and enlistment during the early months of the great war', *War in History*, 14:4 (Nov. 2007), 419.
24 *DJ*, 30 Sept. 1914.
25 *FJ*, 28 Oct. 1914; McConnel, 'Recruiting sergeants', 420–1; Francis Law, *A man at arms: memoirs of two world wars* (London, 1983).
26 J.G. Swift MacNeill, *What I have seen and heard* (London, 1925), p. 236.
27 *DJ*, 18 Nov. 1915.
28 Timothy Bowman, William Butler and Michael Wheatley (eds), *The disparity of sacrifice: Irish recruitment to the British armed forces, 1914–18* (Liverpool, 2020), p. 2.
29 Keith Jeffery, *1916: a global history* (London, 2016), pp 110–11.
30 Okan Ozseker, *Forging the border: Donegal and Derry in times of revolution* (Dublin, 2019), p. 63.
31 Grant, *Derry*, p. 54; McCluskey, *Tyrone*, p. 52; Patrick McGarty, *Leitrim: the Irish Revolution, 1912–23* (Dublin, 2020), p. 21.
32 *County Donegal book of honour: the great war, 1914–1918* (Donegal, 2002), p. 7.
33 Niall Mac Fhionnghaile, *Donegal, Ireland and the First World War* (Letterkenny, 1987), p. 7.
34 Jason Myers, 'Reconsidering Irish fatalities in World War 1', https://www.theirishstory/com (accessed Mar. 2021). Myers' analysis is based on a reworking of the data in Patrick Casey, 'Irish casualties in the First World War', *Irish Sword*, 20:81 (1997), 193–206.
35 *DN*, 21 June 1915.
36 Bowman et al., *Disparity of sacrifice*, pp 34–6.
37 H.E.D. Harris, *The Irish regiments in the First World War* (Cork, 1968), pp 22–3.
38 Terence Denman, *Ireland's unknown soldiers: the 16th (Irish) Division in the Great War* (Dublin, 1992), pp 38–40.
39 CI Donegal, Aug. 1914 (TNA, CO904/94).
40 Ballyshannon Town Commission, 6 Mar. 1916 (DCA, BTC/1/1, pp 447–8).
41 *DJ*, 3 Apr. 1916.
42 Richard Doherty, 'Donegal and the First World War', *DA*, 66 (2014), 40–3.

43 Sporadic efforts were made over the years to recover the gold and most of the bars have been salvaged.
44 Mary Bowden et al., *Along Rathmullan shore: a maritime memoir* (Rathmullan, 2001), p. 25.
45 CI Donegal, Jan. 1915 (TNA, CO 904/96).
46 *Statement giving particulars of men of military age in Ireland, 1916* (Cd. 8,390); Bowman et al., *Disparity of sacrifice*, pp 36–7.
47 CI Donegal, May 1915 (TNA, CO 904/97).
48 CI Donegal, Mar. 1915 (TNA, CO 904/96).
49 CI Donegal, Feb., Mar., May 1915 (TNA, CO 904/96, 97).
50 Ozseker, *Forging the border*, p. 66.
51 Montgomery to Carson, 5 Mar. 1915 (PRONI, Carson (Irish) papers, D/1507/A/11/14).
52 Letterkenny, RDC, 4 June, 2 July 1915 (DCA, RDC 6/1/10, pp 158, 173).
53 Letters from Central Council of Organisation of Recruiting in Ireland, 16, 17 July 1915. Letterkenny RDC, 6 Aug. 1915 (DCA, RDC 6/1/10, p. 186).
54 CI Donegal, Mar. 1915 (TNA, CO 904/96).
55 CI Donegal, Apr. 1915 (ibid.).
56 CI Donegal, May 1915 (TNA, CO 904/97).
57 *DJ*, 21 June 1915.   58 CI Donegal, Apr., July 1915 (TNA, CO 904/96, 97).
59 CI Donegal, Apr. 1915 (TNA, CO 904/96).
60 CI Donegal, Apr., May 1915 (TNA, 904/96, 97).
61 CI Donegal, June 1915 (TNA, CO 904/97).
62 Pauric Travers, 'The Irish conscription crisis' (MA thesis, UCD, 1977), pp 3–7.
63 CI Donegal, Sept. 1915 (TNA, CO 904/98).
64 CI Donegal, June 1915 (TNA, CO 904/97).
65 CI Donegal, Aug. 1915 (TNA, CO 904/97).
66 Letterkenny RDC, 6 Aug. 1915 (DCA, RDC 6/1/10, p. 186); CI Donegal, June 1915 (TNA, CO 904/97).
67 *DJ*, 10 Jan. 1916; Letterkenny RDC, 7 Jan. 1916 (DCA, RDC 6/1/10, p. 274).
68 *DJ*, 10 Jan. 1916.   69 CI Donegal, Feb. 1916 (TNA, CO 904/99).
70 *DN*, 1, 29 Jan. 1916.   71 *Donegal book of honour*, p. 86.
72 Kelly, *Letterkenny*, p. 168.   73 *BN*, 23 Jan. 1915; Kelly, *Letterkenny*, pp 160–1.
74 *Donegal book of honour*, pp 113, 161.
75 Fionnuala Walsh, *Irish women and the Great War* (Cambridge, 2020), p. 23.
76 Caitriona Clear, 'Fewer ladies, more women' in John Horne (ed.), *Our war: Ireland and the Great War* (Dublin, 2008), p. 163; Myrtle Hill, *Women in Ireland: a century of change* (Belfast, 2003), pp 67–8.
77 Catherine Black ('Blackie'), *King's nurse, beggar's nurse* (London, 1939); Claire Chatterton, 'Sister Catherine Black: king's nurse, beggar's nurse', *Bulletin of UK Association for the History of Nursing*, 6 (2017), 50–1.
78 Anthony Begley, 'Letters from the trenches of World War One to families in the Ballyshannon area': https://ballyshannon-musings.blogspot.com/2018/11 (accessed Nov. 2020); Begley, *Ballyshannon and surrounding areas* (Ballyshannon, 2009), pp 331–6.
79 *Donegal book of honour*, pp 40, 103.
80 Medal card of Myles, James Sproule (TNA, WO 372/14/171474).
81 *IT*, 9 June 1917.   82 Begley, 'Letters from the trenches'.
83 Logue to O'Donnell, 11 Mar. 1915 (CÓFLA, O'Donnell papers, XIII).
84 J. McRory diary, book 1, p. 38 (PRONI, McRory D/1868/1).
85 Hugh O'Neill, 'Irish Catholic chaplains in British armed forces during World War 1', *Seanchas Ard Mhaca*, 23:2 (2011), 209.
86 *Cork Examiner*, 14 Oct. 1914.   87 *FH*, 28 Oct. 1914.

88 Mac Fhionnghaile, *Donegal, Ireland and the war*, pp 148–9.
89 John Martin Brennan, 'Irish Catholic chaplains and the First World War' (M.Phil., University of Birmingham, 2011), pp 112–13.
90 Kelly, *Letterkenny*, p. 169.
91 Frank Galligan, 'MacGill, Patrick', *DIB*.
92 Patrick MacGill, *The amateur army* (London, 1915), p. 13.
93 Patrick MacGill, *The great push: an episode of the Great War* (London, 1916), preface.
94 *IT*, 7 Dec. 1915.
95 Army Pension Records, Patrick MacGill (TNA, WO 364/222); letters to Redmond from Lord Derby, Sir Ian Hamilton; Patrick and Margaret MacGill to Redmond, 1915–16 (NLI, Redmond papers, MS 15,180/1; 15,262/9; 15,263/1).
96 Army Pension Records, Patrick MacGill (TNA, WO 364/222); Galligan, 'MacGill, Patrick'.
97 *DJ*, 7 Sept. 1917.   98 *Red Horizon* (London, 1915), p. 1.
99 *Cork Examiner*, 14 Oct. 1914.   100 *DJ*, 31 Jan. 1915.
101 Clare O'Neill, 'The Irish home front, 1914–1918' (PhD, NUIM, 2006), pp 52–3.
102 LGB to DCC, 12 Oct. 1914, DCC, 24 Nov. 1914 (DCA, CC/1/1/6, p. 141).
103 *DJ*, 13 Jan. 1915.
104 Ibid., 15 Jan. 1915; Kelly, *Letterkenny*, pp 166–7.
105 O'Neill, 'Irish home front', p. 200.   106 *DJ*, 28 Apr. 1915.
107 Kelly, *Letterkenny*, pp 166–7; O'Neill, 'Irish home front', p. 86.
108 *DJ*, 5 Apr. 1915; O'Neill, 'Irish home front', pp 53, 63.
109 *DJ*, 4 Jan. 1915.   110 Ibid., 16 Mar. 1917.
111 *BN*, 31 Dec. 1915.
112 Margaret Downes, 'The civilian war effort' in David Fitzpatrick (ed.), *Ireland and the First World War* (Dublin, 1985), p. 28.
113 Walsh, *Irish women*, p. 30.
114 DCC, 11 Jan. 1916 (DCA, CC/1/1/6, p. 284).
115 *DJ*, 13 Dec. 1915, 18, 20 Feb. 1918; *II*, 25 Mar. 1916; *Dublin Daily Express*, 11 Nov. 1916.
116 Walsh, *Irish women*, p. 30.
117 *LS*, 19 June 1917; John Crowley et al. (eds), *Atlas of the Irish Revolution* (Cork, 2017), p. 211.
118 *BN*, 30 Dec. 1915; *DJ*, 13 Dec. 1915.
119 Clara Cullen, 'War work on the home front: the Central Spagnum Depot for Ireland at the Royal College of Science for Ireland, 1915–1919' in David Durnin and Ian Miller (eds), *Medicine, health and Irish experiences of conflict, 1914–45* (Manchester, 2017), pp 155–70; *BN*, 30 Dec. 1915.
120 Walsh, *Irish women*, pp 112–13; Clear, 'Fewer ladies, more women', p. 167.
121 Diarmaid Ferriter, *A nation of extremes: the pioneers in 20th century Ireland* (Dublin, 1999), pp 52–3.
122 *DJ*, 10 May 1915.   123 DCC, 25 Aug. 1914 (DCA, CC 1/1/6, pp 109–10).
124 Caitriona Clear, 'Fewer ladies, more women', pp 165–6; *II*, 16 Oct. 1915.
125 *DJ*, 3 Apr. 1916, 21 Feb. 1919.   126 *II*, 9 Apr. 1915.
127 *DJ*, 8 Jan. 1915.   128 DCC, 15 Dec. 1914 (DCA, CC/1/1/5, pp 155–7, 171).
129 Micks, *The CDB*, pp 54–6; 61; DCA, *From the edge: County Donegal in 1916* (Lifford, 2016), pp 35–6; *DJ*, 8 Feb. 1918.
130 DCC, 20 Apr. 1915 (DCA, CC/1/1/6, p. 201).
131 Robin Fox, *The Tory islanders* (Cambridge, 1978), p. 25.
132 *DJ*, 26 Nov. 1917; Peter Hegarty, *Peadar O'Donnell* (Cork, 1999), p. 40.
133 Sweeney, 'Letterkenny and Burtonport railway', vol. 2, 11–12; *DJ*, 9 Nov. 1917, 2 Aug. 1918.
134 Sweeney, Letterkenny and Burtonport railway', vol. 2, 6; *DJ*, 2 June 1916.

135 *DJ*, 11 June, 19 Sept. 1917, 24 May 1918; Sweeney, 'Letterkenny and Burtonport railway', vol. 2, 8.
136 CI Donegal, Sept. 1916 (TNA, CO 904/101).
137 Curran, *Sport in Donegal*, pp 18, 169; Sweeney, 'Letterkenny and Burtonport railway', vol. 2, 7.
138 Bundoran UDC, Jan. 1917 (DCA, UDC/3/1/4, pp 255, 261); Ballyshannon RDC, Feb. 1917 (DCA, RDC 1/1/13, p. 102).
139 *IT*, 31 Jan. 1917.
140 Beattie, *Donegal in transition*, pp 209–26.

CHAPTER FOUR *'The squabble in Dublin': 1916 and its aftermath*

1 Seosamh Mac Grianna, *An druma mór* (Baile Átha Cliath, 1969), p. 158. '... and there was also talk from time to time about the things that were in the papers: the Great War over in France, and the squabble in Dublin between the Irish and the English.' Seosamh Mac Grianna, *The big drum*, trans. by A.J. Hughes (Belfast, 2009), p. 98.
2 Philip O'Leary, 'Leabhar gur fiú a léamh' in Nollaig Mac Congáil (ed.), *Mo dhá Róisín* le 'Máire' (Dublin, 2010), p. xxxii.
3 Mac Congáil, *Mo dhá Róisín*, pp v–xxv.
4 Madge O'Boyle, *The life and times of Constable Charles McGee* (Dundalk, 2016); Seosamh Ó Ceallaigh, 'Constable McGee and the Easter Rising', *DA*, 68 (2016), 62–6.
5 Seán MacEntee (BMH WS 1052, pp 54–6).
6 Frank Martin (BMH WS 236, p.4); Edward Bailey (BMH WS 233, p. 4); Dónal O'Hannigan (BMH WS 161, p. 24); Patrick McHugh (BMH WS 677, pp 19–21); Eunan O'Halpin and Daithí Ó Corráin, *The dead of the Irish revolution* (London, 2020), p. 34.
7 Patrick McHugh (BMH WS 664).
8 Deirdre MacMahon, 'MacEntee, Seán (John) Francis', *DIB*; *Sinn Féin Rebellion handbook* (Dublin, 1917), pp 111–12.
9 *Census of Ireland, 1911 Donegal*, p. 163.
10 Helen Meehan, 'MacManus, Seumas', *DIB*; Frances Clarke, 'Carberry, Ethna', *DIB*.
11 CI Donegal, May 1913, Apr. 1914 (TNA, CO 904/90, 93).
12 On the GAA in Donegal, see Curran, *Development of sport in Donegal* and *Sport in Donegal*.
13 T.J. O'Connell, *100 years of progress: the story of the Irish National Teachers' Organisation* (Dublin, 1968), pp 334–40.
14 Eithne Coyle and Cumann na mBan (UCDA, Eithne Coyle papers, P61/2/1, p. 1).
15 Anthony Begley, 'Pearse's letter to a Donegal mother', *DA*, 68 (2016), 8–9; Helen Meehan, 'Pearse and the MacManus brothers', ibid., p. 45; Seán Beattie, 'Easter 1916: early reactions in the north-west', ibid., p. 15.
16 *DJ*, 19 May 1905; *Londonderry Sentinel*, 20 May 1905; *Donegal Independent*, 19 May 1905.
17 *DJ*, 3 Oct. 1906.
18 Marie Coleman, 'O'Farrelly, Agnes (Úna Ní Fhaircheallaigh)', *DIB*.
19 On O'Donnell and Irish, see Ó Baoighill, *O'Donnell*, pp 247–83.
20 Begley, 'Pearse's letter to a Donegal mother', p. 8.
21 CI Donegal, Sept. 1914 (TNA, CO 904/94).
22 CI Donegal, Oct. 1914 (TNA, CO 904/95).
23 CI Donegal, Dec. 1914 (ibid.).
24 CI Donegal, Jan. 1912 (TNA, CO 904/86).
25 Daniel Kelly (BMH WS 1004, pp 1–9). McNulty played a leading role in the War of Independence and Civil War, after which he returned to the US with his family.
26 Ibid., pp 9, 14.

27 On the reorganization of the IRB, see Owen McGee, *The IRB: the Irish Republican Brotherhood from the Land League to Sinn Féin* (Dublin, 2005), pp 348–56.
28 Liam Diver, 'The IRB and the Easter Rising', *DA*, 68 (2016), 107–8; Earnán de Blaghd, 'Organizing the IRB in Donegal', *DA*, 7:1 (1966), 41–4.
29 Bulmer Hobson to Blythe, n.d. (UCDA, Blythe papers, P24/1002).
30 Ernest Blythe (BMH WS 939, pp 15–16). 31 Ibid., pp 18–20.
32 Brian Monaghan (BMH WS 879, pp 3–5).
33 Tom Feeney, 'Sweeney, Joseph Aloysius', *DIB*.
34 CI Donegal, Mar. 1916 (TNA, CO 904/99).
35 Daniel Kelly (BMH WS 1004, p. 18). 36 Ibid., pp 19–27.
37 CI Donegal, Apr. 1916 (TNA, CO 904/99).
38 CI Donegal, May 1916 (TNA, CO 904/100).
39 *DJ*, 26, 28 Apr. 1916. 40 *DN*, 29 Apr. 1916. 41 *DJ*, 1 May 1916.
42 *DN*, 6 May 1916; *DV*, 28 Apr. 1916; *DI*, 15 July 1916; Seán Beattie, 'Easter Rising, 1916: early reactions in the north-west', *DA*, 68 (2016), 96–9.
43 Grant, *Derry*, pp 66–7; McGarty, *Leitrim*, p. 37; Terence Dooley, *Monaghan: the Irish Revolution, 1912–23* (Dublin, 2017), pp 54–5; Michael Farry, *Sligo: the Irish Revolution, 1912–23* (Dublin, 2012), p. 30.
44 The minutes of DCC from March 1916 to January 1921 have not survived.
45 *DJ*, 1 May 1916. The minutes of the board of guardians for this meeting (29 Apr. 1916, DCA, BG/75/1/4, pp 314–24) no longer record this resolution.
46 Donegal Board of Guardians, 6 May 1916 (DCA, BG/75/1/4, p. 328); *DJ*, 8 May 1916; *DN*, 15 May 1916. The motion criticizing 1916 was later rescinded. The general minutes containing details of Melly's criticism are missing from the records.
47 Donegal Board of Guardians, 13 May 1916 (DCA, BG/75/1/4, p. 346); *DJ*, 15 May 1916.
48 *DN*, 6 May 1916.
49 Inishowen RDC, 8 May 1916 (DCA, RDC 5/1/9, p. 310). This motion was 'rescinded' in 1920. Beattie, 'Easter Rising: early reactions', p. 16.
50 *DJ*, 10 May 1916. 51 *DN*, 6 May 1916. 52 *DJ*, 10 May 1916.
53 CI Donegal, Apr. 1916 (TNA, CO 904/99).
54 *DV*, 19 May 1916; John Ward, 'The *Vindicator* story', www.vindicator.ca (accessed June 2020).
55 CI Donegal, May 1916 (TNA, CO 904/100). 56 *DJ*, 8 May 1916.
57 CI Donegal, Apr. 1916 (TNA, CO 904/99). 58 Ibid.
59 CI Donegal, July, Aug. 1916 (TNA, CO 904/100).
60 *FJ*, 22 June, 14 Nov. 1916.
61 Meeting of Episcopal Standing Committee, 19 June 1916 (CÓFLA, O'Donnell papers, Arch/10/4/5).
62 Oliver Rafferty, 'The Church and the Easter Rising', *Studies*, 105:417 (Spring 2016), 48; J. Silke and M. Hughes, *Raphoe miscellany*, II (Letterkenny, 2015), pp 67–70.
63 Beattie, 'Easter Rising: early reactions', p. 16; Rafferty, 'The Church and the Easter Rising', 48; O'Donnell, 'The political situation in Ireland' n.d.– [July–Sept. 1916] (CÓFLA, O'Donnell papers, Arch/10/4/5).
64 Meeting of Episcopal Standing Committee, 9 Oct. 1916 (CÓFLA, O'Donnell papers, Arch/10/4/5); Rafferty, 'The Church and the Easter Rising', 48–9.
65 *Fermanagh Times*, 18 May 1916. 66 *DJ*, 1 May 1916.
67 Alvin Jackson, *Home rule: an Irish history, 1800–2000* (London, 2004), p. 181; Gwynn, *Redmond*, p. 493.
68 *DN*, 1 July 1916. 69 CI Donegal, June 1916 (TNA, CO 904/100).
70 *DN*, 15 July 1916. 71 *DJ*, 23 June 1916. 72 *DN*, 17 June 1916.

73 Ibid., 10 June 1916.
74 Devlin to Redmond, 3 June 1916 (NLI, Redmond papers, MS 15,181(3)); MacVeagh to Redmond, 6 June 1916 (NLI, Redmond papers, MS 15,204 (4)); Ó Baoighill, *O'Donnell*, p. 146.
75 Devlin to Redmond, 21 June 1916 (NLI, Redmond papers, MS 15,181(3)).
76 David Miller, *Church, state and nation in Ireland, 1898–1921* (Dublin, 1973), p. 337.
77 Logue to Redmond, 11 June 1916 (NLI, Redmond papers, MS 15,201/9).
78 Letter from 'a northern priest', *DN*, 17 June 1916; F.S.L. Lyons, *John Dillon: a biography* (London, 1968), p. 389.
79 *DN*, 24 June 1916.
80 A.C. Hepburn, *Catholic Belfast and nationalist Ireland in the era of Joe Devlin, 1871–1934* (Oxford, 2008), pp 177–9.
81 UIL meeting, 3 July 1916 (NLI, MS 708).
82 *DN*, 24 June 1916. 83 Ibid., 8 July 1916.
84 Ibid., 1 July 1916; meeting of IPP, 26 June 1916 (NLI, IPP minute books, MS 12,082).
85 Glenties RDC, 24 June 1916 (DCA, RDC 4/1/10, p. 758).
86 Letterkenny RDC, 14 July 1916 (DCA, RDC 6/1/10, p. 411). 87 *DN*, 7 June 1916.
88 *BN*, 13 June 1916; *LS*, 13 June 1916; *DJ*, 17 June 1916; Patrick Buckland, *Irish Unionism II: Ulster Unionism and the origins of Northern Ireland, 1886–1922* (Dublin, 1973), pp 106–7; Jackson, *Home rule*, pp 185–6.
89 UUC statement, 13 June 1916 (PRONI, Carson (Irish) papers, MS D1507/A/17/13A).
90 William Martin to Carson, 13 July 1916, enclosing letter from Saunderson to Monaghan UUC delegates (PRONI, Carson (Irish) papers, D1507/A/18/12,13).
91 Travers Blackley to UUC, 13 July 1916, William Martin to Carson, 13 July 1916 (PRONI, Carson (Irish) papers, D1507/A/18/13,14).
92 Resolution by Donegal UUC delegates, 12 July 1916 (PRONI, Carson (Irish) papers, D1507/A/11/9).
93 *LS*, 20 June 1916. 94 *BN*, 14 June 1916.
95 Leitrim to Carson, 1, 3, 18 July 1916 (PRONI, Carson (Irish) papers, D1507/A/18/1, 4, 24).
96 On the divisions within the Tory party, see Deirdre McMahon, 'The Irish settlement meeting of the Unionist Party, 7 July 1916', *Analecta Hibernica*, 41 (2009), 203–70.
97 Memorandum from Redmond, 18 July 1916 (Parliamentary Archives, Lloyd George papers, E/3/2/1).
98 Redmond to Asquith, 23 July 1916, Asquith to Redmond, n.d. (NLI, Redmond papers, MS 15,165/6).
99 CI Donegal, July 1916 (TNA, CO 904/100).
100 CI Donegal, July, Aug. 1916 (TNA, CO 904/100); *IT*, 11 Aug. 1916.
101 *DJ*, 18 Nov. 1916; *DN*, 18 Nov. 1916.
102 Gwynn, *Redmond's last years*, p. 239.
103 Dooley, *Monaghan*, p. 60; Edith Wheeler to Lady Londonderry, 8 July 1916 (PRONI, Lady Londonderry papers, D2846/1/8/37).
104 Asquith to Redmond, 28 July 1916 (NLI, Redmond papers, MS 15,165/6); Letter from the prime minister to Mr J. Redmond regarding Ireland, 16 May 1917, *Report of the proceedings of the Irish Convention* [Cd. 9,019] (Dublin, 1918), appendix 1, p. 50.
105 For an account of the Convention, see R.B. McDowell, *The Irish Convention, 1917–1918* (London, 1970). For O'Donnell's contributions, see Ó Baoighill, *O'Donnell*, pp 149–53.
106 Plunkett diary, 14 June 1917 (NLI, Plunkett papers, MS 42,222/37).
107 O'Donnell to Redmond, 22 June 1917 (NLI, Redmond papers, MS 15,217/4).
108 Plunkett diary, 14 June, 8 Aug., 11 Sept. 1917 (NLI, Plunkett papers, MS 42,222/37).

109 Confidential report to king (Trinity College Dublin (hereafter TCD), Irish Convention papers, MSS 2986–7, para. 117).
110 *Report of the proceedings of the Convention*, appendix XVII: division lists, pp 140–72; appendix XVIII: attendance, p. 173.
111 Plunkett diary, 24 Jan. 1918 (NLI, Plunkett papers, MS 42,222/38).
112 O'Donnell to Redmond, 3 Oct. 1917 (NLI, Redmond papers, MS 15,217/4).
113 Plunkett, Confidential report to king, para. 69; Gwynn, *Redmond's last years*, pp 298–9.
114 Plunket diary, 11 Sept. 1917 (NLI, Plunkett papers, MS 42,222/37).
115 Ibid., 31 Oct. 1917 (ibid.).
116 Ó Baoighill, *O'Donnell*, p. 152.
117 O'Donnell to Redmond, 14 Jan. 1918 (NLI, Redmond papers, MS 15,217/4); Gwynn, *Redmond's last years*, pp 584–5.
118 Plunkett diary, 2 Mar. 1918 (NLI, Plunkett papers, MS 42,222/38).
119 Ibid., 5 Apr. 1918 (ibid.). *Report of the proceedings of the Irish Convention*, pp 36–43. On Childers's role at the Convention, see Jim Ring, *Erskine Childers* (London, 1996), pp 188–95. O'Donnell remained in contact with Childers and intervened in an attempt to prevent his execution in 1922. O'Donnell to Hooper, 25 Dec. 1922 (CÓFLA, O'Donnell papers, Arch/10/4/25).
120 Miller, *Church, state and nation*, pp 380–3.
121 Ibid., 11 Dec. 1917 (NLI, Plunkett papers, MS 42,222/37); the earl of Midleton, *Ireland: dupe or heroine* (London, 1932), p. 120.
122 Oliver Rafferty, *Catholicism in Ulster, 1603–1983* (London, 1994), pp 198–9; O'Donnell to Redmond, 27 Dec. 1917 (NLI, Redmond papers, MS 15,217/4).

CHAPTER FIVE *'All changed': Sinn Féin, 1916–18*

1 Patrick MacGill, *Maureen* (London, 1920), pp 213–14.
2 Ibid., pp 214–16.
3 Intelligence notes, 1918 (TNA, CO 904/19/48); IG report, Jan. 1918 (TNA, CO 904/105).
4 *Ulster Herald*, 4 Aug. 1917; *DJ*, 21 Sept. 1917.
5 CI Donegal, Sept. 1917 (TNA, CO 904/104).
6 Kelly, *Letterkenny*, p. 183; *DJ*, 28 Dec. 1917.
7 CI Donegal, Dec. 1917 (TNA, CO 904/104).   8 Ibid.
9 CI Donegal, Sept., Dec. 1917 (ibid.).
10 Michael Laffan, *The resurrection of Ireland: the Sinn Féin party, 1916–1923* (Cambridge, 1999), pp 186–7; Report on organisation of Sinn Féin, Dec. 1917 (NLI, Plunkett papers, MS 11,405).
11 Bundoran UDC, 7 Jan. 1918 (DCA, UDC 3/1/2, p. 366).
12 *Fermanagh Herald*, 19 Jan. 1918; CI Donegal, Jan. 1918 (TNA, CO 904/105).
13 Mary Gallagher (neé Kane) (IMA, MSPC, 34REF34890).
14 *Fermanagh Herald*, 19 Jan. 1918; Thomas McShea (BMH WS 782). Teevan, who lived in Ballyshannon, was the son of a small farmer.
15 CI Donegal, Feb. 1918 (TNA, CO 904/105).   16 *DJ*, 18 Feb. 1918.
17 Liam Duffy (BMH WS 1485, p. 2); P.H. Doherty (BMH WS 1516, p. 3); IG report, Feb. 1918 (TNA, CO 904/105). Raphoe was 57 per cent Protestant in 1911.
18 *DJ*, 11, 18, 20 Feb. 1918; Kelly, *Letterkenny*, p. 185; Anthony Begley, *Ballyshannon: genealogy and history* (Ballyshannon, 2011), p. 362; *II*, 19 Feb. 1918; Thomas McShea (BMH WS 782, p. 3).
19 IG report, Feb. 1918 (TNA, CO 904/105).
20 CI Donegal, Feb., Mar. 1918 (ibid.).

21 Patrick C. O'Mahony (BMH WS 745, pp 4–5). On the organization structure of Sinn Féin, see Laffan, *The resurrection of Ireland*, pp 71–3.
22 CI Donegal, Sept. 1917, Dec. 1918 (TNA, CO 904/104, 107).
23 Ernie O'Malley, *On another man's wound* (Niwot, Colorado, 1999 [1936]), pp 99–105.
24 Joseph Murray (BMH WS 1566, p. 3); Patrick C. O'Mahony (BMH WS 745, pp 2–4).
25 CI Donegal, Sept. 1917 (TNA, CO 904/104).
26 Carrying of arms orders, 1917–18 (TNA, CO 904/29/3); *FJ*, 6 Aug. 1917; James McMonagle (BMH WS 1385, pp 1–2).
27 IG report, Feb. 1918 (TNA, CO 904/105).
28 IG report, May 1918 (TNA, CO 904/106; CAB 24/59/323).
29 Patrick C. O'Mahony (BMH WS 745, pp 4–5).
30 *BN*, 11 Apr. 1918; CI Donegal, Jan.–Apr. 1918 (TNA, CO 904/105); Patrick C. O'Mahony (BMH WS 745, p. 3).
31 Eithne Coyle (BMH WS 750, p. 1); Eithne Coyle and Cumann na mBan (UCDA, Eithne Coyle papers, P61/2/1, p. 1).
32 *DJ*, 15 Feb. 1918.
33 CI Donegal, Mar. 1918 (TNA, CO 904/105).
34 CI Donegal, Dec. 1918 (TNA, CO 904/107).
35 *Ulster Herald*, 4 Aug. 1917; *II*, 19 Feb. 1918.
36 Press censor report, Apr. 1918 (TNA, CO 904/166).
37 *Irish News*, 19 Apr. 1918.   38 *DJ*, 27 Apr., 7 June 1918.
39 *DV*, 2 June 1916.
40 Dillon to T.P. O'Connor, 23 Apr. 1918 (TCD, John Dillon papers, MS 468).
41 *FJ*, 18 Jan. 1918.
42 *Hansard (Commons)*, 12 Apr. 1918, vol. 104, cols 1955–60.
43 *Leader*, 3 Aug. 1918; Maume, *Long gestation*, p. 206.
44 Pauric Travers, 'The priest in politics: the case of conscription' in Oliver MacDonagh, W.F. Mandle and Pauric Travers (eds), *Irish culture and nationalism, 1750–1950* (London, 1983), pp 161–81.
45 *FJ*, 22 Apr. 1918.
46 Arthur Samuels to Lloyd George, 2 May 1918 (Parliamentary Archives, Lloyd George papers, F/44/9/2).
47 *DJ*, 27 Apr. 1918.   48 Ibid.   49 Ibid., 19 Apr. 1918.
50 Ibid.   51 CI Donegal, Apr. 1918 (TNA, CO 904/105).
52 IG report, Mar.–June 1918 (TNA, CO 904/105–6); James McMonagle (BMH WS 1,385, p. 2); P.H. Doherty (BMH WS 1,516, p. 4).
53 *DJ*, 26 Apr. 1918; Report of movements and meetings of extremists in the Dublin Police Area during the month of May 1918 (TNA, CAB 24/59/338).
54 *FJ*, 29 June 1918.
55 *Drogheda Argus*, 20 Apr. 1918; *DJ*, 17 Apr. 1918.
56 CI Donegal, Aug. 1915 (TNA, CO 904/97); *Dundee Courier*, 12 Apr. 1918.
57 *Hansard (Commons)*, 10 Apr. 1918, vol. 104, cols 1516, 1569.
58 Intelligence Officer, Northern District, Apr. 1918 (TNA, CO 904/157).
59 *BN*, 22 Apr. 1918.
60 Fiona Devoy McAuliffe, '"The day when Irish labour found itself": the general strike against conscription' in Crowley et al. (eds), *Atlas of the Irish Revolution*, pp 330–3.
61 Grant, *Derry*, pp 81–2.
62 Hegarty, *Peadar O'Donnell*, pp 44–5.
63 CI Donegal, Feb., Aug. 1918 (TNA, CO 904/105, 106).
64 *DJ*, 27 Apr. 1918; CI Donegal, Apr. 1918 (TNA, CO 904/105).

65 CI Donegal, Mar. 1918 (ibid.); Francis Devine, 'A very unpleasant and unsatisfactory dispute: the Letterkenny Lunatic strike, 1924'. I am grateful to Francis Devine for letting me have a copy of this unpublished article.
66 CI Donegal, Apr. 1918 (TNA, CO 904/105).
67 CI Donegal, Sept., Oct. 1918 (TNA, CO 904/107).
68 IG RIC, June 1918 (TNA, CAB 24/59/339).
69 Francis Devine, *Organising history: a centenary of SIPTU, 1909–2009* (Dublin, 2009), pp 1004–5.
70 Intelligence Office, Northern District, July 1918 (TNA, CO 904/157). Francis Devine, 'The Irish Transport & General Workers' Union in Ulster, 1909–30'. I am grateful to Francis Devine for letting me have a copy of this unpublished article.
71 Peadar O'Donnell, *Monkeys in the superstructure: reminiscences of Peadar O'Donnell* (Galway, 1986), p. 28.
72 Fearghal McGarry, 'O'Donnell, Peadar', *DIB*.
73 Hegarty, *Peadar O'Donnell*, p. 41; *DJ*, 13 Feb. 1918.
74 *DJ*, 16 Nov. 1917.
75 Hegarty, *Peadar O'Donnell*, pp 40–1.
76 Grattan Fryer, *Peadar O'Donnell* (Lewisburg, 1973), pp 25–7; Hegarty, *Peadar O'Donnell*, pp 43–4.
77 CI Donegal, Apr., July 1918 (TNA, CO 904/105, 106).
78 CI Donegal, Aug., Sept. 1918 (TNA, CO 904/106).
79 CI Donegal, May, June 1918 (ibid.); *DJ*, 9 Aug. 1918.
80 CI Donegal, Aug. 1918 (TNA, CO 904/106); *FJ*, 19 Aug. 1918; Press censor's report, Aug. 1918 (TNA, CO 904/167/1).
81 CI Donegal, Jan.–Apr. 1918 (TNA, CO 904/105).
82 CI Donegal, Sept. 1918 (TNA, CO 904/107). 83 *LS*, 12 Oct. 1918.
84 CI Donegal, Oct. 1918 (TNA, CO 904/107). 85 Ibid.

CHAPTER SIX *The victory of Sinn Féin: the 1918 general election*

1 CI Donegal, Apr., Dec. 1918 (TNA, CO 904/105, 107).
2 Beattie, 'The AOH in Donegal', 109; J.J. Lee, *Ireland, 1912–1985: politics and society* (Cambridge, 1989), p. 10.
3 Brian Walker (ed.), *Parliamentary election results in Ireland, 1801–1922* (Dublin, 1978), passim.
4 *FJ*, 23 July 1918. 5 *Anglo-Celt*, 16 Nov. 1918.
6 Marie Coleman, 'Law, Hugh', *DIB*; Maume, *Long gestation*, p. 233.
7 *DJ*, 14 June 1918; CI Donegal, June 1918 (TNA, CO 904/106).
8 *DJ*, 18 Nov. 1918. 9 *DJ*, 16 Sept. 1918.
10 Liam Ó Duibhir, *The Donegal awakening: Donegal and the War of Independence* (Cork, 2009), p. 78.
11 Patrick H. Arkinson, 'McHugh, Charles', *DIB*.
12 SF Standing Committee, 16 Oct. 1918 (NLI, P3,269); Kevin O'Shiel (BMH WS 1770, p. 66).
13 Logue to Laurence O'Neill, 6 Dec. 1918 (NLI, O'Neill papers, MS 35,294/4); SF Standing Committee, 4 Dec. 1918. (NLI, P3,269); Michael Collins to Austin Stack, 28 Nov. 1918 (NLI, MS 5,848).
14 *DJ*, 4 Dec. 1918; Elaine Callinan, *Electioneering and propaganda in Ireland, 1917–21: votes, violence and victory* (Dublin, 2020), pp 44–5.
15 O'Donnell to Dillon, 4, 12 Nov. 1918 (TCD, Dillon papers, MS 6,764/106–8).

16 Lyons, *John Dillon*, pp 449–50.   17 *DJ*, 11 Dec. 1918.
18 Ibid., 2, 11 Dec. 1918.
19 CI Donegal, Nov. 1918 (TNA, CO 904/107).   20 *DJ*, 6 Dec. 1918.
21 CI Donegal, Dec. 1918 (TNA, CO 904/107).
22 Rafferty, *Catholicism in Ulster*, pp 193–4; Dooley, *Monaghan*, pp 65–6; Brian Maye, 'Pastor in a time of upheaval', *IT*, 6 Aug. 2018.
23 Pauric Travers, 'The conscription crisis and the general election of 1918' in Crowley et al. (eds), *Atlas of the Irish Revolution*, p. 329.   24 *DJ*, 2 Dec. 1918
25 Ibid., 18 Nov., 6 Dec 1918.
26 CI Donegal, Aug. 1918 (TNA, CO 904/106).
27 CI Donegal, Nov. 1918 (TNA, CO 904/107).
28 *DJ*, 4, 6 Dec. 1918.
29 Charles McGinley (BMH WS 1483, p. 2); Bernard McGinley (BMH WS 1482, p. 2).
30 F. O'Donnell to Bishop O'Donnell, 3 Dec. 1918 (CÓFLA, O'Donnell papers, Arch/10/4/25).
31 Joseph Murray (BMH WS 1566, pp 2–3).
32 Ida Milne, *Stacking the coffins: influenza, war and revolution, 1918–19* (Dublin, 2018), pp 63–5.
33 Seán Moylan (BMH WS 838, pp 63–5).
34 Thomas McShea (BMH WS 782, p. 5).
35 Joseph Murray (BMH WS 1566, p. 4).
36 *DJ*, 21 Dec. 1918; O'Halpin & Ó Corráin, *Dead of the Irish Revolution*, p. 106.
37 Thomas McShea (BMH WS 782, p. 4).   38 *FJ*, 12 Feb. 1919.
39 James McCaffrey (BMH WS 1484, pp 2–3).
40 Michael Sheerin (BMH WS 803, p. 5).
41 CI Donegal, Dec. 1918 (TNA, CO 904/107).
42 Anthony Dawson (BMH WS 1546, p. 3).
43 Travers, 'The conscription crisis', pp 328–9; Callinan, *Electioneering and propaganda*, pp 39–47.
44 *LS*, 31 Dec. 1918.
45 Patrick Maume, 'MacNeill, John Gordon Swift', *DIB*; Coleman, 'Law, Hugh', *DIB*.
46 Devlin to Dillon, 22 May 1919 (TCD, Dillon papers, MS 6,729/226).
47 CI Donegal, Dec. 1918 (TNA, CO 904/107).
48 *DN*, 14, 21 Dec. 1918.   49 *DV*, 10 Jan. 1919.
50 Tomás Ó Fiaich, 'Pádraig Cardinéal Ó Dónaill' in Micheál Ó Mairtín (ed.), *Meascra Uladh* II (Dungannon, 1983), p. 26.
51 *DJ*, 22 Nov. 1918.
52 Dorothy Macardle, *The Irish republic* (Dublin, 1937), pp 842–3.

CHAPTER SEVEN *'Rendering government impossible': the political war, 1919–21*

1 Hegarty, *O'Donnell*, p. 97.
2 For an elaboration of the concept of a counter state and its development under the aegis of Dáil Éireann, see Arthur Mitchell, *Revolutionary government in Ireland: Dáil Éireann, 1919–22* (Dublin, 1995).
3 *DN*, 4 Jan. 1919.   4 *DN*, 11 Jan. 1919.   5 *DJ*, 22 Dec. 1919.
6 Michael Laffan, 'Politics in time of war' in Crowley et al. (eds), *Atlas of the Irish Revolution*, p. 456.
7 CI Donegal, Jan.–Dec. 1919 (TNA, CO 904/108–110).
8 CI Donegal, July 1919 (TNA, CO 904/109).

9   CI Donegal, Oct. 1919 (TNA, CO 904/110).
10 CI Donegal, July 1919 (TNA, CO 904/109).
11 CI Donegal, May 1919 (ibid.).   12 CI Donegal, Mar. 1919 (TNA, CO 904/108).
13 Dooley, *Monaghan*, pp 74–5; Grant, *Derry*, pp 92–3.
14 CI Donegal, Feb. 1919 (TNA, CO 904/108).
15 CI Donegal, Jan., July, Oct. 1919 (TNA, CO 904/108–110).
16 LGB, *Annual report for the year ended 31 March 1920* (Dublin, 1920), pp 98–110.
17 CI Donegal, Jan. 1919 (TNA, CO 904/111).
18 *LS*, 15 May 1920.   19 *DN*, 15 May 1920.
20 Callinan, *Electioneering and propaganda*, p. 226; *FJ*, 12 June 1920; *DJ*, 16 Apr., 31 May 1920; *Fermanagh News*, 5 June 1920; *LS*, 5 June 1920; *DN*, 5 June 1920.
21 *DN*, 12 June 1920.   22 *LS*, 5 June 1920.   23 *LS*, 17 June 1920.
24 DCC minutes, 15 Mar. 1921; 12 Apr. 1921 (DCA, CC/1/1/79, p. 8).
25 *DD*, 18 June 1920.   26 *LS*, 17 June 1920.   27 Ibid.
28 Ballyshannon RDC minutes, 19 June 1920 (DCA, RDC 1/1/15, p. 15).
29 *DD*, 18 June 1920.   30 *DN*, 26 June 1920.
31 *LS* 5 June 1920; *DJ*, 14 June 1920.
32 *DJ*, 14 June 1920; *LS*, 15 June 1920.
33 *BN*, 19 June 1920.   34 *Strabane Chronicle*, 26 June 1920.
35 *DJ*, 26 June 1920; Denis Houston (BMH WS 1382, pp 6–7).
36 *DJ*, 2 June 1920.   37 *DN*, 26 June 1920.
38 Ibid., 16 Oct. 1920; Beattie, *Donegal in transition*, pp 10, 79–80.
39 *IT*, 26 June 1920.
40 Liam O'Duffy (BMH WS 1485, pp 3–6).
41 DCC minutes, 11 Oct. 1921 (DCA, CC/1/1/17),   42 *LS*, 17 June 1920.
43 Laffan, *The resurrection of Ireland*, pp 329–31.
44 Ballyshannon Town Commission, 3 Aug. 1920 (DCA, BTC/1, p. 569).
45 Ibid., 9 Sept. 1920, 7 Mar. 1921 (DCA, BTC/1, pp 573, 582–3).
46 Cosgrave to county councils, 21 Aug. 1920 (Waterford City and County Archives, IE/WCC/GNA/131); reproduced in *Democracy and change: the 1920 local government elections in Ireland* (Dublin, 2020), p. 49.
47 DCC minutes, 22 Feb. 1921 (DCA, CC/1/1/79, pp 17–18).
48 Ibid., 11 Oct. 1921 (DCA, CC/1/1/79, pp 11, 21–3).
49 CI Donegal, Feb. 1921 (TNA, CO 904/114).
50 Ballyshannon Town Commission refused to pay the audit fees, despite objections from one member, 4 Apr., 9 May, 8 Aug. 1921 (DCA, BTC/1, pp 586, 588, 593).
51 DCC minutes, 11 Oct. 1921 (DCA, CC/1/1/79, p. 19).
52 Tom Garvin, *1922: the birth of Irish democracy* (Dublin, 1996), pp 69–71.
53 McGarty, *Leitrim*, pp 103–4.
54 DCC minutes, 11 Oct. 1921 (DCA, CC/1/1/79, p. 17).
55 Monthly intelligence report, no. 3 Brigade (south Donegal) 19 Oct.–Nov. 1921 (IMA, CP/04/17).
56 DCC minutes, 22 Feb. 1921 (DCA, CC/1/1/79, p. 9).
57 Laffan, *The resurrection of Ireland*, p. 314.
58 Mary Kotsonouris, *Retreat from revolution: the Dáil courts, 1920–24* (Dublin, 1994), p. 17. On the experience locally, see John O'Callaghan, *Limerick: the Irish Revolution, 1912–23* (Dublin, 2018), pp 64–7.
59 Cited in Kotsonouris, *Retreat from revolution*, p. 12.
60 Liam O'Duffy (BMH WS 1485, p. 9).
61 Patrick Breslin (BMH WS 1448, p. 15).   62 *IT*, 26 June 1918.

63 CI Donegal, June 1920 (TNA, CO 904/112).
64 *Hansard (Commons)*, 1 July 1920, vol. 131, cols 619–20. 65 *DD*, 24 Dec. 1920.
66 Patrick Breslin (BMH WS 1448, p. 15). 67 *DJ*, 8, 23 July 1920.
68 *DJ*, 20 Aug. 1920; *DN*, 1 Aug. 1920; CI Donegal, June, Nov. 1920 (TNA, CO 904/112, 113).
69 *DN*, 14 Aug. 1920.
70 Liam O'Duffy (BMH WS 1495, pp 9–100); *DN*, 29 Jan. 1921.
71 Síobhra Aiken et al. (eds), *The men will talk to me: Ernie O'Malley's interviews with the northern divisions* (Dublin, 2018), p. 25.
72 P.H. Doherty (BMH WS 1516, p. 7).
73 CI Donegal, July 1920 (TNA, CO 904/112).
74 Patrick Breslin (BMH WS 1448, p. 15). 75 *DN*, 16 Oct. 1920.
76 Ibid.; Liam O'Duffy (BMH WS 1495, p.7); CI Donegal, Aug. 1920 (TNA, CO 904/112).
77 CI Donegal, Aug. 1920 (TNA, CO 904/112); Patrick Breslin (BMH WS 1448, p. 15).
78 IG, Aug. 1920 (TNA, CO 904/112).
79 DI Walsh, Aug. 1920 (TNA, CO 904/112).
80 James McMonagle (BMH WS 1385, pp 6–10); Anthony Dawson (BMH WS 1546, p. 6).
81 CI Donegal, Jan. 1920 (TNA, CO 904/111).
82 CI Donegal, June 1920 (TNA, CO 904/112). 83 CO Donegal, July 1920 (ibid.).
84 Monthly intelligence report, no. 3 Brigade (South Donegal), 19 Oct.–Nov. 1921 (IMA, CP/04/17).
85 O'Malley to Mrs Childers, 26 Nov. 1923, Richard English and Cormac O'Malley (eds), *Prisoners: the Civil War letters of Ernie O'Malley* (Dublin, 1991), p. 80; Richard English, *Ernie O'Malley: IRA intellectual* (Oxford, 1998), pp 79–80.
86 See Linda Connolly, 'Towards a further understanding of the sexual and gender-based violence women experienced in the Irish Revolution' in Linda Connolly (ed.), *Women and the Irish Revolution* (Newbridge, 2020), pp 108–16.
87 *FH*, 15 Jan. 1921 88 *DD*, 7 Jan. 1921.
89 'Ballyshannon raids', *DD*, 24 Dec. 1920.
90 Caroline Carr and Judith McCarthy, *From conflict to division: Donegal, 1919–1925* (Donegal, 2019), p. 32.
91 CI Donegal, Apr., May 1921 (TNA, CO 904/115).
92 *DD*, 13 May 1921.
93 CI Donegal, Mar. 1921 (TNA, CO 904/114); *DJ*, 26 Mar. 1921; O'Halpin & Ó Corráin, *Dead of the Irish Revolution*, p. 349.
94 Patrick Breslin (BMH WS 1448, p. 26).
95 CI Donegal, July 1920 (TNA, CO 904/112); *DN*, 16 Oct. 1920.
96 Ballyshannon Town Commission, 10 Aug. 1920 (DCA, BTC/1/571).
97 *DJ*, 28 Jan. 19211; CI Donegal, May 1921 (TNA, CO 904/115); McAdam to O'Duffy, 27 July 1921 (DCA, Murray papers, P/183/3/7/2). O'Duffy passed the matter on to Murray for investigation.
98 Ballyshannon Town Commission, 4 Apr. 1921 (DCA, BTC/1/586). Report of 1st battalion, South Donegal Brigade, June 1921 (DCA, Murray papers, P/183/3/4/2).

CHAPTER EIGHT *The storm: the War of Independence, 1919–21*

1 Mac Grianna, *An druma mór*, pp 171–2; 'The following year was the year the war broke out. English soldiers were being killed in every glen in the country and Irishmen were being arrested and executed and houses were being burned. Not much of the war came to Ros Cuain.' Hughes (trans.), *The big drum*, p. 105.

2 Peadar O'Donnell, *Storm: a story of the Irish war* (Dublin, 1927); Fryer, *O'Donnell*, pp 37–9; Hegarty, *O'Donnell*, pp 158–60.
3 Patrick Breslin (BMH WS 1448, pp 4–5).
4 Liam Ó Duibhir, *Donegal awakening*, pp 113–19.
5 Niall Mac Fhionnghaile, *Dr McGinley and his times* (Letterkenny, 1985), p. 29.
6 CI Donegal, Jan.–Dec. 1919 (TNA, CO 904/108–110).
7 O'Malley, *On another man's wound*, p. 99; CI Donegal, Sept. 1919 (TNA, CO 904/110); Ó Duibhir, *Donegal awakening*, p. 311.
8 Joseph Murray (BMH WS 1566, pp 7–8).
9 O'Malley, *On another man's wound*, p. 99.
10 Liam O'Duffy (BMH WS 1485, pp 4–5); Thomas Mc Shea (BMH WS 782, p. 5).
11 Thomas Mc Shea (BMH WS 782, p. 5); Joseph Murray (BMH WS 1564, p. 6).
12 O'Malley, *On another man's wound*, pp 99–105.
13 Laffan, *The resurrection of Ireland*, pp 188–92; Ozseker, *Forging the border*, pp 108–9.
14 *DJ*, 5 Sept. 1919; DI Walsh for CI, July 1919 (TNA, CO 904/109).
15 Ibid.; Joseph Murray (BMH WS 1564, p. 5).
16 Thomas McShea (BMH WS 782, p. 6).   17 Ibid., pp 7–8.
18 James McCaffrey (BMH WS 1484, pp 5–6).
19 CI Donegal, Feb. 1919 (TNA, CO 904/108).
20 Patrick Lynch (BMH WS 1515, pp 1–2).
21 CI Donegal, Apr. 1919 (TNA, CO 904/108); *DJ*, 11 Apr. 1919.
22 Michael Doherty (BMH WS 1583, pp 3–4); Ó Duibhir, *Donegal awakening*, pp 111–12.
23 Patrick Breslin (BMH WS 1448, pp 8–11); Patrick ('Kit') O'Donnell (BMH WS 1327, pp 2–4).
24 CI Donegal, Dec. 1920 (TNA, CO 904/110).
25 Denis Houston (BMH WS 1382, pp 6–7); Ó Duibhir, *Donegal awakening*, p. 116.
26 CI Donegal, Jan. 1919 (TNA, CO 904/108).
27 CI Donegal, Feb., Apr., June, Aug. 1919, Sept. 1921 (TNA, CO 904/108, 109, 110).
28 CI Donegal, Nov. 1920 (TNA, CO 904/113).
29 Charles Townshend, 'The Irish Republican Army and the development of guerrilla warfare, 1916–1921', *English Historical Review*, 94:371 (1971), 329.
30 CI Donegal, July 1920 (TNA, CO 904/112).
31 CI Donegal, Sept. 1920 (TNA, CO 904/113).
32 CI Donegal, Apr. 1921 (TNA, CO 904/115).
33 Report by Samuel O'Flaherty, O/C East Donegal Brigade, 3[0–1] Aug. 1920 (IMA, CP/03–06). Only part of the handwritten report survives. The date of the report and the attack are mistakenly given in IMA catalogue as 26 July and 3 August and the location as Dunquinn.
34 Joseph Murray (BMH WS 1566, pp 10–11); My history of events, 1917–21 (original draft of WS statement) (DCA, Murray papers, P/183/1).
35 David Fitzpatrick, 'The geography of Irish nationalism' in C.H.E. Philbin (ed.), *Nationalism and popular protest in Ireland* (Cambridge, 1987), p. 422; Peter Hart, 'The geography of revolution in Ireland, 1917–1923', *Past and Present*, 155 (1997), 159.
36 Henry McGowan (BMH WS 1596, p.10).
37 Brigade activity reports (IMA, MSPC/A40–2).
38 Figures conflated from CI Donegal reports, May 1920–Sept. 1921 (TNA, CO 904/112–16).
39 Charles Townshend, *The British campaign in Ireland, 1919–1921* (Oxford, 1975), p. 213.
40 CI Donegal, July 1920 (TNA, CO 904/115).
41 CI Donegal, Feb. 1920 reported the presence of 17 gunmen from the south and west (TNA, CO 904/114).

42 Townshend, 'The development of guerrilla warfare', 30.
43 Ó Duibhir, *Donegal awakening*, p. 202.
44 Patrick Breslin (BMH WS 1448, pp 18–19).
45 Ibid.; Patrick O'Donnell (BMH WS 1327, p. 5); CI Donegal, Jan. 1920 (TNA, CO 904/114).
46 Ó Duibhir, *Donegal awakening*, p. 207.   47 *An tÓglach*, 15 Mar. 1921.
48 Leonard Roarty, 'Railways in Donegal and the War of Independence', *DA*, 58 (2006), 172–4.
49 CI Donegal, July, Aug. 1920 (TNA, CO 904/112).
50 CI Donegal, Nov. 1920 (TNA, CO 904/113).
51 CI Donegal, Feb. 1921 (TNA, CO 904/114).
52 Activity report, 3rd Brigade 1st Northern Division (IMA, MSPC/A/42 (1)); Brian Monaghan (BMH WS 879), pp 8–9; *DD*, 25 Feb. 1921; O'Halpin & Ó Corráin, *Dead of the Irish Revolution*, p. 310.
53 *DD*, 25 Feb. 1921.
54 Brian Monaghan (BMH WS 879, p. 9); O'Halpin & Ó Corráin, *Dead of the Irish Revolution*, p. 312.
55 CI Donegal, Feb. 1914 (TNA, CO 904/114).   56 *IT*, 2 Mar. 1921.
57 CI Donegal, Dec. 1920 (TNA, CO 904/110).
58 *DN*, 12 Feb. 1921; Lenten Pastoral, Feb. 1921 (CÓFLA, O'Donnell papers, Arch/10/2/1A, folder 3).
59 CI Donegal, May 1921 (TNA, CO 904/115); Anthony Dawson (BMH WS 1546, pp 7–8); O'Halpin & Ó Corráin, *Dead of the Irish Revolution*, p. 433.
60 West Donegal Brigade, Feb. 1921 (UCDA, Richard Mulcahy papers, P7/A/39).
61 Kenneth Griffith and Timothy O'Grady, *Curious journey: an oral history of Ireland's unfinished revolution* (London, 1982), p. 166.
62 Ó Duibhir, *Donegal awakening*, p. 245.
63 Henry McGowan (BMH WS 1596, p. 7).
64 Joseph Murray (BMH WS 1566, p. 15).
65 Liam Ó Duibhir, *Prisoners of war: Ballykinlar internment camp, 1920–1921* (Cork, 2013), pp 50, 286, 303–4.
66 Ó Duibhir, *Donegal awakening*, p. 228.   67 Hegarty, *O'Donnell*, pp 87–95.
68 CI Donegal, May 1921 (TNA, CO 904/115); O'Halpin & Ó Corráin, *Dead of the Irish Revolution*, p. 414.
69 *DJ*, 16 May 1921.
70 O'Donnell manuscript notes on partition, 27 Mar. 1920 (CÓFLA, O'Donnell papers, Arch/10/4/6); *Manchester Guardian*, quoted in *II*, 13 Mar. 1920.
71 *BN*, 11 Mar. 1920.   72 *DJ*, 17 Mar. 1920.   73 *LS*, 10 Apr. 1920.
74 *BN*, 9 Apr. 1920. Born in Lancashire, Wagentreiber was a farmer in Castlefinn; Neely was a merchant from Ballyshannon; Osborne, who was secretary of the Donegal Unionist Association, was a solicitor from Milford and a former commander in the UVF. Moore, an Orangeman, stood for East Donegal in 1918.
75 *FJ*, 8 May 1920; *Evening Mail*, 27 May 1920.
76 *BN*, 27, 28 May 1920; *Scotsman*, 8 May 1920.
77 Malachy Sweeney, *A troubled time* (Donegal, 2014), p. 167.
78 Memo 'in haste' from O/C 4th Brigade, 11 July 1921 (DCA, Murray papers, P/183/3/4/5(2)).
79 Notifications to brigade adjutant, 12 Aug., 9 Oct. 1921 (DCA, Murray papers, P/183/3/8/7, 15).
80 *DD*, 8 July 1921; *DN*, 15 July 1921.

81 DI pp CI Donegal, Aug. 1921 (TNA, CO 904/116).
82 CI Donegal, July 1921 (ibid.).
83 Levy notice, 5 Oct. 1921 (CÓFLA, O'Donnell papers, Arch/10/4/25).
84 O/C, 1st Northern Division to chief of staff, 29 June 1921 (UCDA, Mulcahy papers, P7/A/22).
85 Activity report Apr.–June 1921, A company, 1st Battalion (DCA, Murray papers, P/188/3/6).
86 DI Walsh pp CI Donegal, Aug. 1921 (TNA, CO 904/116).
87 O/C HQ No. 4 Brigade to Officers of Belleek Battalion, 11 Aug. 1921 (DCA, Murray papers, P/183/3/7/5).
88 Townshend, 'The development of guerrilla warfare, 1916–21', 322.
89 On nationalist wishful thinking, see Laffan, *The resurrection of Ireland*, pp 334–5.
90 O'Halpin & Ó Corráin, *Dead of the Irish Revolution*, pp 543, 546.
91 CI Donegal, Aug. 1920 (TNA, CO 904/109).
92 *DD*, 10 Dec. 1920; O'Halpin & Ó Corráin, *Dead of the Irish Revolution*, p. 250.
93 *DD*, 21 Oct. 1921; *DV*, 21 Oct. 1921; O'Halpin & Ó Corráin, *Dead of the Irish Revolution*, p. 534. Con O'Boyle from Dungloe who was wounded in 1921 died later in 1922, *The last post* (Dublin, 1985), p. 157.
94 O'Donnell, *Storm*; Aiken et al. (eds), *The men will talk to me*, p. 25.

CHAPTER NINE *Cogadh na gcarad: the Civil War, 1922–3*

1 'It is a curious thing, not to mention food for thought, to observe two sides in conflict with each other, especially two sides who know each other well. There would be precious little point in saying to either of them that the other side was right, even in the smallest thing. He who fights most manfully for his own side is the most hated by the other.' Mac Grianna, *An druma mór*, p. 118; trans. Hughes, *The big drum*, p. 74.
2 Michael Hopkinson, *Green again green: the Irish civil war* (Dublin, 1988), p. 161.
3 *DD*, 9 Dec. 1921.
4 Griffith & O'Grady, *Curious journey*, pp 264–5.
5 See, for example, Ernie O'Malley's comment on Sweeney's account, Aiken et al. (eds), *The men will talk to me*, pp 32–3.
6 Lee, *Ireland*, p. 54; the earl of Longford and Thomas P. O'Neill, *Eamon de Valera* (London, 1970), p. 175.
7 *DD*, 9 Dec. 1921.
8 Patrick Hugh McDermott, adjutant Ballyshannon company, South Donegal Brigade: Statement re. pension application (DCA, Murray papers, P/183/9/1, p. 23).
9 *DD*, 6 Jan. 1922.
10 *DV*, 9 Dec. 1921, 13 Jan. 1922; Laffan, *The resurrection of Ireland*, p. 358.
11 *DJ*, 9, 19 Dec. 1921; *DN*, 10 Dec. 1921.
12 *DN*, 17 Dec. 1921; *DJ*, 1 May 1922; O'Donnell to John Hagan, 23 Jan. 1922 (Irish College Rome, Hagan papers) cited in Ó Baoighill, *O'Donnell*, pp 160–1.
13 Ó Baoighill, *O'Donnell*, p. 161.
14 *DJ*, 28 Dec. 1921.   15 *FH*, 31 Dec. 1921.   16 *DN*, 7 Jan. 1922.
17 P.J. Ward to Bernard McFadden, secretary, DCC, 30 Dec. 1921 (DCA, CC/1/1/79, meeting 31 Dec. 1921, p. 1).
18 DCC, 31 Dec. 1921, 24 Jan. 1922 (DCA, CC/1/1/79, pp 1–3, CC/1/1/80, p. 1); *DJ*, 2 Jan. 1922.
19 *DJ*, 30 Dec. 1921; *FH*, 7 Jan. 1922.
20 Joe Sweeney interview (UCDA, O'Malley papers, P17b/97/43).

21 *Dáil Éireann debates, 1921–22 (private sessions)*, 22 Aug. 1921, p. 31; 26 Aug. 1921, p. 80.
22 *Dáil Éireann debates*, 7 Jan. 1922, 320–2; *FJ*, 9 Jan. 1922.
23 *Dáil Éireann debates*, 7 Jan. 1922, pp 323–5.
24 O'Carroll, *Finner Camp*, p. 47.
25 Col. Joseph McLoughlin letter of reference: Joseph Aloysius Sweeney (IMA, MSPC, W24SP2913, p. 41).
26 Glennon to vice-commandant, 4th Brigade, 3 Jan. 1922 (DCA, Murray papers P/183/4/4/3).
27 Memorandum from chief of staff, 21 Oct. 1921 (DCA, Murray papers, P/183/3/11/3).
28 Maryann Valiulis, *Portrait of a revolutionary: General Richard Mulcahy and the foundation of the Irish Free State* (Dublin, 1992), pp 124–5; Ronan Fanning, *Independent Ireland* (Dublin, 1983), p. 11.
29 Report from "A" company, 2nd Battalion, 4th Brigade, Jan. 1922 (DCA, Murray papers P/183/45/1, p. 2).
30 Charlie Daly to Tom Daly, 20 May 1922 (UCDA, O'Malley papers, P17b/132/25).
31 Thomas McShea (BMH WS 782, pp 16–31).
32 Dooley, *Monaghan*, p. 103.   33 *FJ*, 9, 10 Feb. 1922.
34 Dooley, *Monaghan*, pp 103–5.
35 *FJ*, 11 Feb. 1922; Craig to Collins, 8 Feb. 1922; Lloyd George to Collins, 8 Feb. 1922 (TNA, CAB 21/254).
36 *FJ*, 11, 16, 24 Feb. 1922; Joseph Dolan (BMH WS 900, p. 7).
37 Thomas McShea (BMH WS 782, p. 27).
38 P.H. McDermott to O/C, 4th Battalion, 15 Feb. 1922 (DCA, Murray papers, P/183/4/3/3, p. 1).
39 *DJ*, 24 Feb. 1922.
40 Michael O'Donoghue (BMH WS 1741, pt. 2, pp 231–2).
41 O'Carroll, *Finner Camp*, p. 46. The first meeting of the county council in 1920 had decided to change the name of the County to Tírconaill.
42 *DV*, 5 May 1922.
43 Fanning, *Fatal path*, pp 318–19, 323–4; Fanning, *Independent Ireland*, pp 25, 28–9.
44 Grant, *Derry*, p. 132; Robert Lynch, *The northern IRA and the early years of partition, 1920–1922* (Dublin, 2006), p. 135.
45 Liam Ó Duibhir, *Donegal and the Civil War: the untold story* (Cork, 2011), pp 83–5; Hopkinson, *Green against green*, pp 67–9.
46 Robert Lynch, *The northern IRA and the early years of partition, 1920–22* (Dublin, 2006), pp 168–9.
47 Mossy Donegan to Florence O'Donoghue, 27 Aug. 1950 (NLI, O'Donoghue papers, MS 31,423 (6)).
48 Mac Suibhne to O/C 4th Brigade, 23 Mar. 1922 (DCA, Murray papers, P/183/4/4/17).
49 Florence O'Donoghue, *No other law* (Dublin, 1954), p. 249.
50 Michael O'Donoghue (BMH WS 1741, pt 2, pp 233–4).
51 Account of evacuation of Finner by P.H. McDermott (DCA, Murray papers, P/183/9/1, pp 32–3).
52 O'Carroll, *Finner Camp*, p. 46.
53 *DV*, 5 May 1922; T. Daly to Brig. J. Murray, 1 May 1922 (DCA, Murray papers, P/183/4/3/6). Tom Daly, younger brother of Charlie, had been O/C Kerry No. 2 Brigade.
54 Grant, *Derry*, pp 134–5.
55 Ó Duibhir, *Donegal and the Civil War*, pp 101–7; Statement by Eithne Coyle, n.d. (UCDA, Eithne Coyle papers, P61/2/1, pp 17–18).
56 Michael O'Donoghue (BMH WS 1741, pp 275–6).

57 Charlie Daly to Tom Daly, 20 May 1922 (UCDA, O'Malley papers, P17b/132/25); Aiken et al. (eds), *The men will talk to me*, p. 70.
58 Michael O'Donoghue (BMH WS 1741, pp 292–9).
59 MacCool (Mac Cumhail) to vice-brigadier, 24 Mar. 1922 (DCA, Murray papers, P/183/4/18).
60 Michael O'Donoghue (BMH WS 1741, pp 293–4); *DJ*, 2 June 1922.
61 Michael O'Donoghue (BMH WS 1741, p. 279).
62 Brian Feeney, *Antrim: the Irish Revolution, 1912–23* (Dublin, 2021), pp 86–7.
63 Ó Duibhir, *Donegal and the Civil War*, p. 91.
64 *II*, 6 Feb. 1922.
65 Eithne Coyle O'Donnell to Minister for Defence, 15 May 1945 (IMA, MSPC, 34REF60256).
66 *LS*, 18 Apr. 1922.
67 *DJ*, 26 Apr. 1922; Eithne Coyle-O'Donnell (BMH WS 750, pp 16–20); Cal McCarthy, *Cumann na mBan and the Irish Revolution* (Cork, 2007), pp 198–200, 209–1.
68 Peadar O'Donnell to Military Pensions Board, 19 Apr. 1945 (IMA MSPC, 34REF60256).
69 The phrase appears in *Belfast Telegraph*, *Northern Whig*, *Dundee Courier*, *Sheffield Independent* and *Sheffield Daily News*, among other newspapers, on 30 May 1922.
70 *BN*, 23 June 1922.
71 John Cunningham, 'The struggle for the Belleek–Pettigo salient', *DA*, 34 (1982), 68–81. The best account from participants – the witness statement by John Travers, James Scollan, Nicholas Smyth and Felix McCabe – is more informative on events in Pettigo than Belleek (BMH WS 711).
72 Nicholas Smyth (BMH WS 721, pp 21–2); Adjutant 4th Brigade to Adjt 1st Northern Division, 26 May 1922 (DCA, Murray papers, P/183/4/1/5).
73 P.H. McDermott, adjutant to O/C 4th Brigade, 2 June 1922 (DCA, Murray papers, P/183/4/1/9, p. 1).
74 John Travers et al. (BMH WS 711, pp 1–2); P.H. McDermott to O/C 4th Brigade, 29 May 1922 (DCA, Murray papers, P/183/4/1/6, p. 1). Some accounts say the USC withdrew to Boa Island, another island in Lough Erne. Travers and Scallan, who were familiar with the area, mentioned Buck Island. Some of the later events did take place on Boa Island.
75 P.H. McDermott statement for pension application (DCA, Murray papers, P/183/9/1, pp 31–2).
76 Ibid.; Nicholas Smyth (BMH WS 721), pp 28–9.
77 P.H. McDermott to O/C 4th Brigade, 29 May 1922 (DCA, Murray papers, P/183/4/1/6/1); Patrick O'Donoghue (BMH WS 1741, p. 279).
78 *Hansard (Commons)*, 31 May 1922, vol. 154, cols 2133–4.
79 P.H. McDermott to O/C 4th Brigade, 1 June – reporting on a visit to Pettigo and a gun battle between USC and 'our men' (DCA, Murray papers, P/183/4/1/6, p. 1).
80 Dan Downing, *Neighbours in Pettigo: living with conflict and division in a border village* (Pettigo, 2018), p. 182.
81 Keith Middlemas (ed.), *Tom Jones Whitehall diary*, iii (London, 1971), pp 204–12; Ernie O'Malley notebooks (UCDA, O'Malley papers, P17B/97).
82 P.H. McDermott to O/C 4th Brigade, 2 June 1922 (DCA, Murray papers, P/183/4/1/9, p. 3).
83 Nicholas Smyth (BMH WS 721, pp 27–31). William Deasley from Tyrone was also killed – apparently shot accidently.
84 Downing, *Neighbours in Pettigo*, pp 276–7.
85 James Langton, *The forgotten fallen: National army soldiers who died during the Irish Civil War*, Vol. 1 (Dublin, 2019), pp 130–3, 184–5, 224–5; Dan Downing, *Neighbours in Pettigo*, pp 182–3.

86 Downing, *Neighbours in Pettigo*, pp 129, 182; Langton, *The forgotten fallen*, p. 96.
87 Ibid., pp 171–9.
88 P.H. McDermott to O/C 4th Brigade, 8 June 1922 (DCA, Murray papers, P/183/4/4/24).
89 Ibid., 9 June 1922 (DCA, Murray papers, P/183/4/1/11, p. 2).
90 Mossy Donegan to Florence O'Donoghue, 15 Sept. 1950 (NLI, O'Donoghue papers, MS 31,423/6); Lynch, 'Donegal and the joint-IRA northern offensive', p. 194.
91 Cited in T.P. Coogan, *Michael Collins: a biography* (London, 1990), p. 366.
92 Fanning, *Fatal path*, p. 330.   93 Garvin, *1922*, pp 175–6.
94 Séamus McCann diary, Private collection – cited in Ó Duibhir, *Donegal and the Civil War*, p. 145.
95 Uinseann Mac Eoin, *Survivors: the story of Ireland's struggle as told through some of her outstanding living people* (Dublin, 1980), pp 342–4.
96 Seán Lehane, 'Summary of activities in division since commencement of hostilities', 19 Sept. 1922 (UCDA, O'Malley papers, P/17a/63).
97 Griffith & O'Grady, *Curious journey*, pp 287–8.
98 Report 12 May 1920 (DCA, Murray papers, P/183/4/5/2).
99 Joseph Murray (BMH WS 1566, p. 11); O'Carroll, *Finner Camp*, p. 49.
100 Lehane, 'Summary of activities', 19 Sept. 1922 (UCDA, O'Malley papers, P/17a/63).
101 Michael O'Donoghue (BMH WS 1741, pp 296–9); Charlie Daly, 13 July 1922 (UCDA, O'Malley papers, P17b/132/20).
102 Statement by Eithne Coyle (UCDA, Coyle papers, P61/2/1, pp 17–18).
103 Michael O'Donoghue (BMH WS 1741, pp 310–12).
104 Ibid., pp 313, 318, 326–7.   105 Ibid., pp 320–5; *DJ*, 21 July 1922.
106 Lehane to chief of staff, 15 Oct. 1922 (UCDA, O'Malley papers, P17a/65).
107 *DD*, 29 Sept. 1922; O'Carroll, *Finner Camp*, pp 50–1.
108 *II*, 28 Sept. 1922; *DD*, 29 Sept. 1922; Begley, *Ballyshannon*, p. 376.
109 Statement by Eithne Coyle (UCDA, Coyle papers, P61/2/1, p. 21).
110 Áodh de Blácam to O'Donnell, 26 Apr. 1922 (CÓFLA, O'Donnell papers, Arch/10/4/25).
111 *DD*, 29 Sept. 1922.
112 Ó Duibhir, *Donegal and the Civil War*, pp 203–4.
113 O'Malley to Lynch, 28 July 1922 (UCDA, Mulcahy papers, P7a/81).
114 Charlie Daly, 20 June, 8 Sept. 1922 (UCDA, O'Malley papers, P17b/132/20, 23).
115 Lehane to O'Malley, 23 Aug. 1922, cited in Ó Duibhir, *Donegal and the Civil War*, p. 190; Daly to O'Malley, 19 Sept. 1922 (UCDA, O'Malley papers, P17a/63).
116 Lynch to O'Malley, 4, 18 Sept. 1922 (ibid.).
117 Lehane to chief of staff, 15 Oct. 1922 (UCDA, O'Malley papers, P17a/65).
118 Lehane, 'Summary of activities', 19 Sept. 1922 (UCDA, O'Malley papers, P/17a/63). These figures did not include volunteers not on active service – in March 1923 their number was put at *c*.380. I/O, Northern Division, 14 Mar. 1923 (UCDA O'Malley papers, P17a/75).
119 *DJ*, 16 Mar. 1922; Ó Baoighill, *O'Donnell*, pp 164–5. For a short dispassionate account of these events, see J.J. Silke, 'The Drumboe martyrs', *DA*, 60 (2008), 167–74.
120 Langton, *The forgotten fallen*, p. 7; National Graves Association, *The last post* (Dublin, 1985), pp 144–68. Hopkinson cites 800 army deaths and suggests republican fatalities would have been higher. Hopkinson, *Green against green*, p. 273.
121 This figure includes Con Boyle who was wounded in 1921 but died some months after; it does not include Donegal deaths outside the county of which there were a number, *The last post* (Dublin, 1985), pp 141, 165, 167.
122 Farry, *Sligo*, p. 110.   123 Ó Duibhir, *Donegal and the Civil War*, p. 108.
124 Griffith & O'Grady, *Curious journey*, p. 306.

CHAPTER TEN *Donegal and the Irish Revolution*

1 Electionsireland.org: 4th Dáil, 1923; Hegarty, *O'Donnell*, pp 144–5.
2 For an account of the background to the Boundary Commission, see Paul Murray, *The Irish Boundary Commission and its origins, 1886–1925* (Dublin, 2011).
3 Fr P. O'Doherty to Bishop Edward Mulhern, 9 Jan. 1923, cited in Paul Murray, 'Partition and the Irish Boundary Commission: a northern nationalist perspective', *Clogher Record*, 18:2 (2004), 209.
4 Geoffrey Hand (ed.), *Irish Boundary Commission 1925 report* (Dublin, 1969), pp 5–6.
5 Ibid., pp 80–1; Submission from Donegal Business Group, 29 May 1925 (TNA, CAB 61/50).
6 *Boundary Commission report*, pp 81–6; Submission from County Donegal Protestant Registration Association, 25 May 1925 (TNA, CAB 61/51).
7 *Boundary Commission report*, pp 90, 101–7, 140–3.
8 Clare O'Halloran, *Partition and the limits of Irish nationalism* (Dublin, 1987), pp 70–1, 113.
9 Margaret O'Callaghan, 'Old parchment and water: the Boundary Commission of 1925 and the copper-fastening of the Irish border', *Bullan*, 5:2 (2002), 45–6.
10 *LS*, 11, 16 May 1922.
11 Terence Dooley, *The decline of the big house in Ireland: a study of Irish landed families, 1860–1960* (Dublin, 2001), p. 287.
12 Ozseker, *Forging the border*, pp 184–5.
13 King, *Memorabilia*, p. 82. See also Samuel Beckton, 'The lost tribe: case studies of southern unionist experiences in post-partition Ireland', (MA thesis, QUB, 2020).
14 David Fitzpatrick, 'The Orange Order and the border', *IHS*, 38:129 (May 2002), 53.
15 The number of Free State born in the 1926 Northern Ireland Census was 64,000, compared to 56,200 in 1911. While Derry, Tyrone and Fermanagh experienced a fall in population, the number of Free State born increased by 2531. NI Census, 1926, Londonderry County Borough report, tables xxiii, p. xxiv; Fermanagh report, xviii, p. 20; Tyrone report, xviii, p. 21; General report, table xxiii, p. 53; David Fitzpatrick, 'Protestant depopulation and the Irish Revolution', *IHS*, 38:152 (Nov. 2013), 662.
16 Terence Dooley, 'Protestant migration from the Irish Free State to Northern Ireland, 1920–25: a private census for County Fermanagh', *Clogher Record*, 15:3 (1996), 87–132.
17 *Census 1926 reports, vol. 3: religion and birthplaces*, tables 8A & 8B, pp 10–11.
18 On the decline in Methodist numbers, see Fitzpatrick, 'Protestant depopulation', 652–8.
19 Robert McDermott and David Webb, *Irish Protestantism today and tomorrow: a demographic study* (Belfast, n.d.), p. 2.
20 David Fitzpatrick, 'Protestant depopulation', 650, 654, 659. See also Marie Coleman, 'Protestant depopulation in County Longford during the Irish revolution, 1911–1926', *English Historical Review*, 135:575 (Sept. 2020), 931–77.
21 *Census 1926 reports, vol. 3, religion and birthplaces*, tables 11 & 12, pp 32–3, 94–7.
22 David Fitzpatrick, *Descendancy* (Cambridge, 2014), p. 165.
23 Katherine Magee, 'Defying the partition of Ulster: John George Vaughan Hart and the Unionist experience of the Irish revolution in east Donegal, 1919–1944' in Brian Hughes and Conor Morrissey (eds), *Southern Irish loyalism, 1912–1949* (Liverpool, 2020), pp 315–32.
24 *LS*, 10 June 1952; Leslie W. Lucas, *Mevagh down the years* (Waterford, 1972), pp 190–1.
25 Jonathan Cherry, 'Adaptive co-existence? Lord Farnham (1879–1957) and southern loyalism in pre- and post- independence Ireland' in Hughes & Morrissey (eds), *Southern Irish loyalism*, pp 293–314.
26 *DD*, 17 Aug. 1923.
27 *IT*, 15 Feb. 1956; www.oireachtas.ie/members/Major-James-Sproule-Myles; www.electionsireland.org, 4thDáil1923. – Myles took the name Sproule from his Tyrone mother. His

first wife Amy Gertrude Drennan whom he married in 1907 was from Dublin and a member of the Church of Ireland; both her parents came from Fermanagh. Her mother was Elizabeth Groves Trimble whose family owned and edited the *Impartial Reporter* in Enniskillen and the Trimbles and Myles remained close friends.
28 Hegarty, *O'Donnell*, pp 97–8.
29 Tom Garvin, *Nationalist revolutionaries*, p. 18. Garvin's model draws on the work of Miroslav Hroch.
30 *DJ*, 24, 31 Mar. 1922.
31 O'Donnell to Hooper, 25 Dec. 1922 (CÓFLA, O'Donnell papers, Arch/10/4/25).
32 See Seamus Cullen, *Kildare: the Irish Revolution, 1912–23* (Dublin, 2020), pp 135–41.
33 Martin O'Donoghue, *The legacy of the Irish Parliamentary Party in independent Ireland, 1922–1949* (Liverpool, 2019), p. 66.
34 Ibid., pp 103, 241–2.
35 Eithne O'Donnell (IMA MSPC, 34REF60256).
36 'A' company (Meenacross), 1st Battalion (IMA, MSPC/CMB/56).
37 I/O 1st Northern Division to assistant chief of staff, 14 Mar. 1923 (UCDA, O'Malley papers, P17a/75).
38 'B' company (Bundoran) (IMA, MSPC/RO/376).

Select bibliography

PRIMARY SOURCES

A. MANUSCRIPTS

Armagh
Cardinal Tomás Ó Fiaich Memorial Library and Archives
Michael Logue papers
Joseph MacRory papers
Patrick O'Donnell papers

Belfast
Public Records Office of Northern Ireland
Carson Irish papers
Personal diary of Lady Lillian Spender
Ulster Unionist Council papers
UVF papers

Donegal
Donegal County Archives
Board of Guardian minutes
County Council minutes, 1912–23
Joseph Murray papers
Miscellaneous Decade of Revolution minutes
Town Commission minutes
Urban and Rural District Council minutes

Dublin
Irish Military Archives
BMH Witness Statements
Brigade activity reports
Collins papers
Cumann na mBan nominal rolls
IRA nominal rolls
Military Service Pensions Collection

National Archives of Ireland
Crime Branch: Returns of Political Organisation in Donegal on 30 September 1919
 CO 904/110
Chief Secretary's Office papers
Dáil Éireann Courts Commission

National Library of Ireland
Boundary Commission papers
Congested Districts Board minutes of proceedings
Bulmer Hobson papers

ITGWU census, June 1918
ITGWU list of branches, June 1918
Maurice Moore papers
William O'Brien papers
Ernie O'Malley papers
Laurence O'Neill papers
Count Plunkett papers
John Redmond papers
Sinn Féin Standing Committee Minute Book

Trinity College, Dublin
John Dillon papers
Irish Convention papers

UCD Archives
Ernest Blythe papers
Eithne Coyle papers
Éamon de Valera papers
Richard Mulcahy papers
Ernie O'Malley notebooks and papers

London
British Library
Balfour papers

National Archives, London
Boundary Commission papers
Cabinet Office papers
Colonial Office papers
Home Office papers
War Office papers

Parliamentary Archives
Bonar Law papers
Lloyd George papers

B. OFFICAL RECORDS

Annual reports of the Congested Districts Board, 1912–21
Census of Ireland 1901, 1911
Census of Ireland (Reports) 1926
Census of Northern Ireland (Reports) 1926
Dáil Éireann. Parliamentary debates
DATI Agricultural Statistics (1912)
Hansard House of Commons parliamentary debates
Royal commission on the rebellion, evidence
Report of the proceedings of the Irish Convention

C. NEWSPAPERS AND PERIODICALS

An tÓglach
Belfast Newsletter
Belfast Telegraph
Derry Journal/Donegal News
Derry People
Donegal Democrat
Donegal Independent
Donegal Vindicator
Fermanagh Herald
Fermanagh Times
Freeman's Journal
Impartial Reporter

Irish Bulletin
Irish Catholic
Irish Freedom
Irish Independent
Irish News
Irish Times
Leitrim Observer
Londonderry Sentinel
National Volunteer
Northern Whig
Sligo Champion
Weekly Irish Times

D. PRINTED PRIMARY MATERIAL

Andrews, C.S., *Dublin made me* (Dublin, 2008).
Birrell, Augustine, *Things past redress* (London, 1937).
Catherine Black, *King's nurse, beggar's nurse* (London, 1939).
Gallagher, Patrick, *My story* (London, 1939).
King, Cecil A., *Memorabilia: musings on sixty-odd years as a newspaper man* (Ballyshannon, 1989).
Lecky, Revd A.G., *In the days of the Laggan presbytery* (Belfast, 1908).
Lloyd George, David, *War memoirs* (London, 1936).
Micks, W.L., *The Congested Districts Board* (Dublin, 1925).
Middlemas, Keith (ed.), *Tom Jones Whitehall diary, III* (London, 1971).
Midleton, the earl of, *Ireland: dupe or heroine* (London, 1932).
O'Donnell, Peadar, *The gates flew open* (London, 1932).
O'Donoghue, Florence, *No other law* (Dublin, 1954).
O'Malley, Ernie, *On another man's wound* (Dublin, 1994).
— *The singing flame* (Dublin, 1978).
Robinson, Henry, *Memories, wise and otherwise* (London, 1923).
Rosenbaum, S., *Against home rule: the case for the Union* (London, 1912).
Ross, John, *The years of my pilgrimage* (London, 1924).
Swift McNeill, J.G., *What I have seen and heard* (London, 1925).

SECONDARY SOURCES

E. PUBLISHED WORKS

Augusteijn, Joost, *From public defiance to guerrilla warfare: the experience of ordinary volunteers in the Irish War of Independence, 1916–21* (Dublin, 1996).
Aiken, Síofra et al. (eds), *The men will talk to me: Ernie O'Malley's interviews with the northern divisions* (Newbridge, 2018).

Beattie, Seán, *Donegal in transition: the impact of the Congested Districts Board* (Dublin, 2013).
——, 'The Dudleys: Donegal's "Penny Nurses", 1903–1923', *DA*, 66 (2014), 16–23.
——, 'The Ancient Order of Hibernians in Donegal, 1904–1927', *DA*, 70 (2018), 107–22.
Begley, Anthony, *Ballyshannon and surrounding areas: history, heritage and folklore* (Ballyshannon, 2009).
——, *Ballyshannon: genealogy and history* (Ballyshannon, 2011).
Bowman, Timothy, 'The UVF and the formation of the 36th (Ulster) Division', *IHS*, 32:128 (2001), 498–518.
——, *Carson's army: the Ulster Volunteer Force, 1910–22* (Manchester, 2007).
Bowman, Timothy, William Butler and Michael Wheatley (eds), *The disparity of sacrifice: Irish recruitment to the British armed forces, 1914–1918* (Liverpool, 2020).
Bury, Robin, *Buried lives: the Protestants of southern Ireland* (Cheltenham, 2017).
Callinan, Elaine, *Electioneering and propaganda in Ireland, 1917–1921: votes, violence and victory* (Dublin, 2020).
Carr, Caroline and Judith McCarthy, *From conflict to division: Donegal, 1919–1925* (Letterkenny, 2021).
Coleman, Marie, 'Protestant depopulation in County Longford during the Irish Revolution, 1911–26', *English Historical Review*, 135:575 (Sept. 2020), 931–77.
Cronin, Sean, *The McGarrity papers* (Tralee, 1972).
Connolly, Linda (ed.), *Women and the Irish Revolution* (Newbridge, 2020).
Coogan, Tim Pat, *Michael Collins, a biography* (London, 1990).
Crowley, John et al., *Atlas of the Irish Revolution* (Cork, 2017).
Cullen, Clara, 'War work on the home front: the Central Sphagnum Depot for Ireland, 1915–1919' in David Durnin and Ian Miller (eds), *Medicine, health and Irish experiences of conflict, 1914–1945* (Manchester, 2017), pp 155–70.
Cunningham, John, 'The struggle for the Belleek–Pettigo Salient, 1922', *DA*, 34 (1982), 38–59.
Curran, Conor, *The development of sport in Donegal, 1880–1935* (Cork, 2015).
——, *Sport in Donegal* (Dublin, 2010).
Devine, Francis, *Organizing history: a centenary of SIPTU* (Dublin, 2009).
Devine, Francis and John B. Smethurst, *Historical directory of trade unions in Ireland* (Salford, 2017).
Doherty, Richard, 'Donegal and the First World War', *DA*, 66 (2014), 39–44.
Dooley, Terence, *Monaghan: the Irish Revolution, 1912–23* (Dublin, 2017).
——, 'The organization of Unionist opposition to home rule in Counties Monaghan, Cavan and Donegal, 1885–1914', *Clogher Record*, 16:1 (1997), 46–70.
English, Richard, *Ernie O'Malley: IRA intellectual* (Oxford, 1998).
Fanning, Ronan, *Fatal path: British government and Irish Revolution* (London, 2013).
Farry, Michael, *Sligo: the Irish Revolution, 1912–23* (Dublin, 2012).
Ferriter, Diarmaid, *A nation of extremes: the pioneers in 20th-century Ireland* (Dublin, 1999)
——, *Lovers of liberty: local government in 20th-century Ireland* (Dublin, 2001).
——, *Between two hells: the Irish Civil War* (London, 2021).
Fitzpatrick, David, 'The geography of Irish nationalism, 1910–21', *Past and Present*, 78 (1978), 113–44.

—— , (ed.), *Ireland and the First World War* (Dublin, 1985).
—— , *The two Irelands, 1912–1939* (Oxford, 1998).
—— , *Descendancy: Irish Protestant histories since 1795* (Cambridge, 2014).
—— , 'Protestant depopulation and the Irish Revolution', *IHS*, 38:152 (Nov. 2013), 643–70.
—— , 'The Orange Order and the border', *IHS*, 33:129 (May 2002), 52–67.
Fox, Colm, *The making of a minority: political developments in Derry and the North, 1912–25* (Derry, 1997).
Freyer, Grattan, *Peadar O'Donnell* (Lewisburg, 1973).
Gallagher, Ronan, *Violence and nationalist politics in Derry city, 1920–1923* (Dublin, 2003).
Garvin, Tom, *1922: the birth of Irish democracy* (Dublin, 1996).
Grant, Adrian, *Derry: the Irish Revolution, 1912–23* (Dublin, 2018).
—— , 'Donegal Labour in the 1923 general election', *DA*, 60 (2008), 275–89.
Griffith, Kenneth and Timothy E. O'Grady, *Curious journey: an oral history of Ireland's unfinished revolution* (London, 1982).
Greaves, C. Desmond, *The IGTWU: the formative years, 1909–1923* (Dublin, 1982).
Gregory, Adrian and Señia Paseta (eds), *Ireland and the Great War* (Manchester, 2002).
Hegarty, Peter, *Peadar O'Donnell* (Cork, 1999).
Hobson, Bulmer, *A short history of the Irish Volunteers* (Dublin, 1918).
Hepburn, A.C., *Catholic Ireland and nationalist Belfast in the era of Joe Devlin, 1871–1934* (Oxford, 2008).
Holmes, William, 'The War of Independence and the Laggan', *DA*, 66 (2015), 22–8.
Hopkinson, Michael, *Green against green: the Irish Civil War* (Dublin, 1988).
Hughes, Brian and Conor Morrissey, *Southern Irish loyalism, 1912–1949* (Liverpool, 2020).
Jalland, Patricia, *The Liberals and Ireland* (London, 1980).
Jeffery, Keith, *Ireland and the Great War* (Cambridge, 2000).
—— , *1916: a global history* (London, 2016).
Jenkins, Roy, *Asquith* (London, 1967).
Kelly, Kieran, *Letterkenny: where the winding Swilly flows* (Letterkenny, 2014).
Kenneally, Ian and James O'Donnell, *The Irish regional press, 1892–2018: revival, revolution and republic* (Dublin, 2018).
Kotsonouris, Mary, *Retreat from revolution: the Dáil courts, 1920–24* (Dublin, 1994; 2020).
Laffan, Michael, *The partition of Ireland, 1911–1925* (1987).
—— , *The resurrection of Ireland: the Sinn Féin party, 1916–1923* (Cambridge, 1999).
Langton, James, *The forgotten fallen; the fallen of the Irish Civil War*, vol. 1 (Dublin, 2019).
Lynch, Robert, *The northern IRA and the early years of partition, 1920–1922* (Dublin, 2006).
—— , 'Donegal and the joint IRA northern offensive, May–November 1922', *IHS*, 35:138 (Nov. 2006), 184–99.
Mac Fhionnghaile, Niall, *Donegal, Ireland and the First World War* (Letterkenny, 1987).

—, *Dr Mc Ginley, his life and times* (Letterkenny, 1985).
MacLaughlin, Jim (ed.), *The making of a northern county* (Dublin, 2007).
MacLaughlin, Jim and Seán Beattie (eds), *Atlas of County Donegal* (Cork, 2013).
McCabe, Anton, '"The stormy petrel of the Transport Workers": Peadar O'Donnell, trade unionist, 1917–1920', *Saothair*, 19 (1994), 41–51.
McCluskey, Fergal, *Tyrone: the Irish Revolution, 1912–23* (Dublin, 2014).
McConnel, James, 'Recruiting sergeants for John Bull? Irish nationalist MPs and enlistment during the early months of the Great War', *War in History*, 14:4 (Nov. 2007), 408–28.
McDowell, R.B., *The Irish Convention, 1917–1918* (London, 1970).
McGarty, Patrick, *Leitrim: the Irish Revolution, 1912–23* (Dublin, 2020).
Maume, Patrick, *The long gestation: Irish nationalist life, 1891–1918* (Dublin, 1999).
Meehan, Helen, 'The Hamiltons of Brownhall', *DA*, 60 (2008), 38–58.
—, 'Cumann na mBan in Donegal', *DA*, 66 (2014), 97–105.
Miller, D.W., *Church, state and nation in Ireland, 1898–1921* (Dublin, 1973).
Milne, Ida, *Stacking the coffins: influenza, war and revolution in Ireland* (Manchester, 2018).
Mitchell, Arthur, *Revolutionary government in Ireland: Dáil Éireann, 1919–22* (Dublin, 1995).
Morrissey, Thomas J., *Patriot and man of peace: Laurence O'Neill, 1864–1924* (Dublin, 2014).
Murphy, Desmond, *Derry, Donegal and modern Ulster, 1790–1921* (Derry, 1981).
Nolan, William, Liam Ronayne and Mairead Dunleavy (eds), *Donegal history and society* (Dublin, 1995).
Ó Baoighill, Pádraig S., *Cardinal Patrick O'Donnell, 1856–1927* (Baile na Finne, 2008).
O'Carroll, Declan, *Finner Camp: a history* (Dublin, 1999).
Ó Corráin, Daithí, '"Resigned to take the bill with its defects": the Catholic Church and the third home rule bill' in Gabriel Doherty (ed.), *The home rule crisis, 1912–14* (Cork, 2014), pp 185–209.
Ó Drisceoil, Dónal, *Peadar O'Donnell* (Cork, 2001).
Ó Duibhir, Liam, *The Donegal awakening: Donegal and the War of Independence* (Cork, 2009).
—, *Donegal and the Civil War: the untold story* (Cork, 2012).
—, *Prisoners of war: Ballykinlar internment camp, 1920–1921* (Cork, 2013).
O'Halpin, Eunan and Daithí Ó Corráin, *The dead of the Irish Revolution* (London, 2020).
O'Neill, Hugh, 'Irish Catholic chaplains in British armed forces during World War 1', *Seanchas Ard Mhaca*, 23:2 (2011), 204–30.
Ó Néill, Séamus and Bernard Ó Dubhtaigh (eds), *Coláiste Uladh: leabhar cuimhne lubhaile leith-chéad blian, 1906–1956* (Donegal, 1956).
Ozseker, Okan, *Forging the border: Donegal and Derry in times of revolution, 1911–1925* (Newbridge, 2019).
Phoenix, Eamon, *Northern nationalism, nationalist politics, partition and the Catholic minority in Northern Ireland, 1890–1940* (Belfast, 1994).
Potter, Matthew, 'The earls of Arran and their estates in Donegal', *DA*, 60 (2008), 102–33.

Rafferty, Oliver, *Catholicism in Ulster, 1603–1983: an interpretive history* (London, 1994).
Privilege, John, *Michael Logue and the Catholic Church in Ireland, 1879–1925* (Manchester, 2009).
Roarty, Leonard, 'The battle of Pettigo, 1922', *DA*, 60 (2008), 242–7.
Silke, John J., 'The "Drumboe Martyrs"', *DA*, 60 (2008), 167–94.
Sweeney, Frank, *That old sinner: Letterkenny and Burtonport railway* (Dublin, 2006).
Sweeney, Malachy, *A troubled time: Donegal from 1914 through the War of Independence* (Donegal, 2014).
Stewart, A.T.Q., *The Ulster crisis: resistance to home rule* (London, 1967).
Townshend, Charles, *The British campaign in Ireland, 1919–1921* (Oxford, 1975).
——, *The republic: the fight for Irish independence, 1918–1923* (London, 2013).
——, *The partition: Ireland divided, 1885–1925* (London, 2021).
——, 'The Irish Republican Army and the development of guerrilla warfare, 1916–1921', *English Historical Review*, 94:371 (1971), 329–31.
Valiulis, Maryann Gialanella, *Portrait of a revolutionary: General Richard Mulcahy and the foundation of the Irish Free State* (Dublin, 1992).
Walsh, Fionnuala, *Irish women and the Great War* (Cambridge, 2020).
Wheatley, Michael, *Nationalism and the Irish Party: provincial Ireland, 1910–1916* (Oxford, 2005).

F. THESES AND UNPUBLISHED WORK

Arkinson, P., 'The political role of Bishop McHugh of Derry during the partition crisis' (MA, University of Ulster, 2000).
Harvey, D., 'The labour movement in Donegal from 1917 to 1923' (MA, Magee College, University of Ulster, 2006).
O'Donnell, Martina, 'The estate system of landholding in County Donegal, 1830–1923: a geographical analysis' (PhD, UCD, 1998).
O'Neill, Clare, 'The Irish home front with particular reference to the treatment of Belgian refugees, prisoners of war, enemy aliens and war casualties' (PhD, NUI Maynooth, 2006).
Sweeney, Frank, 'The Letterkenny and Burtonport extension railway, 1903–47: its social context and environment' (PhD, NUI Maynooth, 2004).
Thompson, Kelly, '"No land worth struggling for": Donegal and partition, 1911–1925' (MA, TCD, 2010).
Tunney, John, 'From ascendancy to alienation: a study of Donegal's Protestant community, 1881–1932' (MA, NUI Galway, 1985).

G. INTERNET SOURCES

Ward, John, The *Vindicator* story, www.vindicator.ca (1 Nov. 2020).

Index

Abercorn, duke of, 4, 9, 24–5; duchess, 13, 24
abstention, 82, 86
Adair, Cornelia, 44
Admiralty, 46, 75
agrarian problems, 10–11, 71, 76–7, 83, 95, 105, 137; *see* land
agriculture: tillage, 5; cattle and sheep, 5; crops, 5
An tÓglach, 106
Ancient Order of Hibernians, Board of Erin (AOH), 9, 10–12, 16–18, 28, 32, 34, 51, 53, 55, 58, 61, 65, 73, 79–80, 83–6, 88, 96, 104, 136, 139; strength in 1917, 66; in December 1918, 79
Anderson, Sir Robert, 103
Anglo-Boer war, 22, 52
Anglo-Irish Treaty, 110, 114–15; Treaty split, 114, 118, 127, 133–4, 138; Treaty debates, 117–18, 120; ratification, 118; local authorities and, 116; pro-Treaty, 118; 127; anti-Treaty, 118, 127; *see* Irish Republican Army
Anglo-Irish truce, 110–12
Annagry, 3, 6, 58, 69, 88, 97
Antrim, County, 30, 59
Apprentice Boys, 23, 26
Archer, Liam, 110
Ardara, 3, 7, 10, 68, 70, 83, 97, 102, 104, 109, 113
Arigna, County Roscommon, 131
Armagh, 81, 99, 106
Arranmore, 47, 76
Ashe, Thomas, 77
Asquith, Herbert, 16, 58, 62
Atkinson, Captain, 119
Audacious, HMS, 33

Baillie, Colonel John Robert, 25
Ballinakillew, 25
Ballindrait, 23, 26, 93
Ballintra, 20, 25, 70, 97, 105

Ballybofey, 3, 18, 25, 26, 29, 53–5, 61, 68–9, 81, 87–8, 97, 105, 109, 121, 127, 129
Ballykinlar internment camp, 108
Ballyliffen, 37
Ballymacool House, 16, 20, 27, 128
Ballyshannon, 2, 3, 6, 8, 10, 12–13, 18, 20, 25, 28, 36–9, 41–2, 45, 66–8, 70–1, 76, 82, 84, 90–1, 95, 97–9, 105, 109, 113, 115, 119, 121, 125, 128–9, 136–7; Board of Guardians, 57; Town Commissioners, 30, 37, 89, 99; 156n; RDC, 91; Sheil Hospital, 121; St Anne's church, 125; the Rock barracks, 130
Barnesmore RIC station, burning of, 93, 97
Baronscourt, County Tyrone, 9, 25, 103
Barrie, Hugh T., (MP)
Barry, Tom, 122
Béaslaí, Piaras, 115
Belfast Newsletter, 74, 92
Belfast, 2, 6, 8, 11, 18, 19, 25, 29, 32, 45, 53, 59, 85, 110; shipyards, 18, 120; boycott, 18, 80, 99–100, 106, 115, 120–3, 128, 135
Belgium, 34, 41, 43; Belgian refugees, 43–4
Belleek, 105, 109, 112, 134; salient, 123–6; fort (the battery), 124, 126
Belleek-Pettigo triangle, 123–6
Birrell, Augustine (chief secretary), 4, 27, 30
Black and Tans, *see* War of Independence
Black, Catherine, 41
Black, John, 92
Blacker Douglass, 119
Blackley, Travers, 60
Blythe, Ernest, 53
Boa Island, 124, 125
Board of Erin, *see* Ancient Order of Hibernians
Bonar Law, Andrew (MP), 13
Bonner, Councillor, 116

173

Bonner, Richard, 50, 52
Boundary Commission, 92, 115–16, 133–6
Bowman, Timothy, 26
Boyce, Bernard, 40
Boyce, Private Hugh, 40
Boyd, Charlotte Agnes, 16, 20, 44, 111
Boyle, Bernard, 39
Boyle, John, 51
Brennan, P.J., 70
Breslin, Patrick, 95
Bridgend, 128, 134
British army, 14, 36, 104, 113, 122, 127, 132; Inniskilling Fusiliers, 25, 36, 40–1, 70; Lincolnshire Regiment, 125; 10th (Irish) Division, 36; 36th (Ulster) Division, 36, 41
Britton, Captain Hugh, 120
Brooke, Captain Basil, 124
Buck Island, 124, 162n
Buckingham Palace conference, 31, 58
Bullock, Stephen, 26
Bunbeg, 77, 97, 104
Buncrana, 3, 10, 29, 37, 45–6, 75, 77, 89–90, 97, 103, 116, 122, 128; UDC, 116
Bundoran, 2, 3, 37, 39, 66, 68, 82–4, 90, 95, 97, 102, 105, 107, 108, 120–1, 124, 129, 130; UDC, 67, 90
Bureau of Military History, 34
Burt, 25, 73, 76, 90
Burtonport, 2, 3, 28, 46, 53, 76, 96–7, 106, 108, 114, 130
Butt, Isaac, 16
Byrne, Joseph (IG), 65, 68–9

Cannon, Fr James, 32
Carndonagh, 3, 51, 58, 67, 73, 96–7, 121
Carney, Frank, 105, 109–10
Carrick, 3, 7, 17, 88, 97, 102
Carrigans, 3, 18, 23, 97, 134
Carrowkeel, 88, 97
Carson, Edward (MP), 13, 19–20, 24, 26, 30, 38, 46, 55, 58, 60–1, 111
Casement, Roger, 1, 3, 15, 50
Cashel, Alice Mary, 71
Cashelnagore, 52, 54
Cassidy, John, 53–4
Castlebellingham, County Louth, 49
Castledawson, County Derry, 18

Castlederg, County Tyrone, 109
Castlefinn, 3, 23, 36, 66, 68, 77, 81, 91, 97, 121, 128
Catholics, 1, 2, 9, 59; attacks on, 18; bishops, 42, 57, 59, 71–2, 78, 115; clergy, 4, 18, 27, 39, 56, 73, 82, 108, 129; education, 8, 30
Cavan, County, 12, 13, 19, 58, 60, 69, 111, 119, 136
Census (1911, 1926), 135–6
Chadwick, Bishop George Alexander, 4, 19, 21, 141n
Chamberlain, Sir Neville (IG), 22, 27
Childers, Erskine, 63, 152n
Church Hill, 84, 97, 128
Churchill, Winston, 125, 127
civil and religious liberties, 19, 21
Civil War, *see* Irish Civil War
Claidheamh Soluis, 28
Clan na Gael, 52
Clarke, Alexander, 110
Clarke, James, 90, 92
Clarke, Tom, 54
Clements, Charles, 5th earl of Leitrim, 16, 22–6, 61, 92, 137
Cliffoney, County Sligo, 102
Cloghaneely, 1, 29, 50, 51, 54, 71
Clogher, 76, 97
Clogher, diocese of, 3, 59
Clones, County Monaghan, 111
Clonmany, 3, 80, 97, 110
Clout, Robert John, 113
Cochrane, Hugh C., 9
Coláiste Uladh, 1, 49, 50–2, 104
Colbert, Con, 66, 81
Cole, Alderman Walter, 67
Colhoun, William, 38
Collins, Michael, 102, 108, 114, 115, 117, 118, 120, 123, 125–7, 130
Compulsory Military Service Act (1918), 71–2
Congested Districts Board (CDB), 2, 4–7, 22, 46, 48, 76–7, 80, 137–8; *see* industry
Connolly, Captain James, 128
Connolly, Jim (James), 66
conscription, *see* First World War
Conservative Party, 60–1, 95
Convoy, 25, 56, 75, 97

Index 175

Cooke, John F., 10, 93, 98
cooperative movement, 7
Cork, County, 71, 106, 121
Cosgrove, W.T., 94
cottage industry, see industry
courts, 95, 96; see Dáil Éireann
Cousins, Margaret, 13
Coyle, Eithne, 50-1, 71, 123, 128-30, 139
Craig, James (MP), 19, 74, 120, 122-3, 125
Craig-Collins pact, 120, 134
Creeslough, 51, 52, 54, 68, 83-4, 97, 103, 131
cricket, 14
Crolly, 6, 106
Crown forces, distribution of, 97; see RIC, Black and Tans
Culdaff, 3, 97
Cully, 25
Cumann na mBan, 3, 50, 67, 69, 70-1, 74, 81, 99 104, 127-30, 139; Lá na mBan, 74; proclaimed, 77; expansion, 104; convention on Treaty, 122-3; membership 1922, 123
Cumann na nGaedheal, 80, 133, 138-9
Curragh, 133; mutiny, 27
Curran, Conor, 14

Dáil Éireann, 87, 90-3, 95-6, 98-100, 116, 118, 127, 133; Dáil loan, 88, 103, 115; department of local government, 98; department of labour, 99; Sinn Féin courts, 95-7, 120; counter-state, 87, 155n
Dáil, An, 99-100
Daily Mail, 21
Daly, Charlie, 121, 124, 128-32
Daly, Tom, 122, 161n
Darney, 20
Dawson, James (Séamus), 69, 70
de Valera, Éamon, 65, 71-2, 102, 114, 116-18, 127, 133; tour of north-west, 67-9; 87
Deasley, William, 162n
Derry city, 2, 6, 8, 14, 25-6, 29, 35, 45, 47, 54, 58-9, 69, 77, 84, 90, 103, 106, 109, 119, 134-5; Trades Council, 75-6; Bogside, 106

Derry Journal, 13, 29, 43-4, 54, 56, 75, 91, 111, 115
Derry People and *Donegal News*, 13, 19, 54, 56, 58-9, 62, 85, 87, 112, 115-16
Derry Weekly News, 14, 99
Derry, County, 2, 3, 11, 13, 17, 19, 23, 30, 33, 36, 52, 74, 76, 78; diocese, 43-4, 59, 81-2, 88, 116, 120, 122, 128, 131, 135
Derrybeg, 73
Despard, Charlotte, 138
Devlin, Joseph (MP), 11, 59, 80, 85
Devoy, John, 52
Dickson, Annie, 40
Dickson, Mary, 40
Dillon, John (MP), 34, 72, 80-1, 85
Doaghbeg police barracks, 92, 97
Doe, 35, 52, 73, 136
Doherty, Councillor William, 44
Doherty, Daniel, 40
Doherty, James, 40
Doherty, John (Ballyshannon), 40
Doherty, John (Letterkenny), 41
Doherty, Patrick H., 73, 96
Doherty, William, 40
Dolan, J.N., 67
Donegal book of honour, 35-6, 40
Donegal County Board, 14, 50
Donegal County Council (DCC), 4, 9, 45-6, 55, 62, 74, 87, 90-2, 94-5, 116, 131, 137, 161n
Donegal County: 17, agriculture, 5, 46-7; constituencies, 10-11, 142n; demography, 2 ; dioceses, 3-4; high sheriff, 9; press, 13-14, 18; militia unit, 36; Technical Committee, 8; topography, 1-2, east, 2, 7, 10, 12-15, 20-1, 23, 25, 28, 34, 39, 44, 46-7, 52, 59, 66, 68, 74-5, 79-86, 88-9, 104, 106, 108, 113, 114, 117, 120, 128, 135; north, 2, 10, 14, 15, 23, 35, 46, 59, 68, 79-86, 117, 134; south, 2, 7, 10, 14, 20, 25, 29, 34, 44, 53, 66, 68, 75, 79-86, 99, 105, 107, 112, 117, 137 ; west, 2, 6, 7, 10, 14, 15, 20, 35, 46-7, 51-3, 65, 72, 79-86, 100, 103, 104, 109, 112-13, 117, 131, 137-9
Donegal Democrat, 14, 98, 111, 113-15

Donegal Farmers' Union, 94
Donegal Independent, 14, 55, 99
Donegal Protestant Registration Association (DPRA), 134, 136
Donegal Town, 3, 9, 20, 25, 36, 53, 68, 70, 76–7, 89, 95–7, 104, 107, 120, 131; Board of Guardians, 55, 91–2, 150n; RDC, 58, 91, 93
Donegal Unionist Association, 159n
Donegal Vindicator, 14, 39, 41, 55–6, 72, 86, 99, 115, 120, 130
Donegan, Mossy, 126
Donnelly, Patrick, 66
Donovan, John, 80, 84
Dougherty, James (under-secretary), 22
Down, County, 30, 81
Downey, John, 14, 115
Downings, 46; Bay, 5
Downpatrick, County Down, 111
drilling, 17–18, 22–5, 28, 66, 74, 77, 88
Drumboe, 128, 130; *see* Civil War
Drumkeen, 129
Drumquin, County Tyrone, 126; *see* War of Independence
Dublin, 2, 8, 26, 38, 49, 51, 55, 57, 60, 83, 105, 114, 122; Castle, 4, 17, 73, 133; Mansion House, 123
Duffy, Captain Joseph, 120
Duffy, James, 40
Dunfanaghy, 3, 10, 51, 91, 97, 104
Dungannon, County Tyrone, 24
Dungloe, 3, 10, 25, 28, 51–2, 68, 76, 95–7, 101, 103, 104, 107–9, 117, 129
Dunkineely, 20, 32, 56, 97
Dunlevy, James, 9, 62–3, 142n
Dunlewey, 131
Dunnion, George, 55
Dunnion, Michael, 83
Dunraven, Lord, 95
Dunree, 10, 103
Dunville, Lieutenant Robert, 49

Erne, Lough, 123–5
Easter Rising (1916), 15, 39, 49, 52–7, 65, 76, 79, 90, 92
Ederney, County Fermanagh, 109
education, 8–9
Elagh border post, 122

elections: by-elections, South Longford, 72; East Clare, 65, 72; South Armagh, 66, 72; Waterford, 72; East Tyrone, 72; East Cavan 77; DCC 9; general election, 1918, 65, 69, 78, 79–86; results, 84–5; municipal and urban districts, January 1920, 89–90; County Council and RDC, 90–1; proportional representation, 91; general election, 1921, 110; Dáil elections, June 1922, 127
emigration, 7, 35, 39, 46, 52, 135, 139; seasonal migration, 7, 28, 36, 46–7, 49, 76, 83, 102; political exiles and economic migrants, 139–40
England, 2, 7, 39, 46
Enniskillen, County Fermanagh, 2, 8, 19, 109, 124
Enright, Daniel, 131

Fahan, 73
Falcarragh, 3, 71, 97, 99, 104, 107, 108
Fanad, 22, 51
farm labourers, 5, 47
Farmers' Party, 133, 139
Farrell, Sergeant, 103
Feetham, Justice Richard, 134; *see* Boundary Commission
female employment, 6, 46
Fenians, 51
Fermanagh Herald, 14
Fermanagh News, 99
Fermanagh, County, 1, 3, 11, 14, 19, 27, 31, 35–6, 58–9, 67–8, 78, 81, 102, 105, 123–4, 134, 136; brigade, 108, 116
Feymore, 52
Finn valley, 2, 129
Finner camp, 10, 35–7, 39, 67, 97, 113, 127–8, 133; handover of, 121, 161n
First World War, 4, 6, 15, 31–48, 50, 103, 119, 123, 135, 138; British Expeditionary Force, 40; chaplains, 42; Voluntary Aid Detachment, 40; War Refugees Committee, 43; War Hospital Supply Committee, 45; Ulster Sphagnum Association, 45; recruitment, 34, 35–40, 46, 77–8; War Office, 36, 42–3; conscription, 34, 39, 40, 47, 71–8, 81; anti-conscription pledge, 72, 76; Donegal

casualties, 35–6; food prices, 38; naval activity, 36–7; War Hospital Supply Committee, 44; woman in, 40–1, 44–6
Fisher, J.R., 134; *see* Boundary Commission
Fitzpatrick, David, 135, 136
Flood, Daniel, 126
Flood, Patrick, 126
flying columns, *see* Irish Republican Army
Foster, CI, 112
Four Courts, 127–8
Foyle, Lough, 37; river, 134
France, 41, 57, 73
Free State, Irish, 118, 126, 134, 136–8, 140; constitution, 127
Freeman's Journal, 33, 35, 62
Freemasons, 12, 143n
French, Lord, 77
Frongoch, 53, 81
Frosses, 102

Gaelic American, 33
Gaelic Athletic Association (GAA), 14, 50, 52, 88
Gaelic football, 14, 47, 88
Gaelic League, 14, 50–1, 82, 80, 88; proclaimed, 77
Galbraith, Andrew, 42
Gallacher, Willie, 76
Gallagher, Danny, 124
Gallagher, Francis, 87
Gallagher, Henry (crown solicitor), 38
Gallagher, James, 120
Gallagher, Mary, 99
Gallagher, P.M., 83
Gallagher, Paddy 'the Cope', 7, 9
Gallipoli, 57
Galway, County, 8
Gannon, Captain Bernard, 131
Garrison, County Fermanagh, 125
George V, King, 31, 41, 110; speech at inauguration of northern parliament, 111
German plot, 77, 81, 85, 88
Gibbons, Margaret, 43
Gillespie, Patrick, 55
Gillies, Harold, 41
Glasgow, 26, 40, 46, 52
Glen, 97, 107

Glencolumbcille, 88, 97
Glennon, Tom, 118, 122
Glenswilly, 53
Glenties, 45, 68, 73, 77, 83–4, 90, 95, 97, 104; RDC, 60, 91
Glenveagh Castle, 44, 123, 128–9
Gonne, Maud, 138
Gortahork, 3, 68–9, 71, 91, 104, 116, 128
Government of Ireland Act (1920), 110, 113, 123
Greencastle, 104
Greenwood, Hamar (chief secretary), 95
Griffith, Arthur, 67, 77, 115, 116
Gweedore and Rosses Teachers' Association, 47
Gweedore, 3, 39, 40, 53, 80, 97, 109
Gwynn, Stephen, 62

hair-cutting, forcible, 98–9
Hamillton, Captain John Stewart, 10, 93, 105
Hamilton, Captain William (Coxtown), 111, 119
Hamilton, Lieutenant John, 42
Harley, Mary, 108, 113
Healy, T.M., 51
Henry McGowan, 105, 108
Herdman, E.C., 23, 92
Heron, Anthony, 83–4,
Hibernian Journal, 79
hiring fair, 7, 46–7
Hobson, Bulmer, 52–3
home rule, 11, 16, 31, 62; home rule all round, 16, 63; home rule crisis, 16–31, 51–2; finance, 17; 63; third home rule bill, 16–18, 22, 29; opposition to, 16–31; Suspensory Act, 31
Hopkinson, Michael, 114
House of Commons, 30–1, 56, 61, 72, 95, 125
House of Lords, 16, 31
Houston, Denis, 76
Howth gun-running 29
Hughes, CI John, 68, 73, 77–8, 84, 97, 103, 104

Impartial Reporter, 14
Inch, 73, 128

indictable offences, 105–6
industrial action (strikes), 75–6
industry, 46, 80; fishing, 5, 37, 46; curing, 5; barrel making, 5; boat building, 6; cottage industry, 46; textiles, 6; knitting, 6, 46; shirt manufacture, 6; linen, 6; lace 6; weaving, 6–7; *see* Congested Districts Board
Inishbofin Island, 49
Inishowen, 2, 6, 10, 37–8, 44, 46, 60, 75, 81, 88, 96, 103, 109, 116, 134; RDC, 55, 90, 116, 150n; Board of Guardians, 94
intermediate zones of development, 15, 137, 143n
Inver, 25, 53
Irish Agricultural Organisation Society (IAOS), 7
Irish American Alliance, 51
Irish Asylum Workers' Union, 75
Irish Civil War, 15, 101, 114–32, 133–4, 140; Newtowncunningham ambush, 122; Northern Divisions, 118, 120, 126–7, 129–30, 139; Southern Division, 121; Western Division, 129, 131; 102; anti-Treaty IRA, 119–22, 124–31; discipline, 122; strength, September 1922, 131, 163n; army convention, 118, 121; demoralization, 128, 130; withdrawal from Donegal, 131; pro-Treaty IRA/National Army, 118, 120–6, 128–31; Drumboe executions, 131–3; cessation of hostilities, 132; fatalities, 132, 163n
Irish Convention, 62–3, 65, 82
Irish Distress Committee, 135
Irish Farmers' Union, 74
Irish Grants Committee, 135
Irish language, 1, 3, 49–51
Irish National Foresters, 12
Irish National Teachers' Organisation, 47, 76
Irish Parliamentary Party (IPP), 4, 10, 13, 16, 17, 30, 32, 38, 45, 53, 55–62, 65–6, 88, 110; impact of conscription on, 71–2, 78; and general election, 1918, 79–82, 83
Irish Republican Army (IRA), 87–8, 90, 92, 96, 100, 105, 137; arms, 103–4, 105, 112, 122, 137; ambushes, 88, 93, 101, 103, 105, 107; arrests, 108; brigade structure, 101–2; brigade, divisional areas, 102; 109; Brigades, 93, 95, 97, 100, 102, 103, 108 109; 125, 128; brigade activity reports, 106; discipline, 102–3, 105, 108–9, 112; social profile, 102, 138; strength, 1919, 101–2; escalation, 103–4; GHQ, 105, 108, 110; Flying columns (active service units), 106–7; and Treaty, 118; Northern Divisions, 109; *see* War of Independence; Civil War
Irish Republican Brotherhood (IRB), 29, 50–4, 81, 84, 108, 114–15, 118, 120
Irish Republican Police (IRP), 96
Irish Revolution, 1, 133–4, 136–40; social aspects of, 118; role of religion, 138,
Irish Times, 24, 27
Irish Trade Union Congress, 74, 76
Irish Transport and General Workers' Union (ITGWU), 75–6,
Irish Volunteers, 14, 28–9, 49, 51–4, 65–8, 79–80, 83–4, 87, 101, 123; composition, 28, 33; split, 33–4; reorganization, 68–70; and conscription, 73–4, 77–8
Irish Women's Franchise League, 13

Jeffery, Keith, 35
Jellicoe, Admiral Sir John, 33
Johnston, Anna ('Ethna Carbery'), 50
Johnston, Captain Patrick, 119–20, 139
Johnston, Major George Hamilton, 77, 113
Joseph Kelly, 54
Jutland, battle of, 37

Kane, Margaret, 67
Kearney, William, 126
Kearns, James, 29
Kelly, Bishop Denis, 42, 57
Kelly, Daniel, 52, 54
Kelly, Edward (MP), 8, 10, 29, 34–5, 79, 80–2, 85, 110
Kelly, H.J., 67
Kelly, William, 88
Kerry, County, 121, 132; Council, 87
Kettle, Lieutenant Tom (MP), 29, 38
Kilcar, 6, 68, 88

Index

Kilcoole, 29
Kilderry, 136
Killea, 134
Killeter, County Tyrone, 69
Killybegs, 3, 6, 10, 68, 96–7, 103, 104, 109
Killygordon, 32, 52
Kilmacrennan, 22, 38, 59, 97
Kilraine, 4, 132
Kinlough, County Leitrim, 102, 119, 128
Kitchener, Lord, 36
Knox, Revd James, 23

labour, 74–6; trade union membership, 75; Labour Association, 73, 75; militancy, 89–90
labourers, 38, 42, 47, 75–6, 83, 102; wages, 38, 75–6
Lafferty, Leo, 103
Laggan, 1
Laghey, 20, 25
Lake Gartan, 129
land: Acts, 4; annuities, 100; estates, 4; landlords, 4, 83; landlessness, 5, 15; ownership, 1, 4, 135; purchase, 4–5; redistribution, 100, 135; small holders, 4; tenants, 4; war, 53; *see* Congested Districts Board
Langton, James, 132
Larkin, Seán, 131
Larne gun-running, 27, 29
Law, Francis, 35
Law, Hugh (MP), 7, 10, 35, 72, 80
Lecky, Revd Alexander, 1
Lehane, Seán, 120–2, 128–31
Leitrim, County, 2–3, 11, 14, 35, 67–8, 129
Leitrim, Lady, 44
Leitrim, Lord, *see* Clements, Charles
Lenan Head, 10
Leonard, Patrick, 119–20
Letterkenny, 2–3, 6, 8, 12, 17, 20–2, 24, 29, 32, 34, 36, 39, 40, 51–3, 55–6, 66, 67–77, 84, 87, 90, 94–5, 102, 103, 104, 107, 108, 109, 112, 117, 120, 128, 136; Board of Guardians, 46, 55; RDC 38–40, 42, 44, 60, UDC, 40, 90
Lifford, 3, 9, 25, 75, 97, 105, 108, 113, 122, 128

literacy, 8
Lloyd George, David, 30, 45, 58, 61–2, 72, 110, 125, 127
Local Government Act (1898), 9
local government: divisions, 89; rural district councils (RDCs), 9; Boards of Guardians, 9; quarter sessions, 10, 113; magistrates, 9; Local Government Board (LGB), 43–4, 92, 93–4
Logue, Cardinal Michael, 42, 59, 72, 81, 115–16, 138
Logue, Rose Anne, 99
Logue, William, 75
Londonderry No. 2 RDC, 91, 92, 94, 134
Londonderry Sentinel, 13, 85, 91, 111, 123
Londonderry, marchioness of, 13, 32–3; Lady Londonderry, 44, 62
Longford, County, 99
Loreburn, Lord, 16
Lough Eske Castle, 9
loyalists, 98, 107
Lynch, Fionán, 67, 69
Lynch, Liam, 130–1
Lyons, F.S.L., 9

Mac Diarmada, Seán, 52
Mac Eoin, Seán, 130
Mac Fhionnghaile, Niall, 36
Mac Fhionnlaoich, Peadar Toner ('Cú Uladh'), 53
Mac Giolla Bhríghide, Niall, 51
Mac Grianna, Seosamh, 49, 101, 114, 140; *An druma mór*, 49, 101, 114, 149n, 157n
MacAdam, Eileen Dalton (Eily), 39, 56, 99–100, 115, 130
MacAdam, John, 14, 39, 55, 56, 72, 85–6
MacArthur, Joseph, 90
MacCumhail, Seán, 122
MacDonagh, Thomas, 51, 54, 56
MacEntee, Seán, 49–50, 67
MacGill, Patrick, 32, 42–4, 65, 140; Socks for the Colonel, 32, 44; A pair of spectacles, 43; *The amateur army*, 42; *The great push*, 42; *Red horizon*, 43; *Maureen*, 65
MacLoone, Fr H, 73
MacManus, Seumus, 50, 52
MacNeill, Eoin, 28, 33, 69, 81, 134

MacNeill, John Gordon (MP), 10, 17, 35, 80, 85
MacVeagh, Jeremiah (MP), 59
Magherameenagh Castle, 124
Malin, 96; Malin Head, 37, 46, 97
Malinmore, 53
Manorcunningham, 25, 97
Mansion House, Dublin, 87; Conference, 71-2, 73, 74, 80
Mayo, County, 2, 8, 85
McBride, Charles, 103
McCafferty Fr John, 12, 32, 34, 72, 73
McCaffrey, James, 84
McCanny, Bernard (aka McKenna), 126
McCarroll, J.J., 13
McCartan, Patrick, 52, 66
McCullough, Denis, 52, 53, 54
McDermott, P.H., 126, 160n
McDonagh, John, 41
McDonagh, Patrick, 41, 42
McFadden, Michael Óg, 139
McGarrity, Joseph, 52
McGee, Constable Charles, 49-50
McGinley, Anthony, 103
McGinley, Bernard, 83
McGinley, Charles, 83
McGinley, Charlie, 129
McGinley, Conor, 53
McGinley, Dr J.P. (TD), 66, 90, 96, 101, 103, 110, 114, 118
McGinley, Eunan, 53
McGoldrick, P.J. (TD), 110, 117
McHugh, Bishop Charles, 30, 59, 61, 81
McHugh, Paddy, 49
McIlhenny, David, 26
McKenna, Bishop Patrick, 59, 82
McKenna, Constable James, 99
McMenamin, Daniel, 80, 82, 85, 139
McMonagle, James, 68-9, 73, 75, 96, 140
McNulty, James, 52, 54, 103, 140, 149n
McQuade, Canon W.J., 21
McShea, Thomas, 84, 102-3, 119-20
Meenacross, 96, 139
Meenmore, 76
Meevagh, 22
Melly, Edward, 55
merchants, 7, 20, 23, 53
Mercier, Cardinal, 43

Michael, Revd W., 21
Middletown, 99
Midleton, Lord, 63, 64
Milford, 2-3, 22, 25-7, 29, 40, 67, 91, 97
Miller, David, 63
Milroy, Seán, 67, 101, 102, 103
Mitchell, Arthur, 87
modernization, 15, 143n
Molenan, 122
Monaghan, County, 12, 13, 17, 19, 27, 58, 60, 88, 106, 111, 119, 136
Montgomery, Dr Henry, 19
Montgomery, J.A.L. (high sheriff), 38
Moore, Colonel Maurice, 28, 69
Moore, DI, 103
Moore, Major Robert Lyon, 82, 85, 111, 122, 124, 159n
Moore, William (MP), 24
Morrell, H.B. (CI), 10, 18, 22
Morton, Alexander, 6, 93
Mountcharles, 34, 53, 97, 107
Moville, 3, 10, 25, 97
Moylan, Seán (TD), 83
Moyne, 25
Muff, 3, 25, 88, 97, 134
Mulcahy, Richard, 108, 118, 121
Mulroy, 5-6; 22-3, 25, 137
Murdoch, Charles, 110
Murphy, Desmond, 6
Murray, Joseph, 83, 102, 108, 112, 121, 125-6, 128, 140, 157n
Myles, James Sproule, 12, 14, 16, 18, 25, 41-2, 57, 90, 111, 119, 133, 137, 143n, 164-5n

National Amalgamated Union of Labour, 75
National army, 118, 120-6, 128-9, 131; estimated strength, September 1922, 131, 139
National League, 139
National Volunteer, 33-4
National Volunteers, 33-7, 42, 57, 69, 73
nationalists: 9, 16, 32-3; cultural nationalism, 52; divergent nationalism, 88; Protestant nationalists, 10; radical nationalism, 14, 15, 49-64; 66-7, 71, 133; Nationalists (constitutional), 90-1

Index

naval bases (coast guard), 36–7, 97
Neely, Robert, 111, 159n
Newtowncunningham, 3, 26, 97, 120, 122, 132
Ní Fhaircheallaigh, Úna (Agnes O'Farrelly), 51
Northern Ireland, 123–4, 127, 134
northern offensive, 120–1, 126–7; arms for, 122, 126, 128
nursing, 40–1, 129

Ó Grianna, Séamus ('Máire'), 49–50, 140; *Castar na daoine ar a chéile*, 49; *Mo dhá Róisín*, 49
O'Boyle, Con, 160n
O'Boyle, Éamon, 53
O'Connell, W.H. (Deputy IG), 31
O'Connor, Rory, 127
O'Connor, Úna, 127
O'Doherty, Joseph (TD), 81, 84–5, 133
O'Doherty, Philip (MP), 10, 35, 59–60, 80–1, 117
O'Donnell, Bernard, 71
O'Donnell, Bishop Patrick, 3–4, 8, 11–12, 14, 16–17, 27–8, 30, 32, 33–4, 39–40, 42–5, 51, 56–7, 59, 62–5, 110–11, 138, 152n; and conscription, 72–3, 75; and general election, 81–3, 85–6; and War of Independence, 107, 112; and Treaty, 115–16; and Civil War, 130–2, 134, 138
O'Donnell, Frank, 113, 128
O'Donnell, James, 46
O'Donnell, Peadar, 47, 76, 81, 87, 95, 100–101, 106, 109–10, 113; and Treaty, 118; and Civil War, 120–1, 123, 127–8; and the Irish Revolution, 133, 137–40; *Storm: a story of the Irish war*, 101, 113
O'Donoghue, Michael, 128
O'Duffy, Eoin, 100, 114, 121, 157n
O'Duffy, Hugh, 116
O'Duffy, Liam, 93, 95–6, 102
O'Farrell, Michael, 124
O'Flaherty, Sam, (TD), 77, 81, 85, 88, 102, 105, 110, 117
O'Flanagan, Fr Michael, 82
O'Leary, Philip, 49
O'Mahony, Patrick C., 69–70, 101

O'Malley, Ernie, 69, 98, 101, 102–3, 128, 130
O'Shannon, Cathal, 76
O'Sullivan, Timothy, 131
Omagh, County Tyrone, 3, 10, 35, 37–8, 97, 107
Orange Order, 4, 12, 19, 20, 22, 29, 63, 68–9, 136; Donegal Grand Lodge, 12; Londonderry Grand Orange Lodge, 12; Orangemen, 18, 122, 124
Orr, Revd S.H., 21
Osborne, Rosabelle, 40
Osbourne, J. Allan, 25, 27, 111, 159n

Pain, Colonel George William Hacket, 24, 26
Parliament Act (1911), 16
Parnell, 4, 50
partition, 15–16, 24, 30–1, 62, 82, 105–6, 110, 113–14, 120–3, 128; Lloyd George negotiations, 58–62; Anti-Partition League, 61; impact of, 135–7
Pearse, Emily, 51
Pearse, Margaret, 66
Pearse, Patrick, 1, 28, 51, 53–4, 66
Pettigo, 23, 102, 105, 109, 123–6, 132, 134
Pine Coffin, Major, 25
Plunkett, Horace, 4, 62–3
Plunkett, Joseph Mary, 51
poverty, 15, 52, 71, 76, 131, 137–8
press, the, 13–4, 40, 41, 54–5
Protestants, 1, 2, 15, 20, 23–4, 44, 99; clergy, 21, demography 2–3, 135–6; education, 8; farmers, 39; fears, 17, 19, 21, 24; established church, 9, 20, 136; Episcopalians, 3, 20, 40, 136; General Synod, 4; Methodists, 3, 18, 20, 136; Presbyterians, 3, 9, 19–20, 23, 25, 40, 90, 112, 136; Protestant anti-conscription pledge, 74; attacks on, 128, 135; population decline, 135–6; after partition, 135–7; migration, 135
Provisional government, 118, 125, 128

railways, 1–3, 52, 107; Lough Swilly railways, 75, 106, 107
Ramelton, 24–5, 40–1, 45, 97, 120

Raphoe, 6, 10, 20, 24–5, 29, 36, 68, 75, 91, 97, 103, 128, 152n; diocese 3–4, 32, 42–4, 57, 59
Rathmullan, 10, 46, 97
Red Cross, 44–5
Red Hand, 125
Redmond, John E. (MP), 16–17, 28, 31, 33–4, 37–8, 41–3, 46, 51, 55–6, 58–63, 70, 80, 139
Regan, Thomas (acting CI), 53, 56
Representation of the People Act (1918), 79
republic, 70, 82, 105, 114, 118; republicanism, 133
Ricardo, Captain Ambrose, 25, 111
Richardson, Sir George, 24, 25
Roberts, A.A. (CI), 23, 26–7, 29, 39, 47, 51, 56–7
Robinson, Sir Henry, 43
Rooney, Thomas, 113
Rosserly, Lord, 24
Rosses, the, 6, 35, 76, 101, 109
Rossnowlagh, 21, 23, 25
Royal Irish Constabulary (RIC): 26, 28, 49, 66–7, 70, 75, 77, 84, 87, 97, 102, 103, 113; barracks, 97, 121; barracks closed by July 1921, 97, 105, 107; establishment, 10, 142n; police districts 9, 97; County Inspector, 10, 97; resignations, 104; see War of Independence
Russell, George (AE), 7
Ryan, Bernard (Bunny), 66, 70

Salonika, 40
Samuel, Herbert, 31
Satchwell, Constable Thomas, 107
Saunderson, Major Somerset, 60–1
Scallan, Jim, 124
Scanlon, Canon, 82
Scotland, 2, 7, 8, 14, 29, 35, 39, 40, 42, 46, 47, 52, 103
Semple, James, 75
Shankey, DI John, 17–18
Sheila Humphreys, 127
Shinwell, Mannie, 76
shopkeepers, 6, 7, 8, 10, 18, 29, 99
Sinclair, Thomas (MP), 19

Sinn Féin (SF), 14, 39, 50–1, 55–6, 62, 64–5, 76, 80–4, 101, 110, 137; growth after 1916, 66–7, 69–70; and conscription crisis, 72–3; proclaimed, 77; membership December 1918, 79; and the political war, 88, 90–100; and Treaty, 116–17, 118; Sinn Féin courts, see Dáil Éireann
Sion Mills, 23, 25, 103, 111
Sligo, County, 2, 14, 19, 67, 102, 129, 131, 132
Smith, F.E. (MP), 24
Smyth, Nicholas, 124
soccer, 14, 47
social revolution, 137–8, 140
Soloheadbeg, 101
Somme, 41–2, 57, 60, 62
Spanish Flu, 83
St Enda's, Rathfarnham, 51, 53
St Eunan's cathedral, 7, 21, 32, 51, 72
St Eunan's college, 8, 42, 53, 56, 73
St Johnston, 3, 20, 22, 25, 26, 29, 134
St Patrick's College, Drumcondra, 76, 81
Stafford jail, 53–4
Stephens, Cecil, 14
Stewart estate, 75
Strabane No. 2 RDC, 90, 92, 94, 134
Strabane, County Tyrone, 24, 47, 69, 102, 107, 109, 122, 134
Stranorlar, 4, 18, 25, 53, 94, 108
Stubbs, Alfred, 18
suffrage, opposition to, 13; suffragettes, 21
Sweeney, Daniel, 106
Sweeney, Jack, 129
Sweeney, John (Johnny Rua), 51, 53
Sweeney, Joseph (TD), 53, 81, 83, 85, 91, 102, 104, 106, 109–10, 112; and Treaty, 114, 117–18; and civil war, 120–2, 125–6, 128–32; later career, 138–9
Swilly, Lough 10, 33, 37, 46
Sydney, William, 3rd earl of Leitrim, 22

Teelin, 5
Teevan John, 67, 152n
temperance, 45–6
Templecrone Agricultural Cooperative Society, 7
Termon, 22

Tierney, Fr Cornelius, 66, 71
Tipperary, County, 88, 101, 106
Tirconaill, 1, 120, 137, 161n
Tory Island, 1, 3, 5, 37, 46
Townshend, Charles, 104, 106, 113
Trainor, Fr J., 82
Travers, John 124
Treasury, 44, 100
Trimble, Samuel Delmege, 14
Trimble, William, 14
Trinder, Revd G.N., 21
Trinity College, 54, 62; estates, 2, 105
Tullaghan, County Leitrim 102, 120, 130; Ladies' SF club, 67
Ture, 37, 75
twelfth celebrations, 12, 18, 23, 29
Tyrone Herald, 14
Tyrone, County, 3, 11–13, 17–19, 23, 27, 31, 35–6, 58–9, 78, 81, 96, 105, 116, 122–4

Ulster Covenant, 4, 19–22, 60–1, 111; women's declaration, 19–21; Ulster Day, 18–21
Ulster Plantation, 2
Ulster Special Constabulary (USC), 119, 120, 122, 124–5, 127–8; B Specials, 132
Ulster Unionist Council (UUC), 16, 19, 22, 58, 60–2, 111, 122
Ulster Volunteer Force (UVF), 22–9, 35–6, 39, 51, 68, 77, 79, 103, 119–20, 123, 125, 159n; social composition, 25; arms 26–7, 103
Ulster Women's Unionist Council (UWUC), 13, 20–21, 26, 32, 45, 62
Unionist Party, 13; unionists: 16, 19, 32, 33, 60–3, 74, 79, 83, 85, 88, 90–2, 106, 111, 114, 135; unionist clubs, 16, 19, 22–4; liberal unionists, 9, 20; southern unionists, 63; kidnappings of, 119–20; boundary petition, 1934, 135
United Irish League (UIL), 9, 10–12, 16–17, 34, 65, 73, 79, 88, 110; membership, December 1918, 79
University College Dublin, 53, 81

Vaughan Hart, Colonel John, 136
Von Clausewitz, Carl, 101

Wagentreiber, Captain, 111, 159n
Walker, Fr Morgan, 82
Wallace, Colonel, 63
Wallace, DI, 103
Walsh, DI Patrick, 96, 112
Walsh, Lieutenant, 39–40
Walter, Lavinia Edna, 6
War of Independence, 41, 76, 87, 101–13, 126, 128, 132, 136, 139–40; pattern of activity, 105; attacks on police, 88, 96, 101, 103–5, 107, 110; boycott of police; 96–9, 104; burning of barracks, 104; Meenbanad, 101, 106; Rampart ambush, 88, 93, 101, 103; attack on Drumquin barracks, 96, 105, 158n; reinforcements from the south, 106; Black and |Tans, 104, 107; reprisals, 107; prisoners, 88, 108, 119–20; fatalities, 113; malicious damage claims, 91–3; collection of rates, 93–4; non-combatants, 98–9; *see* Irish Republican Army
Ward, Edward, 84
Ward, Fr J., 82
Ward, P.J. (TD), 81, 84–5, 90, 92, 94, 102, 107, 116–18
Waterford, County, 8, 69–70, 85
Watson, Margaret Rita, 40
Wheeler, Edith, 62
White, Captain Henry, 9
White, Captain Jack, 28–9
White, John, 139
Wilkinson, Andrew, 103
William Ward, 91
Williamson, W.R., 25
Wilson, Sir Henry, 127
women, 6, 12, 21, 26, 40–1, 44–6, 67; anti conscription pledge, 74; attacks on, 98–9; and the Irish Revolution, 139
Woodenbridge, County Wicklow, 33, 35
Wormwood Scrubs, 90, 93
Wright, Revd J. Jackson, 41–2
Wylie, T.C., 111